THE GUIDE TO

HIGH-PERFORMANCE
POWERBOATING

THE GUIDE TO

HIGH-PERFORMANCE POWERBOATING

From Racecourse to High-Speed Pleasure Boat

Joanne A. Fishman

with photographs by
Forest Johnson

Hearst Marine Books

NEW YORK

Library of Congress Cataloging-in-Publication Data

Fishman, Joanne A.
    The guide to high-performance powerboating : from racecourse to high-speed pleasure boat / Joanne A. Fishman.
        p.   cm.
    ISBN 0-688-08209-2
    1. Motorboat racing—United States.   2. Motorboats.   I. Title.
GV835.F57   1989
797.1'4'0973—dc19   89-31243
                                                                        CIP

Printed in the United States of America

First Edition

1 2 3 4 5 6 7 8 9 10

BOOK DESIGN BY PATRICE FODERO

To my dad, Hugh V. Alessandroni,
whose love of powerboats
was contagious

Preface

People have been drawn to the joys of crossing the water at high speed for more than a hundred years, ever since yachtsmen discovered the thrill of racing their steam-driven yacht tenders. However, the original motive for harnessing power afloat was not for speed as such but to end dependence on the wind, whose fickleness was often costly to captains of merchant ships. But unlike cars and planes that operate on land or in the air, a boat travels on the ever-changing boundary between air and water. Because a boat is an interface craft, its speed is considerably lower than speeds achieved by craft on land and in the air. The search through the years for an ever-faster boat—the ultimate means of traveling the difficult boundary between water and air—has proven to be a constant and intriguing challenge.

In writing about high-performance powerboats, it seemed reasonable to set parameters defining high performance. First, I sought to define performance strictly by a speed minimum of 40 miles per hour, because at such speeds and greater a boat can be expected to handle differently than a craft at slower speed. But with the significant engine developments of recent years, power is available to push a variety of hulls to much higher speeds. There are ski boats and small family cruisers capable of cruising at 50 mph. There are open console fishing boats that can reach the offshore canyons at 70 mph. And with growing financial rewards giving anglers a strong incentive to be first to the fish, the bass boats of the inland lakes and rivers are topping 70 mph.

While high performance can be defined by the purpose of the boat, such as a ski boat or bass boat, over the years it has generally related to an offshore powerboat, one that performs well in the open waters of the oceans, Great Lakes, or Mediterranean Sea. And offshore high performance is the primary focus of this book, "offshore" as it evolved through racing and then split into the Unlimited Hydroplane and Offshore circuits. High performance is the driving factor in the development of propeller-driven engine technology and hull construction today, as well as one of the strongest segments in the boating industry. High performance is the hotrod of the seas, and as increasing numbers of boatmen are discovering, fast is indeed fun.

Acknowledgments

I am grateful to those in the sport and the industry for their support and generous assistance. They include: Gus Anastasi, Wellcraft Marine; Bonnie Anderson, Hydroplanes, Inc.; Craig Barrie, Cigarette Racing Team; Jerry Berton, Global Marine; Bob Black, Bob Black & Associates; Allan "Brownie" Brown; Phil Buck, Unlimited Racing Commission; Chris Craft; Jack Clark, Jaguar Marine; Betty Cook, Kaama Marine; John Crouse, John Crouse Associates; Dan Fales, *Motor Boating & Sailing*; John Henry Falk, New York Offshore Powerboat Racing Association; Fred Farley, Unlimited Racing Commission; Stan Fitts, Offshore Racing Commission; Dick Genth, Donzi Marine; Tom Gentry, The Gentry Companies; Bob Gowens, Cigarette Racing Team; Bob Idoni, Popeyes Racing Team; Peter Janssen, *Motor Boating & Sailing*; Val Jenkins, Cigarette Racing Team; Mike Jones, American Power Boat Association; Fred Kiekhaefer, Kiekhaefer Aeromarine; Clem Koehler, Mercury Marine; Joe Langlois, Denison Marine; Bobby Latham, Latham Marine; Chris Lavin, Jesse James Racing Team; Mariner's Museum of Newport News, Virginia; Roger Marshall, N.A.; Dave Roycroft, Outboard Marine Corp.; Jerry Stansfield, U.S. Marine; Walter Sullivan, BUC International; Ted Theodoli, Magnum Marine; Jim Wynne, Wynne Marine, Inc.

Contents

Contents

Contents

Contents

Part 1

History

The craze for speed, even at a sacrifice of safety, comfort and everything else that goes to make boating a pleasure, seems to have taken possession of the yachting fraternity.

—*Motor Boat* magazine, 1904

Chapter 1

The First Powerboats

Reliance III, an early single-step hydroplane built by the legendary Christopher Smith, reached an average speed of 37 mph on the race course. *(Courtesy of the Mariner's Museum, Newport News, Virginia)*

One hears the boat long before it's visible. The distant buzz becomes a roar as the boat leaps out of the summer haze of Long Island Sound and heads for the harbor. Five years ago, this would have been a unique sight, but no more. From Boston Harbor to Key West to Lake Michigan to San Francisco, there is a renaissance of high-performance powerboats. Perhaps not since the early days of racing with Gar Wood have performance boats, both race and pleasure boats, been so popular. And in tandem with that popularity, new developments in engines, drives, and hull construction are emerging as well as new uses for the boats themselves.

It's not uncommon now, for instance, to drive for lunch from Miami to Bimini, a distance of some fifty miles, and return. Why not when one is cruising at 70 mph? Production builders today are turning out high-performance offshore boats capable of reaching 70 mph, even 100 mph. While the engines are mainly gasoline, diesels—especially turbocharged diesels—are coming on strong. And whereas twenty years ago the choice was largely between an outboard or an inboard engine, today sterndrives, which use an inboard engine attached to an outboard drive, are the dominant power choice for performance boats.

The original wooden displacement hulls gave way to deep vee planing hulls of wood and then fiberglass in the 1960s, and now hulls run the gamut from wood-epoxy to fiberglass to a host of axial fibers and unidirectional fiberglass to exotic materials of carbon fiber, Kevlar and sandwich construction with lightweight core materials. On the race circuits in the later 1980s, the Unlimited Hydroplanes began running with helicopter turbine engines instead of the traditional aircraft engines, and speeds have edged upward. The Unlimiteds, which race on calm inshore waters, are capable of reaching 200 mph, with two-and-a-half-mile lap speeds hovering around 150 mph. Meanwhile, in recent years the catamaran, or tunnel hull, has come to dominate the Offshore powerboat races held on the open ocean or the Great Lakes, where superboats running on four engines set a blazing pace, with average course speeds of 110 mph and straightaway speeds in excess of 140 mph. On the drawing boards now are offshore boats capable of running 150 mph and faster.

While the boats may be able to run that fast, there is some question whether the racers can handle them. Increased speeds have resulted in increased risk, and accidents and deaths have prompted greater safety precautions. Nonetheless, when traveling at 120 mph or so, there is little time to make corrections, and even if the racer reacts quickly, the boat may not respond to the correction in time to avert catastrophe. One sponson dipping too low, one rogue wave upsetting the boat's attitude, and it is nearly impossible to prevent the boat from rolling over or the bow from stuffing. Consequently, Offshore racers are outfitting their craft with F-16 cockpit covers—as the Unlimited drivers already have done—as well as oxygen supplies and escape hatches, all to gain that extra fraction of a knot of speed, to be able to ride on that hairy edge without falling off.

Today the sport basks in the chrome glow of success and recognition as one of the strongest segments of the recreational boating industry, and it has been gaining stature as race circuits provide a marketable sports commodity with sponsorship dollars to sustain the costs of competition. This is a long way from where it all started.

Beginnings are always cloudy. Powerboating is no exception, although some elements are clearer than others. The basic elements of marine propulsion, and even the concept of planing hulls, have been known for nearly a hundred years or so, but the ideas evolved, taking new shape and form as dictated by the marketplace and converging technologies. Aside from the commercial benefit of being independent of the wind, factors that influenced the development of fast boats were the evolution of the internal-combustion engine, the development of motor torpedo boats by the European and American navies, and the sport of motorboat racing.

Throughout the evolution of high-speed powerboats, though, runs the constant thread of human achievement: audacity and sheer nerve, amazing innovation and skill, and above all the competitive spirit that still fuels the drive for speed on the water.

The first internal-combustion motor was designed and built in Europe in 1678 by the Abbé Jean Hautefeuille. His motor operated on gunpowder and performed the task of pumping water to propel the boat, although not reliably. In the next twenty or so years there were several unsuccessful attempts to improve on the design of the Hautefeuille machine. Meanwhile, the steam era was getting under way.

The patents for the first engine-propelled vessel reportedly were taken out as early as 1737 in England. The patented vessel had rear paddles connected by belts or rope to large wheels driven by a steam engine. The purpose of the craft apparently was to tow sailing ships in a calm from the dock to the harbor entrance where they might catch a breeze. The projected speed has been estimated at 2 mph.

The first commercial steamboats began operating on the Clyde River in England in 1801, with Robert Fulton's *Clermont* following on the Hudson River six years later. From this point on, steam was developed in commercial ships and pleasure boats, primarily for the purpose of freeing seamen from dependence on the wind, rather than increasing speed. Queen Victoria's first steam yacht, *Victoria and Albert*, was completed in 1843. On the other side of the Atlantic Ocean, during the summer of 1875, the first two steam yacht races were conducted under the auspices of the New York Yacht Club. The era of the steam yacht was beginning and probably more famous vessels of this type flew the burgee of the New York Yacht Club than that of any other club, with the exception of Britain's Royal Yacht Squadron. The huge steamer *North Star* was built for

Cornelius Vanderbilt in 1853, and in 1864 the steamers *Bijoux* and *Clara Clarita* appear listed together as a group separate from the sailing yachts in the club yearbook. By 1897 there were 4 napthas, 12 launches, and 156 steam yachts in the club fleet. A number of club members lived on the shores of the Hudson River or Long Island Sound and would use their steamers and launches to commute to Wall Street.

For small craft, the steam engine, requiring large boiler spaces and coal lockers, was simply too slow and heavy to produce much speed. Another form of propulsion was needed for small boats. In 1823 Englishman Samuel Brown built the first internal-combustion engine to be installed in a boat. In an 1825 demonstration for the British Admiralty he ran a 36-foot boat some 7 mph on the Thames River. Brown's gas-vacuum engine condensed the products of combustion by using a jet of water, thus creating a partial vacuum. However, his engine was clumsy and unwieldy. A couple of years later American Samuel Morey of New Hampshire tested an internal-combustion engine in a 19-footer. He also is credited with developing the first effective carburetor. Yet the first internal-combustion engine that provided a viable alternative to steam power made its debut in Paris in 1864 as Jean Joseph Etienne Lenoir, an automobile pioneer, launched the first motorboat, driven by a 2-horse-power gasoline engine.

About the same time in Europe the self-propelled torpedo, the predecessor of the motor torpedo boat or fast patrol boat, was being developed by the Austrian Lupis from 1864 to 1866 and then improved by the Englishman Whitehead in 1872. The steamships being built by all navies at that time to carry the self-propelled torpedoes were slow, heavy displacement ships, and their lack of speed limited the effectiveness of the torpedoes. Because of the torpedo's limited range and slowness, compared to artillery fire, its success depended on surprise attack at close quarters at night or in using large numbers of torpedo boats to distract the enemy in daylight. In search of a suitable ship, the English shipyard owner Sir John Thornycroft in 1871 conceived of building smaller, faster steamboats to carry the torpedoes. His first design was *Miranda*, 13.7 meters long with a speed of 16.4 knots, the forerunner of all high-speed patrol boats. *Miranda* was equipped with a 3.95-meter towing torpedo attached to the top of the funnel. In 1873 Thornycroft built the first torpedo boat for the Norwegian navy, and in the next few years the boats became more powerful and more efficient by having the torpedo fired from a tube.

While all the torpedo boats were heavy-displacement ships with round bilges, in 1872 an Englishman, the Rev. C. M. Ramus, approached the British Admiralty with a plan for a 360-foot "stepped" ship, a 2,500-ton planing vessel. A step is a crosswise break in the planing surface intended to reduce friction. Ramus estimated the ship, with 1,500 hp, would reach 30 knots or nearly 35 mph. Ramus's plan was rejected as unrealistic by William Froude, an expert on resistance and the first to test ship models in tanks, who had been commissioned by the Admiralty to analyze the Ramus design.

The principle of planing without a step had been established in England some years prior to the Ramus design. In 1852, Joseph Apsey became the first person to patent the idea of a planing shape. The first planing boat was built by Escher Wyss in Zurich in 1887 from designs by a Frenchman, Pittet. *Le Rapide*, with 400 hp, was 23.5 meters overall and displaced 47 tons. It did not really get up on a plane, however, because it weighed too much for its horsepower.

The first boat that did plane was apparently built in 1905 by the Frenchman Campet who then wrote to the young engineer Techel, one of the pioneers of the German U-boats, that if larger motorboats "are built successfully which perform well, the use of high-speed motorboats as coastal torpedo boats will also be possible."

The rise of the planing boat, which skims across the water's surface rather than riding through it, occurred when S. E. Saunders of Cowes, Isle of Wight, developed the 1908 patent ideas of William Henry Fauber, a Chicago engineer who had become wealthy from his bicycle patents. Saunders put a number of longitudinal steps in his hull and gave it a vee section.

At the time the word *hydroplane*, which today refers to a type of raceboat, was used for all planing craft. Fauber defined a hydroplane as a craft "equipped with planes or surfaces presenting an upward angle to the direction of movement, and designed to act on the water in a manner to lessen the displacement and skin friction of the boat, for the purpose of accelerating the speed, or securing desired speeds with a lesser expenditure of power."

Although planing craft only emerged in the early part of the twentieth century, the last two decades of the nineteenth century had been a fertile ground on both sides of the Atlantic for powerboat development.

In America, two brothers, Henry and Christopher Columbus Smith of Algonac, Michigan, were busy carving duck decoys and building flat-bottomed duck skiffs for use on the flats and marshes of the St. Clair River. Later they also created rowing and sailing boats, known for their quickness. Word of the brothers' boats spread, resulting in the first recorded sale of a recreational boat in 1874. A number of years later Chris heard that a marine gasoline engine had been built by Charlie Sintz of Grand Rapids. He bought one, installed it in one of his rowboats, and blazed up the St. Clair River at the unheard-of speed of 9 mph. This is believed to be one of the first American powerboats.

In fact, key features of one of the most creative drive systems today—surface-piercing propellers—actually date back to a 1869 patent issued to a C. Sharp of Philadelphia. Shortly after the development of the marine screw propeller, Sharp proposed the partially submerged or surface-piercing propeller as an alternative to the paddle wheel. His patented unit incorporated features found in current systems, such as cupped blades for improved performance, and multiple blades to reduce the unsteady forces of the propeller working on the surface.

The early models of the internal-combustion engine were created to power boats rather than cars. The German Nicholaus Otto, however, perceived the significance of compression prior to combustion and built engines that resemble ones in use today. In 1872 Gottlieb Daimler teamed up with Otto, who four years later developed the four-cycle concept of intake, compression, power, and exhaust. Daimler, along with his protégé Wilhelm Maybach, who became a renowned engine designer, split with Otto in 1882 to pursue their own design theories. They produced the first known in-line engine, with cylinders arranged in a single row, in a four-cylinder machine designed specifically for marine and industrial use. At 620 revolutions per minute, the 330-pound engine developed only 5 hp. Nonetheless, this engine is regarded as the predecessor of all marine power plants since.

By 1890 the first motorboats in regular use were operating in Hamburg, Germany. Used by the police, they were wooden craft powered by Daimler internal-combustion engines. In 1889 the popularity of the Daimler engines in Europe led to their being shipped to the United States for marine use and later as automotive power. The Daimler engines were a vast improvement over the steam power plants, then used to produce the same amount of power but weighing at least twice as much and requiring a heavy load of water and fuel plus considerable space.

In 1887, the 103-foot 4-inch *Turbinia* made a grand entrance on the yachting scene by powering through an international naval review in honor of Queen Victoria's Diamond Jubilee at 39 mph, then an unheard-of speed. This was the first experimental steam turbine boat and it set the pace for development of larger craft. Its triple-shaft turbine, generating 2,000 hp, turned nine propellers, three on each shaft. The turbine engine continued to evolve for use in naval ships while smaller boats turned to the internal combustion engine and a variation on this theme, the outboard engine.

The idea for the outboard came to Ole Evinrude on a hot afternoon on Wisconsin's Okauchee Lake. Wanting to impress Bess Cary, whom he would later marry, Ole rowed across the lake for ice cream. On the slow row back, though, the ice cream melted, something Ole decided wouldn't happen again. Intrigued with the internal-combustion engine, Ole spent his spare time working on one that could be attached to the stern of a rowboat. Completed in 1907, his design established the basics for the standard outboard engine: horizontal cylinder, vertical crankshaft, and drive shaft with the direction-changing gears housed in a submerged lower unit. Ole's 1½-hp, single-cylinder outboard motor would make rowing across the lake a thing of the past.

As creative efforts in the marine field continued in America and Europe, the evolution of power on the water found expression in competition.

The Origins of Racing

It probably was a natural progression that the French, the original creators of the racecar, should be in the vanguard of transferring the venue from land to the water. The French were the first to take the automobile engine out of a chassis and install it in a hull, creating a new form of craft that closely followed the lines of the torpedo boat. Propelled by light gasoline engines, these craft were capable of 15 miles per hour or more on the Seine and other inland waters. Naphtha boats, an interim phase between steam and gasoline engines in which the fuel used was this derivative of crude petroleum, won the international motorboat races in Paris in 1898, while in 1900 a boat with a gasoline engine won.

The sport took on a more organized shape as associations were formed: the Marine Motor Association in Britain in 1902, followed a year later by the American Power Boat Association and in 1907 by the German Motor Yacht Verband in 1907.

Until 1902, however, the English "—always unbelievers in any maritime affair which emanated from France—refused to take the new departure seriously," according to a writer in a 1904 issue of *Motor Boat* magazine. To a Britisher, "any vessel which could not successfully hold its own in the turbulent water of the Channel or the North Sea was a toy, was something a Frenchman might favor, but an English seadog, never!" according to the writer.

At this point, a strange chain of events served to change the British outlook. First, the American sailing yacht *America* beat the cream of the British fleet in a race around the Isle of Wight in 1851 to win The Queen's Cup, known now as the America's Cup. The British began to realize they no longer were rulers of the seas, a lesson hammered home after they had lost nine America's Cup matches by 1901.

When James Gordon Bennett, owner of the New York *Herald* and a former commodore of the New York Yacht Club, moved to Paris, he didn't forget the club or the *America*. In 1899 Bennett offered a ten-thousand-dollar challenge cup for a world automobile championship, and in the deed of gift he duplicated the conditions of the America's Cup, essentially making the automobile take the place of the yacht and shifting the competition to land. With England having won the race in 1902 from the French, the venue moved to Ireland, as the conditions called for the defense of the cup over the roads of the country that held the cup.

Then, Sir Alfred Harmsworth, later Lord Northcliffe, the wealthy British newspaper owner and sportsman, sought to transfer the international contest back to the water. The Harmsworth International Cup for Motorboats was first contested in powerboats up to 40 feet long in Queenstown Harbor, Ireland, on July 11, 1903, during the week of the James Gordon Bennett auto race. Fastest over the eight-and-a-half-mile course from the Royal Cork Yacht Club to Glanmire was *Napier Minor*, a 40-foot displacement craft owned by S. F. Edge and powered by a 75-hp, four-cylinder Napier engine turning a two-bladed propeller. Driven by Campbell Muir, *Napier Minor* ran at an average speed of 19.5 mph with a top speed of 23.5 mph, easily defeating the launches entered by F. Beadle and J. E. Thornycroft.

Napier Minor awakened the British to the potential of the autoboat, which also became known as the speed launch, and the British made plans to defend the trophy. The Harmsworth trophy race also aroused America's competitiveness. As *Motor Boat* magazine observed, Americans had regarded the speed launch with "small favor until their life-long antagonists, the Englishmen, took it up and by the winning of the Harmsworth Trophy, gave America another excuse for foreign conquest. The result has been the phenomenal vogue of the high-powered, swift-traveling racing launch in this country which will continue to expand until the great American question of 'How fast can I go?' is answered in finality, which in the present instance will not be in your day or mine."

In America, it had become fashionable just before the turn of the century for a yacht to carry on board a small launch powered by gasoline. Originally, it was a novelty and luxury. In a matter of several years, though, a yacht was not considered properly fitted out unless it had a powerboat on its davits. A number of yachtsmen who owned small racing craft also owned powerboats to tow them from one regatta to another. During the races the powerboats followed the sailors over the course to be on hand in case of a mishap or to tow the sailboat back if it became becalmed. This sort of activity led to the formation of the United States Power Squadrons.

As gasoline motors were improved and enlarged they were placed in boats of 70 and 100 feet long which then were used as yachts. "The evolution of the gas motor may be largely credited to the yachtsman," wrote Henry J. Gielow, a prominent designer of sail and power boats in 1904. "If the yachtsman had not used the motor when it was in its infancy, it would never have been developed to such an extent that it would be profitable for commercial purposes. . . . Just now the fad is to have a fast boat, one that can race and win races and the efforts of makers of motors and designers of boats are turned towards speed."

Following the first Harmsworth race in Ireland, the next international contest of note followed in April 1904 in Monte Carlo's Bay of Hercules. There were four classes of raceboat, based on length of hull and the power of the motors.

Of the 76 entries representing five countries, 38 were racers, 29 cruisers, and 9 "others." Among the racers were entries representative of the leading European car racers such as Fiat from Italy, Napier from England, Germain from Belgium, Mercedes from Germany ("Daimler" apparently sounded too Teutonic for its French importer who renamed the car for his daughter, Mercedes). French entries included the Paris Automobile Company, Société des Automobiles Peugeot, Darracq, and Richard-Brasier.

The placing of powerful engines in lightweight hulls made for some interesting competition. After racing a series of ten heats around the 12.5-km course, the 33-foot *Trèfle-a-Quatre* won top honors for the meet as well as winning the Prince of Monaco's nautical-mile contest with a speed of 25.1 mph. *Trèfle-a-Quatre* was powered by a 84-hp engine designed by Henri

Two vintage bathing beauties show off a 1920s Elto (an acronym for Evinrude Light Twin Outboard), also known as the "rudder-twin" model because it was steered by the large rudder rather than by turning the engine and propeller. *(Courtesy of Outboard Marine Corp.)*

Brasier. The event was marred by several mishaps, however, prompting the correspondent for *Motor Boat* magazine to comment, "It would seem that the foreign makers have not sufficiently recognized the importance of the intimate relation between motor and boat. They seem to have taken no special pains to adapt the latter to the former, but have gone on the principle that a motor is a motor, and provided it was powerful enough, they let it go at that."

The misfortunes of the 52-foot racer *Parisienne II*, with its triple 80-hp engines, illustrated the problems. During the practice runs the boat lost one of its three screws and in a race the starboard propeller fell off, which not only slowed it down but also made it difficult to maintain a straight course. At the first mark, one of three pipes connecting the motors became disconnected and escaping gasoline caught fire, igniting the 800 liters of fuel. The fire blazed out of control and the three on board jumped into the water.

While some of the boats were criticized as being unstable, the commentator goes on to say, "Undoubtedly some of the accidents were caused by unpardonable lack of care shown by those entrusted with the management of the boats. The motors in many cases were far from clean and sadly in need of oiling and polishing. It is needless to say, however, that the winning boats were all in perfect order."

The Monte Carlo races caused a stir in yachting circles, giving an impetus to organized competition. Later that same spring organized powerboat racing was initiated in America on the western end of Long Island Sound.

Until 1903, when the American Power Boat Association was formed at a meeting of representatives of yacht clubs at the Columbia Yacht Club at the foot of West 86th Street in New York City, motorboat racing in the United States had not been conducted on a formal basis. But make no mistake, there had been racing already for several years in a few areas of the country, such as on the northern New Jersey shore. Speed launches were racing on the Shrewsbury and Navesink rivers with a measurement rule to handicap the different boats. Spectators watched from shore and even placed bets on the outcome.

For several years the queen of the rivers was the 25-foot

motorboat *Annie*, owned by Charles N. Peterson and driven by an 8-hp Buffalo motor. But *Annie* met its match in 1904 when it was dethroned by *Blue Streak*, which covered the sixteen-mile course on the Shrewsbury River at an average speed of 17.46 mph. The 26-foot 4-inch *Blue Streak*, powered by a 20-hp Mohler and DeGress engine, was built for John M. Richards by the Seaman Launch and Skiff Co. of Branchport, New Jersey. It was similar in design to the "autoboats," boats with automobile engines that featured a sharp entrance and long, flat run aft with a rounded stern.

The same Seaman firm was one of several local builders that also turned out the famous Sea Bright skiffs for both the rum-runners and the U.S. Coast Guard during Prohibition. The Sea Bright skiffs, forerunners of the Jersey Speed Skiff Class of raceboats, were a distinctive style of lapstrake shoal-water boat that fishermen originally launched off the beach at Sea Bright, New Jersey.

Meanwhile, there were the beginnings of powerboat competition at the turn of the century on the inland lakes of the Northwest. In America, 1904 was a watershed year as the first races organized by the American Power Boat Association (APBA) got under way with a full summer of competition at prominent yacht clubs not only in the Northeast, but also at the Chicago Yacht Club and the Southern Yacht Club in New Orleans. Other races were held by the Eastern Yacht Club in Marblehead, Massachusetts; by the Hartford (Connecticut) Yacht Club; and by the Larchmont, Knickerbocker, and Manhasset Bay yacht clubs in New York. The New York Yacht Club also hosted two races at its stations in Newport, Rhode Island, and Glen Cove, New York.

Spurred by the improvement of gasoline engines and the great popularity of the automobile, sailors began fitting the powerful engines into narrow, light launches so they could race when the lack of wind prohibited sailboats from competing. Soon people were building autoboats for the pleasure of running rings around every other craft on the water. One of these was Albert C. Bostwick, vice commodore of the Larchmont Yacht Club in New York, who used to take particular delight in passing any launch he encountered. Bostwick entered his boat in races, too, but since there was no means of handicapping the diverse boats properly, there was little sport in the contests.

The designer Henry Gielow, the first APBA measurer, framed a measurement rule that reportedly worked so well that a small launch 20 feet in length having a 4-hp motor could be put on terms of equality with a 150-foot torpedo boat destroyer that could make 30 mph. Under this rule yachts were rated for classification and time allowance by a rating determined by taking fifteen times the cube root of the square root of the waterline multiplied by the horsepower and divided by the area of the midship section.

Nonetheless, the autoboat—the launch that evolved into a raceboat—had grown in popularity to the point that the owners of these boats didn't want to race other types of boats, which were built primarily for day cruising. The APBA elected to create a special class for autoboats, the first class created for raceboats per se. Here an autoboat was defined as one whose rating exceeded ten times the square root of its load waterline. The boats were required to be fitted with a reverse gear sufficient to drive them at the rate of 4 miles an hour.

The "new power racing fleet" was to make its debut on Memorial Day 1904 in the first race of the first season of organized competition. The race was hosted by the Manhasset Bay Yacht Club on the western end of Long Island Sound. All that morning a stream of boats, large and small and both power and sail, converged on Manhasset Bay while other spectators arrived by car as well as by railroad from New York City. The *Delaware*, flagship of the New York Yacht Club with Commodore Frederick G. Bourne on board, arrived and lowered its steam launch so that the commodore and his party could watch at close range. The flagships of other clubs, including the Columbia and American yacht clubs, also were on hand. And William K. Vanderbilt, Jr., arrived in his magnificent *Tarantula*, a 152-foot steel yacht with triple turbines capable of bringing Vanderbilt from his home in Great Neck, Long Island, to his office in New York at 33 mph. Vanderbilt had planned to compete in his new speed launch *Hard Boiled Egg*, which he had towed in fresh from its City Island yard with mechanics still working on it. However, in the crowd of boats milling around before the start, Vanderbilt swerved to avoid a collision, which bent the rudder and caused *Hard Boiled Egg* to be withdrawn.

The starting line was located near the Manhasset Bay Yacht Club in Port Washington, and two hours before the 2:30 P.M. start the clubhouse and dock "were crowded with interested spectators, while the harbor was filled with yachts of all classes," wrote the *Motor Boat* correspondent. Of the fifteen entries, twelve actually started. The larger yachts ran a distance of nineteen and a half miles out into Long Island Sound and back, while the smaller launches traveled nine and a half miles. *Japansky*, owned by F. H. Waldorf of New Rochelle, New York, won the large-boat class with an average speed of 20.2 mph.

For a race the following month, the Columbia Yacht Club had provided a perpetual challenge cup, designed by Tiffany's, known as the American Power Boat Association Challenge Cup. Since there was no time to accept a foreign challenge for it in 1904, as the new sport was just getting started, it was agreed that any member of a club in the association could enter his boat and the club winning the cup would then defend it against all comers. What started as the Association Cup in a matter of weeks became known as the Gold Challenge Cup, now shortened to the Gold Cup which today is the foremost trophy in Unlimited competition. The first race was held June 23, 24, and 25 on the Hudson River from the Columbia Yacht Club to Piermont, New Jersey, a distance of eight miles, and back.

While there were nine entries for this banner event in powerboat racing, only three showed up. Some of the new powerboats were not yet completed, but others apparently had been intimidated by the so-called Phantom of the Hudson. This boat, a narrow 58-foot launch built of double-planked, copper-riveted mahogany and having a 7-foot 3-inch beam, had arrived on the Hudson that spring with no name or home port on its transom. The speed launch had the disconcerting habit of pulling alongside a steam launch, and as the fires in the steamboat's boilers were being stoked for an impromptu contest, the nameless boat would leap ahead, cut across the steam launch's bow and power on.

By the time the Gold Cup began, all on the Hudson had

learned the identity of the mystery craft. It was the *Standard*, built to promote the Standard Special Engine built by the United States Long Distance Automobile Company. The *Standard* was a racer, an autoboat. Carl C. Riotte, who designed its engine, believed, as did engine builders with Mercedes, Fiat, Lozier, Panhard, Napier, Peugeot, and others, that success on the race-course would increase sales of both marine engines and auto-mobiles.

The *Standard*'s engine weighed nearly 3,200 pounds, pro-ducing 110 hp at 420 rpm. Riotte's monstrous 3,016-cubic-inch engine was 7 feet long and over 4 feet high. After installing the engine in the hull in the fall of 1903, Riotte apparently decided to do some on-the-water testing in the spring of 1904 by taking on the river steamers.

Under clear skies, with a warm breeze sweeping up the river, only two other autoboat owners had the courage to com-pete against the *Standard*: C. H. Tangeman of the Atlantic Yacht Club with his launch *Fiat I*, and Frank Seaman of the Yonkers-Corinthian Yacht Club with *Water Lily*. On the first day *Fiat I* was eliminated after hitting a submerged log and damaging its rudder. At the helm of *Standard*, representing Columbia Yacht Club, Riotte along with his brother Eugene won all three races by "darting up the river at a tremendous pace" while *Water Lily* "hung on like grim death," according to one correspon-dent. In the second race, *Standard* averaged 23.63 miles per hour, which was considered the highest speed reached by any autoboat up to that time.

So anticlimactic was this first race for the Gold Cup that another was set for later that season in September. *Standard* had dropped out of competition by then, having been sold for use as a pleasure launch on the St. Lawrence River. However, in this second Gold Cup race of 1904 ten boats competed on a white-capped Hudson River, with *Vingt et Un II* capturing the trophy. Built by the Smith & Mabley Company to promote its light, four-cylinder motors for cars and launches, *Vingt et Un II* carried a 75-hp prototype Smith & Mabley engine. Its hull was designed by Clinton H. Crane, whose hulls would win five of the next nine races.

Meanwhile, during the summer of 1904 powerboat racing

was spreading throughout Europe. In June the German Automobile Club sponsored a race for motorboats in Kiel Harbor that was watched by King Edward VII of England and the German Kaiser Wilhelm II. S. F. Edge's *Napier Minor*, the first Harmsworth Trophy winner, handily won against *Blitzmaedel*, a Daimler company entry. In France, there was the second running of the 207-mile race from Paris to the sea with thirty-six boats competing. *Mercedes IV* won the racer class, up to 39 feet in length, with an average speed of 27 mph. And England's *Napier Minor* captured the second Harmsworth Trophy race held on the Solent, defeating the American boat *Challenger*, a Clinton Crane design that developed engine problems. *Challenger* later went on to set a new world speed record of 29.3 mph on Florida's Lake Worth in February 1905.

Actually, *Napier Minor*'s victory was short-lived. In a belated decision, officials declared *Trèfle-a-Quatre*, the French entry, the winner because England's *Napier Minor* had earlier been defeated by *Napier II* in the elimination trials. As each country was entitled to one entry and England had selected *Napier II*, the last-minute substitution of *Napier Minor* was protested. In the race, the French boat ran a slow third, but wound up the victor on this technicality.

American interest in the Harmsworth Trophy was sparked again in 1907 when the first of the famous series of boats named *Dixie*, designed by Clinton Crane and owned by E. J. Schroeder of Jersey City, New Jersey, was sent to England with Capt. S. Bartley Pearce and engineer Albert Rappuhn. *Dixie* won the race with an average speed of 31.8 mph, bringing the trophy, and the race, to the United States.

In general, the designers of the high-speed powerboats at this time relied heavily on the concept of an "easily driven" form, which tended to be molded after the steam torpedo boats. There was little agreement on what shape constituted this ideal, as the torpedo boats from Thornycroft, Norman, Yarrow, and Herreshoff varied substantially, sharing little more than rounded cross sections, extremely sharp entries, and the narrowest of forms possible with some shred of lateral stability. In fact, Crane admitted that his early boats became "cranky," exhibiting severe lateral rolls that terrified the uninitiated at speeds of 25 mph.

While Crane was aware of "skimmers," he also was aware that their flat forms pounded heavily and thus required heavier construction, which in turn negated the advantage of the lesser wave-making resistance when skimming. The bow of Crane's first *Dixie*, though, showed signs of struggling to lift clear of the water. In consecutive models of the *Dixie* series between 1905 and 1909, Crane widened the stern and flattened the run aft. He also discovered that by ballasting one of the *Dixie*s with 900 pounds in the stern, it ran faster than before. With this bit of knowledge, he promptly moved the engine back in the hull and removed the ballast.

Schroeder, commodore of the Motor Boat Club of America, had commissioned Crane to design a second *Dixie* on the condition that it reach 35 mph. Crane agreed and in 1908 *Dixie II* was built to defend the Harmsworth Trophy off Huntington, Long Island. *Dixie II*, a similar but more powerful version of *Dixie I*, defeated the British boats *Daimler II* and *Wolseley-Siddeley* with a dramatic finish. Captain Pearce drove *Dixie II* across the line while holding engineer Rappuhn, unconscious because of the engine fumes, in his arms.

By the time *Dixie II* made its debut in the Gold Cup challenge, it had set a new water speed record of 36.6 mph, Crane's guarantee to the commodore fully met. With its 2,394-cubic-inch, 220-hp V8 engine, *Dixie II*, which never was defeated in its racing career, swept all three thirty-mile heats over its rival, *Chip III*. The technological pace was swift. In four years, heat speeds had increased 31 percent and the weight needed to generate one horsepower had dropped 66 percent from the 29 pounds-per-horsepower of *Standard* to the 10 pounds per horsepower of *Dixie II*.

The displacement-hulled *Dixie*s continued to win the world's most prestigious races. *Dixie*s also won the Gold Cups of 1909 and 1910 against local competition. But Crane knew something was amiss when *Dixie III* met the British challenger *Pioneer* in defense of the Harmsworth Trophy on Long Island Sound in 1910 (no race was held in 1909). *Pioneer*, a hydroplane, proved far faster than *Dixie III*. It started with a tremendous rush while *Dixie III* plodded along at what seemed a hopelessly slow pace. Unfortunately for its backers, *Pioneer* broke down with a clogged water-intake pipe when it was half a lap ahead of *Dixie III*, and the Americans retained the trophy. After *Pioneer*'s loss due to a momentary problem, the rules were changed to provide for a series of three races rather than one, in the interest of fairness. In the interest of winning, Crane knew a faster defender was needed.

The stepped form clearly was emerging. By 1910 George Crouch announced in *Motor Boat* that "the day of the hydroplane has arrived." By "hydroplane" he wasn't referring to the patented Fauber multistep hydroplanes or to a particular school of naval architecture, but rather to the designs of Fitzmaurice Hunt, a former St. Lawrence fishing guide.

The ill-fated *Dixie IV* encountered one of Hunt's hydroplanes the next year in the Gold Cup. Powered by two huge V8 engines rated at 270 hp, the 40-foot *Dixie IV* promptly set a new water speed record of 45.21 mph. In the Gold Cup, it ran the first twenty-eight-mile heat faster than its nearest competitor by nine minutes. A bearing failure kept it out of the second heat, and the cup that year was won on points by Hunt's hydroplane *Mit II*. *Dixie IV* went on to defend the Harmsworth at Huntington Bay. Later that year, though, *Dixie IV* crashed into a crowd of spectators on shore, injuring several and killing a boy. Crane subsequently stopped designing hydroplanes as he "saw no way of making them useful."

The picture was changing. Great Britain sent over *Maple Leaf III* in 1912 for the Harmsworth. By proving to be a better rough-water boat than any of the American defenders, *Maple Leaf III* won the series of three races and took the Harmsworth Trophy back to England.

As for Crane, it wasn't as if he or his designs had disappeared from sight. To the contrary, his influence on the sport was so strong that his designs won the Gold Cup in 1912 and again in 1913. The 1912 Gold Cup victor was a stock Crane design named *PDQ II*. Although its heat speed was no greater than that of the 1911 winner, *PDQ II* reached this speed in an entirely different manner. The Crane design had been modified by the addition of a single step by St. Lawrence River builder Fred Adams, who also rode as mechanic. Of the eight starters for the 1912 Gold Cup, half were Crane designs, including *Ankle Deep*, a boat new to racing. Its owner and driver, Count Mankowski, had never driven a raceboat before and capsized *Ankle Deep* on the first lap. The count recovered to race again and to win the Gold Cup the next year, making *Ankle Deep* the last of the old speed-launch style of craft to win the Cup.

In the 1912 Cup race, the 32-foot *Ankle Deep* had dwarfed a 20-footer known as *Baby Reliance*, which also did not finish. *Baby Reliance* backfired loudly, exploded its crankcase, and caught fire. No one paid much attention to it at the Gold Cup. But the boat had terrorized its competitors in the Mississippi River regattas earlier that year. And it was a sign of things to come, for the obscure *Baby Reliance* had been built by the Smith-Ryan Boat Company of Algonac, Michigan.

The ideas that would revolutionize the sport had been brewing for several years, both in America and Europe. In addition to Fauber and the St. Lawrence contingent, two Illinois brothers, William and Larned, had been studying hydrofoils for twelve years, finally receiving a patent for a design of their own in 1910. Their concept was of three planing surfaces, one forward of a central hull and two to the rear on outriggers with the engine in the central hull. Other concepts were being studied by the brothers Orville and Wilbur Wright. Once they got their first airplane off the ground they began thinking about how to fly a plane off water and tested steel hydroplanes on the Miami River in Dayton, Ohio. During this period, John Hacker of the Detroit Launch and Power Co. was busy on the Detroit River. First he designed and tested *Kitty Hawk*, the first stepped vee bottom hydroplane with a single engine, followed by a hydroplane having a bow rudder.

In France by 1906, Count C. A. de Lambert had developed a multiplane catamaran craft, powered by a 50-hp engine, that reached 34 mph. What he called his *glisseur* (skater) became the fastest boat on the Seine. In Paris, meanwhile, Paul Bonnemaison received a patent for a single-step hydroplane. His first boat of this design, *Ricochet Nautilus*, was a single-seater that reached 29.8 mph with a 10-hp motor.

While the ideas for faster hulls took shape, powerboat racing expanded into new courses and contests. The first ocean race became a twenty-two-mile jaunt over the English Channel from Calais, France, to Dover, England, on August 8, 1904. *Mercedes IV* of France, powered by a single 80-hp Daimler engine, topped the twenty-one-boat fleet. *Mercedes IV*'s winning time was one hour flat, with England's *Napier Minor*, driven by its owner, S. F. Edge, finishing second.

The first regular offshore powerboat race in Britain was the London to Cowes event which was held annually from 1906 to 1938. The boats used were seagoing cruisers, as the planing boats of today did not exist, and prizes were given for first to finish as well as for predicted times.

In America, powerboat racing was becoming fashionable in yachting circles and was drawing spectators. "New England to Have Great Regatta," announced the headline in *Motor Boat* regarding the races in Boston Harbor. Races were being run from St. Augustine, Florida, to Seattle. And the July 4, 1911, Mississippi Valley Power Boat Association regatta at Dubuque, Iowa, billed itself as "the first important event in this country in which hydroplanes will participate." This marked the debut of *Red Top III*, the 32-foot Fauber design owned by W. E. Hughey, commodore of the MVPBA. *Red Top III* and *Oregon Wolf*, the latter designed with metal plates on its hull bottom, later were the stars of the Pacific Coast championship which drew several thousand spectators. With speeds approaching 40 mph, *Oregon Wolf* emerged victorious.

Flatbottoms, vee bottoms, one-steps, multiple-steps, hydrofoils, catamarans, and all their variations mixed with engines from more than twenty-four manufacturers—all were converging to reshape the sport. This ultimately was done by Garfield Arthur Wood, the man known as The Grey Fox.

Chapter 2

In Search of Speed: The Gar Wood Era

FIAT II, a 26-foot-long autoboat powered by a 35 hp Fiat automobile engine, competed in the American Power Boat Association's first race held on May 31, 1904, on Long Island Sound. *(Courtesy of the Rosenfeld Collection, Mystic Seaport Musuem, Inc., Charles Edwin Bolles , photographer)*

Gar Wood was named for the President and Vice-President inaugurated in the year he was born, 1880. He was one of thirteen brothers and sisters whose father had run away from home at the age of fourteen to become a drummer boy in the Civil War. After the war, his father, Walter, married and pursued various jobs, winding up as a ferryboat operator on Lake Osakis, Minnesota.

There was an intense rivalry between Walt Wood and the captain of another ferry, *Belle of Osakis*, and *Belle*'s captain was determined to prove that his boat was the fastest on the lake. One day these wood-burning steam paddleboats met in a race that was to have ramifications far beyond the world of the upper Lake Country. Walt Wood ran short of fuel. *Belle*'s captain chugged ahead, "giving a Minneapolis cheer as he went by," according to a *Nautical Quarterly* account. Walt Wood shouted back and then asked his crew, his young son Gar, to help him break up the boat's furniture. In a wild chase to the finish, they fed the furniture to the boat's boiler and won.

Decades later Gar Wood hadn't lost the taste of that victory. "I still feel the thrill of winning that race. . . . I resolved right then that someday I was going to build and race boats of my own."

As a youngster Gar Wood learned a lot about boats by making a series of toy boats with clockwork motors, and after the family moved to Duluth on the shores of Lake Superior, Wood became a professional captain at the age of thirteen, running the first gasoline engine craft in Duluth. He later explained to a reporter that his first "speed" boat was a 16-footer with a 3-hp engine. "With it I succeeded in getting eight miles an hour running up and down the harbor at Duluth near my home, merely by squirting raw gasoline into the bell of the motor with an oilcan."

Soon after, Wood built his first boat, which made 15 mph with a 10-hp engine, fast enough to beat all the other boats on Minneapolis's Lake Minnetonka. Wood then spotted a faster boat, *Fritz*, and after going to St. Paul to talk to the builder, Fred Dingle, he later decided to move to St. Paul with his new wife, Murlen. Here Wood journeyed around town fixing cars and stopping by Dingle's shop to talk speedboats. In 1912 this Lake Country mechanic spotted a truck driver laboring to unload two tons of coal with a hand-operated lift. "Mrs. Wood and I had just two hundred dollars between us at the time," he later said. He told her he had a new idea, a mechanical device for dumping trucks, and wondered if he should put money in it. "She was a good sport and said go ahead." Using half their savings, Wood built the first hydraulic truck hoist in a backyard garage. There was an immediate demand for Wood's device. He patented it and started the Wood Hydraulic Hoist and Body Company, whose success made Wood wealthy for the rest of his life and able to indulge his passion for fast boats.

In his early racing days, Wood appropriated his wife's stuffed teddy bear to use as a mascot on his 1912 racer, *Little Leading Lady*. The boat won all the races in its class that year at the Mississippi Valley's big regatta. Mrs. Wood then bought a second teddy bear, which found its way to Wood's boat also. For the next twenty years Wood would not race unless his two stuffed mascots, Teddy and Bruin, were aboard. This fixation grew. Murlen Wood soon was making tiny cork life jackets, bathing caps, ear mufflers, and rubber-soled shoes for these treasured racing companions. As speeds escalated and Wood set his sights on breaking the 100-mph barrier, he placed his trust in his good-luck teddy bears. As he once said, and believed, "They are the captains of my fate."

Wood, his wife, the teddies, his family, and the business moved to Detroit in 1914. At this point, the paths of Gar Wood and Chris Smith crossed and powerboat racing was never the same again. Smith, the waterman turned builder from Algonac, forty miles north of Detroit, had been turning out raceboats since 1911. He went into partnership with John "Baldy" Ryan, a high-stakes gambler from St. Louis and Cincinnati, after Ryan had bought Smith's first raceboat, a 29-footer. The next boat, guaranteed to reach 40 mph, was built for J. Stuart Blackton, the silent movie pioneer and commodore of the Atlantic Yacht Club in New York. This was *Baby Reliance I,* whose hull split on impact with a wake shortly after Blackton acquired it. The commodore then ordered two more boats, *Baby Reliance II,* which won all its classes at the Mississippi Valley championships, and *Baby Reliance III,* which set a new measured-mile speed off 53.7 mph.

"I don't care about displacement. All I need is enough water to cool the engine," remarked Smith at one point during his boatbuilding career. Actually, the combination of engine advances and hull design was the key to Smith's boats, which dominated Gold Cup competition and most other open races, including the Harmsworth, through 1921.

There had been tremendous progress in reducing engine weight and increasing output. For instance, weights had fallen to some 7 to 8 pounds per horsepower and would drop to 5 pounds per horsepower by 1915 with the Model R Sterling which produced 275 hp at 1,700 rpm and weighed 1,400 pounds. Power now existed to push the single-step boats fast enough to enable the design to perform efficiently. There was more than enough power to get a boat up on a plane and the payoff was becoming evident.

In the construction of his boats, Smith carefully used a variety of woods to their best advantage. The topsides were half-inch Philippine mahogany copper-nailed to continuous elm ribs. The bottoms were single-planked, in butternut usually, and decks were butternut covered with canvas. A typical Smith racing boat weighed 3,000 pounds.

As the Smith-built boats achieved increasing success, they became enveloped in secrecy, eventually with skirts hiding their bottoms and guards on duty. A key member of the yard in Algonac was Jack Beebe, a self-taught mechanic who met Smith

In 1912 Gar Wood (left), shown here with his riding mechanic, Jay Smith, took his wife's Teddy to use as a mascot and won all his races that year. For the next twenty years Wood would not race unless "Teddy" and later "Bruin" were on board. *(Courtesy of the Mariners' Museum, Newport News, Virginia)*

when he sold him small engines for rowboats. Later Beebe prepared the Sterling engines used in the Smith boats. The single-step *Miss Detroit* was designed by Beebe as were some earlier Smith raceboats. Beebe went on to design and built his own raceboats, including *Whip-Po'-Will* which set a 70-mph record in 1917.

The Miss Detroit Powerboat Association, one of a number of groups that had formed to organize local races, could not raise the money to build a second *Miss Detroit* for the 1916 Gold Cup, and the victory went to another Smith boat, *Miss Minneapolis*. The association now had to sell the obsolete *Miss Detroit I* to the highest bidder. This was Gar Wood. The impulsive and fiery Wood also bought into Smith's boatbuilding firm and commissioned *Miss Detroit II*. With Jay Smith aboard as mechanic, Wood won the 1917 Gold Cup, with a formidable average speed of 56.6 mph. And after winning the cup, *Miss Detroit II* blazed through a measured mile at 61.273 mph, making the mile-a-minute barrier a thing of the past. Wood, the inventor and racer, was at the top and he never looked back.

For the next Gold Cup, Wood became the first person to install an aircraft engine in a boat, much to the annoyance of powerboat officials. *Miss Detroit III* was equipped with a twelve-cylinder Curtiss aircraft V12 engine. Despite being burned by flames shooting out of the exhaust stacks, Wood defended the cup. During the next couple of years, marine engineers and designers studied the aircraft engines, tuning them up and properly placing them in the hulls. These aircraft engines became the leading edge of Gold Cup technology and remained the primary power plants until the early 1980s when gas turbine engines first appeared.

The aircraft engines represented a great leap forward, bringing the weight-to-power ratio from the Sterling's 4 to 5 pounds per horsepower to the 2 pounds per horsepower of the Liberty V12 aircraft engines. The Liberty V12 engines, whose prototype was built by the Packard Motor Car Co., produced more power than the Curtiss engines. The Liberty 1,650-cubic-inch 400- to 450-bhp motor had been designed in a crash program during World War I. After the war, the Liberty engines initially found their way into raceboats via a former Government inspector, Howard Grant, who had purchased supposedly scrap and defective parts when manufacturing ended and then assembled the engines from his stocks. By 1919, both *Miss Detroit II* and *III* had been refitted with Liberty engines. With *Miss Detroit III*, Wood again defended the Gold Cup in 1919 and then set his sights on the Harmsworth International Trophy.

Wood's success with the Liberty engines made them popular among racers, who included Carl G. Fisher, founder of the Indianapolis Motor Speedway and the Allison Engineering Co., and developer of Miami Beach and promoter of the first powerboat races in Miami. Fisher also competed in his Miami races. Together he and Wood formed the Detroit Marine Aero Engine

Company to purchase aircraft engines from the United States Government along with Liberty engines built by Packard, Ford, and others; they also bought engines such as Fiat, Mercedes, and Benz in Europe. The engines then were resold to boatbuilders and racers.

To recapture the Harmsworth Trophy, Wood had Chris Smith build him *Miss America*, a 26-footer with the now conventional single step and driven by two Liberty engines providing 900 hp. This was his smooth-water boat. Wood also had Smith build a rough-water boat, *Miss Detroit V*, also equipped with two Liberty engines, and he brought both to Southampton Water, England, in 1919 for the first Harmsworth race since the war held in 1920. Using *America I*, Wood decimated the field, winning the two heats needed to bring the bronze international trophy home to Detroit.

With barely a pause between races, Wood took the wheel of *Miss America* and defended the Gold Cup on the Detroit River, setting a blazing 70-mph average for three heats, a Gold Cup record that would stand until after World War II. Next he ran the One-Mile Championship of North America on Lake George, setting a new world water speed record of 77.89 mph. He was now the preeminent powerboat racer in the world, the winner of all the top races and the fastest man afloat. He had demolished the competition and in the process become a celebrity. But it wasn't enough.

Early in 1921 the slender, 5-foot 4-inch Wood decided to take on another project. To demonstrate the effectiveness of a 50-foot express cruiser that he had developed to run with a pair of his Liberty engines, he embarked on the first significant distance runs, grueling tests of endurance. On February 12 Wood set a world cruiser record for the 129-mile distance from Miami Beach to Palm Beach, averaging 32.8 mph for four hours. The next week he went on to win the Miami-to-Key West cruiser race with an average speed of 38.2 mph over the 157 miles. And two months later Wood embarked on what has become the best-known endurance run: Miami to New York. Wood did it in his own style, racing the Havana Special, the fastest train on the Atlantic coast. With his friend Charles F. Chapman, editor of *Motor Boating* magazine (now *Motor Boating & Sailing*),

Wood drove his cruiser *Gar II Jr.* 1,260 miles up the unpredictable and at times rough Atlantic Ocean. With five fuel stops, *Gar II Jr.* arrived in New York 47 hours 23 minutes after leaving Miami, and 23 minutes ahead of the express train.

In his report on the Miami races, the *Motor Boat* correspondent observed, "Despite the prognostications of the rocking chair fleet, [Wood] proceeded to go out and prove that he could build the world's fastest express cruiser, just as he had built and raced the world's fastest hydroplane. This man Wood is a fiend for speed and accuracy. He does little or no talking, just goes out and builds a boat and then asks the whole darned world to come and beat him—if it can."

In this period, Wood was not the only one to reach high speeds on the water, although he certainly was the best-known and most successful. In 1916 *Vibora*, a Sea Sled design (known also as an inverse vee) owned by James Deering, competed in the Miami regatta. In the rough waters, *Vibora* sank while rounding a buoy. Nonetheless, the Sea Sled design, as conceived in 1914 and patented by Albert Hickman, was refined into a viable high-speed craft, essentially the first effective tunnel hull. To create it, Hickman cut a vee bottom boat in half lengthwise, pulled the halves apart and then switched the sides, creating a tunnel between the two in the forward section of the boat. The two came together in midsection and swept down to a flat bottom. Instead of a narrow bow, the Sea Sled had a wide one. Hickman's idea was to trap water inside the tunnel to give the boat lift. He also fit his craft with surface-piercing propellers.

The Sea Sled *Orlo II*, owned by George Leary, Jr., and driven by Hickman, competed in the 1921 Miami races, marking the first time a Sea Sled using the principles of surface propellers was entered in a big race. Noting this, the *Motor Boat* correspondent went on to say, "had it been possible to give more time to tuning up the power plant, the Sea Sled would quite likely have won the series of races. . . . The combination of the Sea Sled type of design plus surface propellers is still somewhat novel to the average motor boat fan, but it had more than one man thinking hard down in Miami." Indeed, derivatives of Hickman's concepts can be seen on today's raceboats.

That summer at a race in Buffalo, *Orlo III*, powered by two

Gar Wood and Jay Smith speed to victory in the 1918 Gold Cup Race aboard *Miss Detroit III*. *(Courtesy of the Mariner's Museum, Newport News, Virginia)*

300-hp Murray & Tregurtha engines, smashed the existing displacement boat speed record by more than 10 miles an hour, averaging 57.8 mph for six runs. Although *Orlo III* finished the race third, the boat was now considered the fastest displacement craft and Hickman was ready to challenge Wood.

They met August 27 in the 1921 Gold Cup competition, and the outcome was anticlimactic. *Orlo III* had no chance against Wood's *Miss America* or the third entry, the hydroplane *Miss Chicago*. After an accident in the third heat, Hickman skipped the final heat, leaving the other two with the formality of finishing. This was Wood's fifth Gold Cup victory in five years and it would be his last, although he made attempts at winning it once more in later years. And Hickman left competition to concentrate on building Sea Sled pleasure craft.

On the heels of the Gold Cup followed the race for the Harmsworth International Trophy, which Wood had won from the British in 1920. Held in the United States, the race was the climax of a series of prestigious powerboat races on the Detroit River. To defend the trophy Wood had upped the ante, packing more horsepower in a raceboat than ever before. His new 32-foot *Miss America II* built by C. C. Smith & Sons was equipped with four Grant-Liberty engines totaling 1,800 horsepower. The challenger was *Maple Leaf VII*, the latest *Maple Leaf* fielded by Baron Edgar of Chalfont which was powered by four Sunbeam aircraft engines developing a total of 1,800 hp.

Following the example of Chris Smith, *Maple Leaf*'s builder had equipped the craft with a bow rudder and other elements of American design. *Miss America II* won the Harmsworth in a single heat, however, as *Maple Leaf*'s bottom, forward of the step, gave way causing a bad leak; the boat sank before it reached its slip. Soon after, *Miss America II* was clocked at 80.57 mph in the North American Mile Championships.

Gar Wood became the victim of his own success, though. There was concern that Wood's domination of the sport and his unlimited spending was killing off the competition. In the 1921 Gold Cup, for example, only two of the twelve entries showed up for the first heat. "This classic event," wrote the *Motor Boat* correspondent, "has descended into little more than a circus performance for the grandstand. . . . *Miss America* would have won regardless of the number of starters for she is faster by far than anything in the country with the exception of *Miss America II*, which was held out to defend the Harmsworth Trophy. . . . even a procession would have been more in keeping with the dignity of this historic old trophy."

During that winter, the APBA changed the game. By a committee decision, a decade of high-speed powerboat development was eliminated from the Gold Cup competition. The APBA decreed that in future the Gold Cup would be limited to displacement boats of more than 25 feet and with engines not exceeding 625 cubic-inch displacement. The intent was to encourage the development of more practical, seaworthy boats that would have use beyond the racecourse. It also broke Wood's hold on the cup. This ushered in the era of the so-called gentlemen's runabouts.

In 1922 thirteen new boats entered the competition, the

largest field to compete in years, but speeds dropped dramatically, barely reaching 40 mph. The victor was Col. Jesse G. Vincent's Packard Chris Craft, built by Chris Smith, also the builder of *Baby Gar*, which Wood drove to third place. Wood was angered that Smith would build a faster boat for someone else, and they wound up parting company in 1923. With the speed limitations, the Gold Cup became just another race in a series of races held by the Detroit Yacht Club each year.

During the next decade, Wood became obsessed with defending the Harmsworth Trophy against increasingly powerful competition and defending his title as holder of the world water speed record. The Harmsworth became one of the premier sporting events in North America, with half a million people converging on the banks of the Detroit River each year to watch four boats (at most) dash around a course.

Runabouts from the famed builder C. C. Smith & Sons compete in a 1929 regatta on the Detroit River. *(Courtesy of the Mariner's Musuem, Newport News, Virginia)*

In 1925 Henri Esdres challenged with *Excelsior-France* and Wood responded by building *Miss Americas III* and *IV*. However, *Excelsior-France* burned and sank in a test on Lake Geneva and the Harmsworth was canceled that year. Esdres built another boat and challenged again in 1926. In turn, Wood built *Miss America V*, which won after *Excelsior-France II* broke down.

Then followed two challenges by Betty Carstairs, a wealthy Englishwoman. In 1928 she arrived with *Estelle I* and *Estelle II*, powered by single Napier Lion engines. Wood had intended to defend with *Miss America VI*, a 26-foot-long power package containing two Packard V12 aircraft engines developing 1,060 hp each. Two weeks before the race, *Miss America VI*, traveling at an incredible, although unofficial, 105 mph, disintegrated, nearly killing Orlin Johnson, the mechanic. Divers retrieved the engines, which were cleaned and overhauled and installed in the newly completed *Miss America VII*. Riding with the bandaged Johnson, Wood again successfully defended the trophy while Miss Carstairs capsized. She returned the following year with *Estelle IV*, powered by triple Napier Lion engines generating 3,000 hp. Wood defended with *Miss America VIII*. This time Miss Carstairs retired with engine trouble, but spectators watched an awesome display of power in the close finish between Wood in his newest raceboat followed by his brother George driving *Miss America VII*.

The scenario was repeated in 1930. Two new *Estelles*, *IV* and *V*, challenged *Miss Americas V, VIII*, and the new *IX*. *Estelle V* retired with engine problems in the first heat, followed by *Estelle IV* in the second, leaving the race to a duel again between the brothers. At this point, Betty Carstairs, nearly $400,000 poorer due to her racing efforts, retired from further challenges.

Later in 1930 England's Sir Henry Segrave set a new world water speed record of 98.76 mph on Lake Windermere with *Miss England II*. However, on a subsequent run *Miss England II*, powered by two 3,600-hp aircraft engines, cartwheeled, killing Segrave. To regain the record, Wood took *Miss America IX* to Indian River in Florida. He had had the Packard engines supercharged, a process in which power output is boosted by forcing air or a mixture of air and fuel into the combustion chamber of an engine under pressure. This boosted the output

50

from 1,060 hp each to 1,400 hp each. Here Wood toppled another barrier, becoming the first man to break officially 100 mph in a boat. And once again, he ruled as the fastest man on the water. It was a brief reign, though.

Miss England II had been resurrected and modified. Within four months of Gar's record, the English automobile racing driver Kaye Don took the helm of the rejuvenated *Miss England II* and bumped the record to 104 mph, and then up to 110 mph. Kaye Don next headed for Detroit in an attempt to reclaim the Harmsworth Trophy for the British.

That 1931 Harmsworth race, one of the most controversial, was between Don in *Miss England II*, Gar Wood with *Miss America IX*, and his brother George, as usual, driving the older boat, *Miss America VIII*. It was generally believed that the British boat had superior speed, but as it happened, there was no opportunity to prove it. Initially, Don had refused to allow Gar Wood a forty-five-minute postponement for repairs, contending that the oil in his engines already was warm. At great risk, one of Wood's mechanics then crawled under the deck of the boat and soldered up the full but cracked fuel tank. Wood was now furious at his competitor and determined to "show Don a trick or two."

There is no way of knowing whether what happened next was deliberate or accidental. *Miss America IX* led *Miss England II* over the line before the starting gun sounded. Both were disqualified. *Miss England* then made a sharp turn and rolled over at high speed while *Miss America IX* was flagged off the course. Meanwhile, George Wood ambled by in *Miss America VIII* and won the heat. Brother George cruised around the course the next day, also, to win the Harmsworth. The events led journalists to dub Gar Wood "the wily grey fox of Algonac." But Wood wasn't through with Don yet.

Their duel for the world speed record continued into 1932. In February *Miss America IX* nudged the record up to 111.712 mph. Five months later on Loch Lomond in Scotland, Kaye Don and *Miss England III*, a new craft built by the famous hydroplane firm of John I. Thornycroft & Co. and powered by a new generation of aircraft engine, unleashed 4,400 hp to reach a new record high of *119.81* mph. And only a few months later, the Grey Fox fought back, driving a new boat, *Miss America X*, to a new world water speed record of 124.91 mph.

Miss America X, "while a marvel of construction and mechanical perfection, is not a freak. . . . She is the utmost pinnacle of boat and engine construction and represents all the finest that America can offer," enthused a correspondent for *Rudder* magazine. Actually, there never before was anything like *Miss America X*.

Don's *Miss England III* was the product of some five million dollars spent by the British Air Ministry in developing a more powerful Rolls-Royce aircraft engine. Because of Harmsworth rules, which prohibited Wood from using engines other than ones from his own country, and because America had not developed any new technology, Wood was left with a slower boat. His solution was simple but dangerous. He took the four aircraft engines from the *Miss America*s *VIII* and *IX*, supercharged them to the hilt, and then put all four into a new 38-foot boat—*Miss America X*.

The new British boat was regarded as a distinct improvement over the old one, with "a better planing bottom and better suited to making turns and being kept under control than her predecessor." The twelve-cycle engines were the lightest engines for their power ever designed, weighing only 12 ounces per horsepower. Each engine drove its shaft through a clutch and forward gearbox, with the motors built to operate in opposite rotation. The challenger was nearly 5 feet shorter than *Miss America X* and both boats were similar in hull design. *Miss America X* came to the line with 6,000 horsepower, however, nearly 2,000 more horsepower than *Miss England III*'s. This was no small achievement.

The four motors were linked in tandem in the mahogany hull. One day Wood and a friend had been playing Ping-Pong when Wood threw down his paddle and started sketching diagrams on a large piece of paper. He drew *Miss America X* and then a line down the center, explaining that he believed a beam installed down the center would eliminate the shimmy of the four engines. He and his friend Perry Deakin went to his Algonac, Michigan, boatyard and Wood told Nape Lisee, his builder, and Orlin Johnson, his engineer, what he wanted. As Deakin recalled in a *Nautical Quarterly* article, both said "it wouldn't work; so Gar says to them, 'Well, do you like your job?' 'Yeah,' Nape replies, 'Well that beam goes in here.' And it was put in and it did stop the shimmy. Now that was Gar. He was thinking every minute of how he could do a little better."

This time, in the 1932 Harmsworth, it was just the British challenger against one American defender, *Miss America X*. In the first heat, England's Kaye Don led for four laps before faltering with engine problems and Wood passed him to win by more than a mile.

"It's an old story to Detroiters who have become accustomed to seeing British challengers sink, capsize and break up during the past years. Too much speed in rough water has done its work," wrote the *Motor Boat* correspondent.

The water was rougher in the second heat. Soon after the start *Miss America* leaped ahead while *Miss England II* was "belching great clouds of smoke . . . evidently in some kind of trouble." With the port engine seized up, Don finally threw in the towel and accepted a tow. And the Harmsworth Trophy remained in Detroit.

Gar Wood by now was an American hero, a multimillioniare and the fastest man in the world on the water. His palatial estate called Grey Haven, on Lake St. Clair near Algonac, had among other things a huge indoor swimming pool and a lounge that could seat seventy-five persons. He also had a boat well and a little dry dock, which was home to the *Miss America*s.

The tenth, and last, *Miss America* particularly reflected the precise attention to detail that had caused Gar, the mechanical whiz and inventor, to become a success both on and off the water. The world's fastest boat, weighing seven and a half tons, was perceived to be a typical Wood single-step design. The step was sheathed in quarter-inch Duralumin held in place by steel bolts running up through the frames. But between the metal covering and the hull bottom was a wedge. Rather than the traditional fixed planing step, this step was adjustable, enabling the angle of attack to be varied until the best angle was found. The hull frames were constructed of Michigan rock elm, closely spaced and bolted and screwed together with steel bolts and screws. They were first fastened to a Michigan oak keel and

Miss Detroit III was the first boat fitted with an aircraft engine, a 12-cylinder Curtiss. Wood's idea of using World War I aircraft engines represented a great leap forward in lowering the weight-to-power ratio. *(Courtesy of the Mariners' Museum, Newport News, Virginia)*

supported by four Oregon spruce longitudinal girders running from step to stern. The girders, acting as engine beds, were reinforced the entire length by quarter-inch Duralumin plates bolted along the bearers with angle pieces on top. Wood's builder, Lisee, believed that with this method of construction the hull would have great strength and weight and that hull vibrations would be distributed throughout.

In 1928, when Wood originally received the Packard engines used in the boat, each overhead cam V12 engine was rated to

750 hp at 1,800 rpm, with top engine speed at 2,100 rpm, according to the Packard engineers. By 1932, the original power output had been more than doubled by Wood and Packard engineers, reaching 1,600 hp at 2,600 rpm. Superchargers accounted for most of the increase. Wood installed the four engines as two power plants of twenty-four cylinders each on each side of the boat. The two engines functioned as a single unit by being synchronized and turning as one shaft. Since a gearbox didn't exist that could handle power set in tandem, Wood designed one himself and had it made at his Wood Hydraulic Hoist and Body Company.

Wood faced one more Harmsworth challenge. This came in 1933 when the small 24-foot single-step hydroplane *Miss Britain III* arrived in Detroit. Built of lightweight aluminum and driven by its owner, Hubert Scott-Paine, a wealthy powerboat enthusiast, *Miss Britain III* was a clean aerodynamic form powered by a supercharged 1,375-hp Napier Lion engine. While Wood retained the trophy, the challenger gave a strong showing despite its outmoded single engine.

The rivalry with England that Wood fired when he went to England in 1920 to win the Harmsworth drew to a close. The 1933 race was the last time the Harmsworth Trophy was contested until after World War II. And after spending about ten million dollars for his ten *Miss Americas*, Wood's interest shifted to aviation. His boatbuilding firm, GarWood Boats, Inc., shifted from building pleasure cruisers to landing craft. A few years later, he sold his conglomerate of factories and businesses and retired to Florida. His world water speed record was eclipsed by England's Sir Malcolm Campbell, who progressively boosted it to 126 mph and eventually 142 mph.

Wood pursued a variety of inventive projects in his later years, from helping Howard Hughes build the *Spruce Goose* to building the world's fastest golf cart. By the time he died in 1970 at the age of ninety, the powerboat racing scene had shifted. The game had changed again, with new boats and new races. But before that happened, the Gold Cup boats, those "gentlemen's runabouts," would lose their gentlemanly ways and go for speed.

Chapter 3

The Growl of Thunder: The Unlimiteds

It's a Wonder, one of the first Unlimiteds to have sponsons, was powered by a 1914 vintage Hispano-Suiza aircraft engine. Although a non-prop rider, *It's a Wonder* could run 127 mph on the straightaway and sped to victory in races in 1953 and 1957. *(Courtesy of Fred Farley)*

The gentlemen's runabouts of the 1920s cruised to speeds to 50 mph or so, no faster than they had been in 1916. To rejuvenate spectator interest, the APBA decided to allow steps on the hulls but to keep the 625-cubic-inch engine limit. The Depression came and went, and interest waned further. It was hard to become excited about raceboats whose top speeds were less than half of the 124.9-mph record runs that Gar Wood was producing with *Miss America X*. Gold Cup competition simply paled next to the exploits of the Grey Fox.

In fact, after the 1934 Gold Cup, the *Motor Boat* correspondent was moved to write, "The Gold Cup affair, for the last few years, has become the annual old home week for a select coterie of sportsmen who date back to the days when women swam in bloomers and skirts."

By 1936, rules were changed to allow engines up to 12 liters, which then made Gold Cup boats the same as those in international competition. A year later, the beautiful *Notre Dame*, the first of a series of boats with that name owned by Herbert Mendelson and named after his alma mater, took advantage of the larger engine size and showed the way to the future with brute power, optimized equipment, and flat-out speed.

The craft, which won the 1935 and 1937 Gold Cups, was considered to have one of the most elegant engines ever installed in a boat—a twenty-four-cylinder supercharged Duesenberg. The idea for the engine came from Horace Elgin Dodge, son of the founder of the Dodge Motor Company, whose lifetime pursuit was to win the Gold Cup, a feat he never did achieve. In 1926, though, he hired Fred and August Duesenberg to create the best Gold Cup engine. The brothers delivered two for $25,000, a tidy sum then. Dodge later sold one to Mendelson, a large General Motors stockholder who turned the engine over to the top engine men in GM's research department, mechanic Bert MacKenzie and engineer Paul Miller. Their assignment was to debug the engine and boost the power. They eliminated assorted problems such as crankshaft vibration. Miller designed a centrifugal supercharger with an 8-inch rotor that turned at 32,500 rpm, with the engine itself winding up to the then remarkable speed of 4,600 rpm. The supercharger boosted the intake pressure by 15 pounds per square inch and was the biggest single factor in raising the power output. As built by Duesenberg, this superb engine, having three banks of eight cylinders, developed 400 hp. By the time the GM whizzes were through, it produced a mighty 900 hp.

The first of Mendelson's boats sank in the 1938 Gold Cup race. The famous engine, though, was retrieved and installed in a second *Notre Dame*, which had a series of design flaws. At this point, Mendelson commissioned Dan Arena, a young driver from California who favored the new three-point hull. Mendelson's more traditional views prevailed, and instead they built the third *Notre Dame* as a stepped hydroplane along the lines of the two-point type built by the Fred Jacoby Boat Works of North Bergen, New Jersey, which had become dominant in outboard hydroplane racing. The 22-foot-long gleaming mahogany craft with a 3-foot overhang beyond the transom was regarded as one of the most beautiful raceboats. It also made speed fashionable again. In 1940, Arena drove *Notre Dame* to 100 mph, the first Gold Cup boat to reach this speed. But it no longer was enough. The era of the three-point hydroplane was beginning.

The 1938 Gold Cup saw the arrival of *My Sin*, a three-point hydroplane designed by Arno Apel, who had been developing these hulls for more than twenty-five years. His first effort toward sponsons was *Tech Jr.* in 1912, a boat that was fast in a straight line but had trouble turning. Twenty years later Apel's designs dominated the popular 225-cubic-inch class with speeds

With Jack Regas at the helm, *Hawaii Kai III* set a mile straightaway record of 187.627 mph in 1957 and went on to win the national high-point championship. Built in 1956 by Les Staudacher and Ted Jones, the rose- and coral-colored Unlimited had a plywood hull sheathed in metal and powered by a supercharged Allison airplane engine. *(Courtesy of Fred Farley)*

running higher at times than in the supposedly faster Gold Cup boats. Apel knew that air trapped under the hulls of his three-point hydroplanes generated lift, and he shaped the forward sections to benefit from this. *My Sin* was Apel's adaption of this concept to Gold Cup boats. In the 1941 Gold Cup on the Navesink River in Red Bank, New Jersey, *My Sin* cruised around the course to win as the only entry. The two other competitors didn't show up. War was approaching, and racing came to a halt as World War II took first priority.

When the Gold Cup races resumed in 1946 on the Detroit River, the rules had been changed to allow the Gold Cup boats once again to use unlimited engine power; hulls could be as long as 40 feet. This was the beginning of the modern-day class of Unlimiteds, the fastest raceboats in the world.

The durable Dan Arena arrived for the 1946 race with a new and untested *Miss Golden Gate III* and went on to shatter the speed records for seven consecutive laps. Wrote the *Yachting* correspondent, "Her thunderous roar and tremendous spuming wake brought the crowd to its feet and it never occurred to anyone to sit down." But suddenly the boat stopped dead in the water with oil-circulation problems, and bandleader Guy Lombardo went on to an easy victory in his *Tempo VI*. Arena's new weapon was a twelve-cylinder General Motors Allison aircraft engine, the same engine used in such fighter planes as the Lockheed P-38 Lightning and the Curtiss P-40 Warhawk. This was the first time a modern aircraft engine was used to propel a powerboat.

Since the rule change allowing unlimited engine power, competitors quickly picked up at bargain prices surplus World War II aircraft engines that could turn out twice the horsepower of *Notre Dame*'s Duesenberg. Engines costing $45,000 new were being unloaded at $2,500 or so each.

Although Arena never did win the Gold Cup, three of his designs did and, in all, his boats set twenty world records, capped by the 1962 run made by *Miss United States* with Roy Duby driving. On Lake Guntersville, Alabama, this craft topped 200 mph on a straight run, a record for piston-engined propeller-driven boats that remains unbroken.

Dan Arena's racing career spanned the transition in which Gold Cup competition once again emerged into an all-out contest for speed. Advancement continued in the late 1940s and early 1950s with John Hacker's designs for *My Sweetie* and *Miss Pepsi*. But it was Stanley Sayres of Seattle who revolutionized the sport.

The Unlimiteds now had power. Sayres, with the design talents of Ted Jones, provided the boat to go with it. In 1940, Sayres, a competitor in the outboard division for many years, bought *Tops III*, one of the most successful three-point hydroplanes in the smaller 225 class. This became the first *Slo-Mo-Shun*. During the early 1950s, the *Slo-Mo-Shuns IV* and *V* made

Bill Muncey won more Unlimited races than anyone else in a twenty-five-year career that ended with his death in 1981. He won a total of 62 victories, 7 national titles, and 8 Gold Cups. (*Courtesy of Fred Farley*)

all other types of hull configuration obsolete. Sayres swept the Gold Cup five times, from 1950 through 1954, with drivers Ted Jones, Lou Fageol, Stan Dollar, and Joe Taggart, wrenching the cup and the competition from Detroit to Seattle.

Sho-Mo-Shun IV was the model for the thunderboats racing today. Jones had driven the three-point outboard hydroplanes originally conceived by Apel, boats which ran on a few inches of twin sponsons forward and the edge of the bottom at the transom. With the increased power of the aircraft engines, Jones finally had the power to get the boat riding higher off the water with almost no wetted surface, riding on half of the high-revving propeller alone instead of on the transom bottom. *Slo-Mo-Shun IV*, the first Jones boat of this design, blasted to a world straightaway speed record of 160.32 mph in 1950 and upped it to 178.49 mph two years later.

"I found out the thing would idle at a hundred miles an hour," said Jones of his early tests with *Slo-Mo-Shun IV*. "I'd just punch it and it would go up to a hundred and ninety mph before I even got my foot off it." The 28-foot-long craft had a mahogany hull with Duralumin and an oak frame. In addition to its design, *Slo-Mo-Shun IV*'s success was due to its weight-to-horsepower ratio of 3:1, meaning the boat weighed 4,600 pounds compared to the 1,600 horsepower of its Rolls-Allison engine. The propeller spun three times for every revolution of the engine. Indeed, this was the design to harness the full power of the aircraft engine.

When he first tested his design, Ted Jones also discovered the dilemma that still confronts Unlimited teams today. At 75 mph the boats start to become airborne. Around 100 mph they rise up to ride on the propeller and sponson tips. And beyond 150 mph they *are* airborne. To keep them from flying out of control and blowing over, or lifting up and flipping upside down, requires tremendous skill and sometimes just plain luck.

Slo-Mo-Shun IV brought the Gold Cup to the Northwest, to the protected waters of Lake Washington, far from the treacherous Detroit River where boat wakes ricochet from shore to shore. Seattle became the capital of Unlimited powerboat racing. The Seattle fans were then, and still are, fervent in their support, with hundreds of thousands of people showing up for the Unlimited events. When *Slo-Mo-Shun IV* was destroyed in a 1956 crash in Detroit, the pieces were flown back to Seattle and parked on a truck next to a scaffold erected to accommodate the mourners.

As the boats and the costs of campaigning them became increasingly expensive in the postwar years, the owners searched for sponsors willing to pay to have their names flashed before tens of thousands of spectators. Some of the first "floating billboards" included *Miss Pepsi* and *Such Crust*, the latter entered by Schafer Bakeries of Detroit. Sayres also received corporate support. With Mobil Oil as his main sponsor, he had assistance from twenty-four other companies, mainly from the Seattle area.

The Gold Cup trophy succeeded the Harmsworth in importance in North America, and the international trophy remained idle until it was rejuvenated as a prize in international competition for offshore powerboats, which emerged in the 1950s.

For pure speed over water, *Slo-Mo-Shun IV* in 1952 was the only Unlimited to set the pace. Then England's Donald Campbell, the son of Sir Malcolm Campbell, carried on his father's tradition of speed with a series of craft called *Bluebird*. Sir Malcolm's speed records prior to World War II had been lost to *Slo-Mo-Shun IV*. Donald Campbell retrieved them in 1955 with *Bluebird*, the first jet-propelled boat to break the 200-mph barrier. In a series of *Bluebirds*, Campbell progressively raised the world record, reaching 276.3 mph in 1964. Campbell, who had been forced to mortgage his home to continue financing his dreams of even-greater speed, also was the first person to break the 300-mph barrier. On January 4, 1967, Campbell had been clocked at 328 mph on Coniston Water in the English Lake District. Then his starboard sponson rose up, hit the water, and flew off. *Bluebird* somersaulted and disintegrated on hitting the water, killing Campbell.

The trouble with records is that they tend to be fleeting; there always seems to be someone fighting to climb to the top and claim a new Mount Everest. Three months after Campbell was killed, his old record was superseded by a new one of 285.2 mph set by Lee Taylor of Bellflower, California. Taylor's fas-

In 1979, on Seattle's Lake Washington, *Miss Budweiser* accelerated through the 200 mph "twilight zone" and then cartwheeled in a shower of spray and debris. (*Photo by Gary Tollman*, Seattle Post-Intelligencer)

cination with speed began when as a teenager he saw a raceboat in a movie. A 1964 crash before his first record attempt left him in a coma for eighteen days, but his desire remained intact. By 1978, Taylor's record had been replaced by Ken Warby of Australia, who upped the ante to 317.6 mph.

On November 13, 1980, Taylor was poised to snatch the record back. His 40-foot rocketboat called *Discovery* was constructed of aluminum and stainless steel and powered by hydrogen peroxide fuel that could generate 8,000 pounds of thrust, developing an amazing 16,000 horsepower. The forty-six-year-old Taylor, in fact, believed *Discovery* was capable of speeds surpassing 600 mph. In tests the spring before with his remarkable $2.5-million boat, which he described as "a piloted water missile," he was clocked at 350 mph; he believed he was close to 400 mph. On that November day on Nevada's Lake Tahoe, the incredible missile-shaped boat was demolished in two, maybe three, seconds. Traveling at 330 mph, the boat disintegrated and disappeared under the lake's smooth surface.

"In five seconds, everything was gone," said an observer. "Lee's helmet was floating in the water. The helicopter flew right to it, but there was nothing else to see but some bubbles."

Films of the accident show that the left sponson seemed to rise and then land hard enough to submerge. Hooking the water at that speed, the boat barrel-rolled, turning over and simultaneously going backward. "Danger is something that goes with the territory, and Lee probably knew it as well as anybody," said Dave Severson, Taylor's longtime friend.

In Unlimited competition, higher speeds brought higher risk. One driver, though, seemed to belie this. Bill Muncey, who left his father's Chevrolet dealership in Detroit to become a professional powerboat driver, raced for nearly thirty years. The length of his career and his unparalleled number of victories were remarkable in a sport noticeable for its lack of "veterans."

"There has always been the recognition of risk within the sport, but somehow Muncey seemed beyond that," remarked John Love, then executive director of the APBA.

Muncey drove his first Unlimited, *Miss Great Lakes* (the former *Miss Golden Gate III*), in 1950 at the age of nineteen after meeting with success in a smaller class of boats. It was not an auspicious beginning. Muncey, anxious to prove himself, drove *Miss Great Lakes* hard, passing the veterans. After he moved up to fourth place, *Miss Great Lakes* started to fall apart. The boat slowed and sank and Muncey was picked up by a rescue boat. It would be five years before he would be asked to drive another Unlimited. Then he received two offers, one from Horace Dodge, a member of the automobile family, and the other from Willard Rhodes of Seattle, the owner of *Miss Thriftway*, a new three-point hydroplane, whose offer he accepted. His first success was at the helm of *Miss Thriftway*, designed for the owner of Thriftway Stores by Ted Jones and built by Les Staudacher, who was in the business of manufacturing church pews and built racing hulls on the side. With *Miss Thriftway*, Muncey won eighteen races, starting with the Gold Cup in 1956 and ending with the Diamond Cup in 1963.

One of the odder moments in *Miss Thriftway*'s distinguished career was the 1958 Seattle Gold Cup competition, which had drawn a tremendous crowd of 750,000 spectators. As Muncey entered a turn leading at 160 mph, the rudder disappeared. He was headed straight off the course with no control at an unstoppable 160 mph. *Miss Thriftway* cut across the boats coming up from behind and ran straight into a Coast Guard patrol boat, sinking it in less than a minute.

For Muncey this meant another trip to the hospital. He was becoming philosophical about his injuries. "Anything less than death is a minor injury," he remarked at one point. And another time, he said, "Kidneys are amazing. I happen to have ruptured mine four times and still they perform remarkably well."

Muncey's career was distinguished by its ups and downs. "Sure, he won more races than anyone else," said Unlimited historian Fred Farley. "He also lost more than anyone else."

Not until the 1960s did Muncey's racing style develop to the point where he could win three heats in one day. And after reaching the top, he stumbled. From 1973 to 1975, Muncey lost thirty races in a row. "People thought he was over the hill," recalled Farley. "Then he went out and bought the *Pay 'n Pak* team, became an owner and went on to some great years. He had the quality of being able to rebound and perform brilliantly."

Muncey tended to stay with one team at a time rather than hop from one to another. His racing career was primarily with Rhodes, Lee Schoenith, owner of the Gale boats, and O. H. Frisbie, chairman of Atlas Van Lines. Muncey teamed up with Frisbie in 1971 and would drive the Atlas Van Line boats to fame.

The Thriftway boats had replaced the Allison aircraft engines with Rolls-Royce Merlin engines, which during the war had powered the Spitfire and Hurricane fighter planes. The Merlin proved superior to the Allison because of its two-stage supercharging. Those used in Unlimiteds were built by Packard under an agreement worked out with Rolls-Royce during World War II. When the war started in Europe in 1939, it was clear fighter plane engines were going to be a critical factor. America was producing the Allison engine while England had the Rolls-Royce Merlin. However, England's factories were being destroyed by German bombs. In desperation, the English arranged for the Merlin to be built in America by Packard, and the engines subsequently were used in both American and English planes. Rolls-Royce sent Packard the plans for its engines. The companies agreed no Rolls-Royce engineers would accompany the drawings to avoid friction, as the Packard engineers would have to adapt the drawings to their tooling and manufacturing procedures.

The first Packard-built Rolls-Royce Merlin came off the production line only a year later, a time span regarded as an engineering feat. It was these American-built Merlins that found their way into Unlimited competition. The Unlimited teams had developed the Merlin to the point where it put out 2,500 hp, which could be boosted to 3,000 hp when the driver pushed a button on the steering wheel to inject nitrous oxide into the engine. Nitrous oxide, also known as laughing gas, can increase engine output considerably but at the same time it puts a great strain on the engine. The Merlin would power the Unlimiteds until the 1970s when the Rolls-Royce Griffon engine, with 1,000 to 1,200 more horsepower, became the power plant of choice.

As speeds nudged upward, the chance of blowovers escalated. Muncey, who spent his racing life on the hairy edge, went some twenty years without a severe accident. Then, dur-

Dean Chenoweth, the top Unlimited driver at the start of the
1980s, was killed in 1982 when his *Miss Budweiser* somersaulted
and crashed during a qualifying run on the Columbia River.

ing the final heat of the world championship race in Acapulco in October 1981, *Atlas Van Lines* was tearing down the back-stretch at 180 mph when it blew over, killing Muncey at the age of fifty-two. He had won more races than anyone else: seven national titles, eight Gold Cups, and sixty-two career victories.

Before the race, Muncey had been playing catch-up all season with *Miss Budweiser* and its powerful Rolls Griffon engine. Muncey did not take kindly to losing. "I have never been able to come to grips with myself about losing," he had said. "It's just unacceptable. But I don't see anything wrong with being a poor loser as long as you remain a good sport."

Driver Chip Hanauer, who would later be tapped to take Muncey's place at the wheel of *Atlas Van Lines*, recalled Muncey's last heat. "He drove incredibly well. He made the finest start of his life. He had that boat so wrung out. . . . He hit the line at least fifty miles an hour faster than anybody else, right on the button. . . . The problem was, and this is something I battle with, that he was driving with his emotions. If at some point he'd been analytical about it and said, 'Look, I've got a handle on this now,' he would have survived; but no, he was out in front, and he was just going to rub their noses in it. He was angry. And he just drove the boat over backwards. If he hadn't let emotion take completely over, he'd have won that race, he'd have beaten the Budweiser."

Miss Budweiser, new in 1979, was designed by Ron Jones, the second generation of the talented Unlimited design family. In addition to the Rolls Griffon engine, the boat featured a new cabover design with the driver's cockpit placed ahead of the engine, and a custom horizontal stabilizer wing to propel the craft through tight corners. Budweiser team owner Bernie Little had entered Unlimited competition in 1962 and by 1988 he had become the most successful owner in the history of the sport. Success has not come without a price.

With his super new *Miss Budweiser* and the Griffon engines, driver Dean Chenoweth became the second Unlimited racer in history to crack the 200-mph barrier on October 23, 1979. Then, with the boat's speed climbing toward 220 mph, submerged debris sheared off the rudder and propeller. *Miss Budweiser* soared skyward, dumping Chenoweth into the water a split second before crashing in a shower of wreckage. His survival, with fractured ribs and pelvis, was considered a miracle. In August 1980 Chenoweth flipped again during a qualifying run for a Seattle race, this time breaking more ribs and a shoulder blade. In 1982, Chenoweth, who began racing in 1968, brought *Miss Budweiser* up to 175 mph on the Columbia River for a qualifying run in the Columbia Cup Race when its bow lifted. The boat somersaulted, crashing upside down and killing Chenoweth.

Within a year, the sport's top two drivers had been killed on the racecourse. As the sport moved into the 1980s the emphasis was on safety, as a new engine, the Lycoming helicopter turbine, started to challenge the World War II aircraft power plants.

Chapter 4

Pushing to the Limits: The Don Aronow Era in Offshore Racing

Kiekhaefer Aeromarine #3 (right) heads for another victory while being pursued by airborne press photographers in 1971. *(Courtesy of Kiekhaefer Aeromarine, Inc.)*

"Riding in a boat at seventy miles an hour is like jumping off of a building from the seventh floor," Rocky Marciano once said. The heavyweight fighter never suffered a knockdown in his boxing career. However, as the story goes, he hit the deck thirty-two times in a Bahamas 500 race in the mid-1960s riding as crew with Dick Genth. When Genth stopped in Nassau, the halfway point, Marciano got out of the boat. Genth explained the race wasn't over. "For me it is," Marciano replied.

In another race in the 1960s Don Aronow and Knocky House, his longtime riding mechanic, jumped into the water and scrambled aboard their inflatable after their boat caught fire off Nassau Harbor. While pushing out from under the lee of the burning boat, House cut his arm and spilled a considerable amount of blood over the raft. Aronow, noticing the blood dripping into the water, said "Stop bleeding, Knocky. There are sharks around here."

The offshore powerboat racing that emerged in South Florida was a rough sport, attracting a colorful cast of characters. They were individuals who liked their racing wild and crazy, who purposely scheduled races during the windiest months of the year, and who thought nothing of delaying a start until the wind picked up over 10 knots to make crossing the Gulf Stream interesting. They were men, and a few women, who enjoyed pushing 25-foot boats over 10-foot seas, the wind and spray in their faces, and didn't seem daunted when their boats burned and sank or delaminated en route. They were the pioneers, the inventors, the adventurers.

In the process of creating the sport, they created the offshore powerboat—today's deep vee hull—as well as the revolutionary sterndrive form of propulsion. They were the test pilots for the new hull material called Fiberglas, for new propellers, steering systems, and a host of other developments. They raced production boats taken off the showroom floor and when they broke, they glued them back together; when they needed a special part, they made it.

The most colorful of these personalities was Donald Joel Aronow. Before he retired from racing in 1969, after winning two world and three national championships, this Brooklyn-born real estate developer of Russian-Jewish ancestry had created the long, needlenose racing machines and the sexy, macho image that essentially established the market for high-performance boats. He then set out to fill that market. After he had purchased a tract of land on the Intracoastal Waterway at N.E. 188th Street in North Miami Beach, Aronow carved boat companies out of the pinellas pines over the next twenty-five years. In all, he created six companies, starting with Formula, which began operations in Miami Beach, followed by Magnum, Donzi, Cigarette, Squadron XII, and USA Racing Team. In the intervening years, Cigarette, named after a Brooklyn rumrunner, has become virtually a generic name for high-performance boats, and the block-long N.E. 188th Street has been nicknamed Fleet Street after its most famous resident. Don Aronow defined the sport.

The sport, however, started without him. The first rough water offshore powerboat race of the modern era in the United States was the Miami-to-Nassau race created by Capt. Sherman "Red" Crise, a flamboyant promoter, and first held in 1957. Offshore racing already had been launched in California: In 1955, offshore outboard racing was inaugurated with two races in Long Beach, another in La Jolla, and the longest, a 120-mile, three-lap competition, in Paradise Cove-Ocean Park. By 1956, these bluewater races were being praised by *Yachting* magazine: "There is nothing like these ocean distance races to test inherent

Don Aronow's racing career peaked in 1969 with his 32-foot offshore design, the Cigarette, powered by twin 475 hp MerCruiser engines. *(John Crouse photo)*

strengths and weaknesses of stock outboard runabout and cruiser hulls and engines."

In South Florida in the early 1950s, there were some pickup races, coastal skirmishes including a dash from Key West to Havana. Adventure, drama, and ultimately sport arrived at the hands of Crise, whose earliest success dated to the mid-1930s when he ran midget-auto races in the New York area. Crise had made a tidy sum in car racing and by 1956 he was running an annual sports-car contest in Nassau, sponsored by the Bahamas tourism authority which had hired him. In offshore powerboat racing he saw the potential for an exciting promotion, and with backing from the Bahamian authorities, Crise became the self-appointed impresario of the new sport. His first Miami–Nassau Ocean Powerboat Race, which made its debut in 1957, was won in 9 hours 20 minutes by Sam Griffith, a charismatic United States Army Air Corps veteran from Miami who dominated the early years of the sport.

Griffith had nerves of steel, driving into 6-foot seas at 50 mph without blinking, an attitude undoubtedly conditioned by his days as a flier in which he narrowly escaped death several times. (Once in North Africa he had to bail out of his plane but his parachute didn't open. Griffith was saved by landing in the only river for miles around.) Griffith won the race again in 1958, while Gordon Hoover (of the Hoover vacuum company), in one of the first fiberglass raceboats, took first place in 1959.

The 1960 race shaped the future of powerboating not just in the United States but throughout the world. Richard A. Bertram, a Miami yacht broker and sailor, won with a new 31-footer named *Moppie* powered by two 275-hp Interceptor engines. With him, as reported by *Yachting*, "were Carleton Mitchell, twice winner of the Newport–Bermuda race with the yawl *Finisterre*, as navigator, and Sam Griffith, a fearless Miami co-pilot. . . . The fiberglass inboard was designed by C. Raymond Hunt of Boston, distinguished naval architect in sail and power." *Moppie*, the forerunner of the Bertram yachts of today, set a course record of 8 hours flat in the stormy 184-mile passage across the Gulf Stream. Second to finish was a smaller Hunt design similar to *Moppie* and driven by Jim Wynne; it was powered by the first two production Volvo sterndrives, built from Wynne's design. The rest of the fleet straggled in the next day.

"We totally outclassed the field because of the deep vee and, in my case, the sterndrive," said Wynne. "This started the development of boats that would run much faster." That development quickly followed in 1961 with the Bertram Yacht Company's production run of the Bertram 31.

To place in perspective the elements of that pivotal 1960 race, one has to back up a bit. Dick Bertram was a sailor and a first-rate crewman in offshore ocean racing. During 1958, when he was serving as foredeck crew on *Vim* during the America's Cup selection trials, Bertram admired *Vim*'s tender, a 23-foot prototype designed by C. Raymond Hunt and owned by Jakob Isbrandtsen. Hunt, a Boston naval architect, had been experimenting with the deep vee hull form in the late 1950s, based on his experience with earlier craft of his design coupled with the new possibilities inherent in the lightweight, powerful engines that had started coming out of Detroit. He also was a student of Lindsay Lord, another Boston naval architect who was the author of the classic text *The Naval Architecture of Planing Hulls*.

The first Hunt deep-vee was a 23-foot wooden prototype with surface propellers built by Charlie and Sam Wharton in Jamestown, Rhode Island. This was followed by four fiberglass versions made by Bill Dyer for Essex Fiber Boat, one of which was sold to Isbrandtsen. Bertram eventually bought the tender from Isbrandtsen and then asked Hunt to design a 31-foot wooden version. The Hunt design had a deep-vee section to the underbody, which allowed it to knife through the waves. Horizontal planing strips on each side of the bottom, running fore and aft, lifted the hull so it could plane efficiently. Impressed by *Moppie*'s performance on Biscayne Bay, Bertram decided to enter it in the 1960 Miami–Nassau Race. Before climbing aboard this odd vee-shaped hull for the start, Griffith said disdainfully, "looks like a damn sailboat."

"All those early races were rough-water races," Bertram later recalled. "If there had been a flat-water race, I might have lost interest. . . . I wanted to see how different hulls and gear stood up to rough water. . . . I'm oriented to the performance of boats, and that's why the sport grabbed me."

In the meantime, Wynne powered to the starting line in a 24-foot Hunt deep-vee built by Marscott Plastics in Fall River, Massachusetts, and fitted with two 80-hp Volvo sterndrives.

"The boat would only do thirty to thirty-three miles an hour," said Wynne. "But because of the roughness of the race, we kept going full speed all the time. The only other boat to beat us was Dick Bertram with the bigger *Moppie*. We outlasted everybody else because of the roughness. That was fun. And the publicity that ensued was good for me, for Volvo, and for the deep vee."

Because of its success in the Miami–Nassau race, the Hunt deep-vee was acclaimed as a breakthrough and the resulting publicity established his hulls. But his deep-vee was not the first. Lindsay Lord in Boston and Harold C. "Pappy" Seaman of Long Branch, New Jersey, were designing deep vee hulls for the rumrunners during Prohibition, and others such as John Hacker were moving in that direction. As Pappy Seaman once explained, he started moving the vee section aft to soften the ride because the pounding the flat-bottomed skiffs were taking in the surf was causing the bottles to break. "I just kept moving the vee back until it reached the transom and I had the first dihedral [deep vee] hull," Seaman said. In the late 1920s, Seaman also was the first to take the outboard engine inboard, installing it ahead of the transom in a covered well to protect it from the ocean spray. Years later, Jim Wynne, then a young Miami marine engineer, was also motivated to move the power inside the boat and in the process created a new propulsion system.

Wynne had worked for Mercury Marine for five years after graduating from the Massachusetts Institute of Technology in 1953. He left at the end of 1957 to form his own consulting business. Wynne had raced inboard hydroplanes and runabouts since high school and while working for Mercury competed in the first Miami–Nassau race, finishing fourth in a boat powered by four Mercury outboards.

As a result of his experience with big outboard motors, Wynne concluded there had to be a better way. In the spring of 1958, working in his mother's garage in North Miami, Wynne assembled a new type of power plant, the first successful sterndrive. He attached a four-cylinder, four-cycle Volvo marine inboard engine through the transom to an outboard drive.

"I wanted to combine the advantages of an inboard, specifically an engine inside the boat that would be protected, and still have the steering and tilting drive of the outboard, which was more effective," Wynne explained. "They had been around before but there hadn't been one that worked properly." Wynne tested his prototype that summer, patented it, and then licensed Volvo to produce it. Wynne devoted the next seven years to "real serious racing activity" to further develop the Volvo sterndrive.

The sterndrive, also known as the inboard/outboard or simply I/O, opened up an entirely new segment of the boating industry between the outboard and the conventional big inboard. That segment has been the most rapidly growing portion of the boating field since 1960. For use in pleasure boats, the sterndrive offers the advantage of being able to steer with the trimming device, and its tilting drive allows a boat to be run up on the beach or onto a trailer.

The 1960 race set the crazy, inventive pace the sport would take during the decade. In 1961 Bertram and Griffith returned with a fiberglass version of the 31-foot *Moppie* named *Glass Moppie*. They dashed across the long stretch of the Bahamas Bank in calm water, stopping briefly at Frazier's Hog Cay to pick up a 55-gallon drum of gasoline. Refueling on the run, they finished in a breathless 4 hours 20 minutes.

The following year Aronow arrived on the scene as did the crusty Carl Kiekhaefer, the legendary engine manufacturer who founded Mercury Marine. Kiekhaefer wasn't enamored of ocean racing. He felt it didn't prove anything, but he couldn't abide sitting on the sidelines. After successfully campaigning stock cars and seeing his Mercury motors dominate outboard racing in the 1950s, he entered a small fleet in the 1962 Miami–Nassau race. Aronow entered a 27-foot wooden boat, named *Claudia* after his daughter and built by Howard Abbey of Miami.

Kiekhaefer won with *AOKone*, a 25-foot Bertram hull driven by Johnny Bakos and powered by a MerCruiser sterndrive. AOK stood for Alumni of Kiekhaefer, presumably a tongue-in-cheek reference to Wynne and others who had worked for Mercury. By merging his company with the Brunswick Corporation of Chicago, Kiekhaefer got around some of Wynne's patents and produced his 310-hp MerCruiser sterndrive, which was based on the Chevrolet truck engine. Kiekhaefer put two MerCruisers into *AOKone* and Bakos raced across the mirror-calm course to lower the record to 3 hours 42 minutes 20 seconds. *Claudia* crossed the line fourth. But the race was enough to move Aronow to action, both on and off the water.

Before taking up the sport at the age of thirty-four, Aronow already had seen considerable action. Lying about his age, he had enlisted in the United States Merchant Marine as a teenager during World War II and was assigned to a supply ship making the run across the North Atlantic to Murmansk, Russia. German

Don Aronow and Jim Wynne toast their victory in the 1977 Palm Bay Offshore Invitational race for stock boats. This was the first time the two former world champions rode in the same cockpit. *(John Crouse photo)*

submarines and aircraft in the North Sea made this run one of the deadliest. Yet at nineteen Aronow emerged from the war unscathed and went on to attend Brooklyn College, earning letters in football, wrestling, and track.

Somewhere along the line, recalled John Crouse, Aronow's publicist for twenty-five years, the 6-foot 3-inch, 210-pound, ruggedly handsome Aronow with the square jaw and wide smile was offered a screen test for the role of Tarzan, but declined. Aronow's first wife Shirley was the daughter of a successful New Jersey real estate developer and Aronow took the same path, first working for his father-in-law and then leaving to form his own company.

While building garden apartments on the Jersey shore, Aronow owned a series of four Jersey Speed Skiffs all built by the respected Hans Pedersen & Sons yard in Keyport. He raced the skiffs in Sandy Hook Bay and the Shrewsbury River and started learning about fast boats from Pappy Seaman. As fate would have it, Aronow himself would become Seaman's modern counterpart—building high-speed offshore boats for both the drug runners and the Coast Guard.

By the age of twenty-eight Aronow was a millionaire. By the age of thirty-one he had retired and moved to Florida. Three years later, he was bored and hanging around the waterfront. The Miami waterfront at that time was an exciting place. Red Crise's Miami–Nassau race was drawing international attention, the competition was tough, and the equipment was evolving.

Aronow was intrigued by the race, which seemed a lark compared to the runs across the cold Atlantic to Murmansk. But it was generally believed that "everything he knew about boatbuilding wouldn't fill a thimble," as John Crouse put it.

"This is no discredit to Don, but Don was not a boatman, as such," said Jim Wynne. "He was not adept at handling boats and did not have a feel for design in the early days. But he learned very rapidly."

Indeed, he did.

"Despite the fact that everyone, including me, thinks Don didn't know a thing about boats, Aronow had so many breakthroughs because he was a bright, ballsy guy," observed Allan "Brownie" Brown, a former racer and builder and now an inventor and consultant who has been a part of the sport since the 1961 Miami–Nassau race.

In his first Miami–Nassau race, Aronow learned from his experience with *Claudia*, a modified vee-hull built of plywood, that the deep-vee and fiberglass were the keys to speed offshore. Within a year after the race, Aronow had founded Formula Marine and hired Jim Wynne and his partner Walt Walters to design a 23-foot offshore machine. This was the highly successful Formula 233 hull. Next Aronow sold Formula to Thunderbird Marine. At this time, Dick Genth, who had entered offshore competition via a misadventure during the 1963 Miami–Nassau race, was a salesman for Thunderbird. Genth went on to head Chris-Craft and Wellcraft and later purchase and rejuvenate Donzi. Donzi, now located in Televast, Florida, was the second boat company created by Aronow and the first located on N.E. 188th Street.

Genth, a U.S. Air Force test pilot for many years, received a call at the airbase one day from Dick Pope, who had owned Cypress Gardens in Winter Haven, Florida. Pope was looking for a navigator for the Miami–Nassau Race and told Genth that he was offering a two-week paid vacation in Nassau in exchange. Genth volunteered. He found himself crossing the Gulf Stream in a 20-foot boat in huge, stormy seas. "I had never ridden in a boat before," Genth related. "The driver said we had to go back. I said we couldn't, the seas were too big. He literally quit driving, so I took the wheel. We went from Miami to Cat Cay, fifty miles across. It took us seven and a half hours and just beat the hell out of us. Then we left there to go to Nassau and sank at midnight that night. A cucumber freighter out of Andros picked us up. The next morning we arrived back at Cat Cay. I got off, chartered this little plane, and went to Nassau. I had my vacation coming. As it turned out, I went into the hospital in Nassau for a couple of weeks and had a big hospital bill to pay." Despite the bashing he took, Genth has been involved with fast boats since that first race.

Meanwhile, Aronow's Formula hulls performed beautifully and proved formidable on the racecourse. But it wasn't until his record-smashing victory in the 1965 Miami–Nassau race at the helm of the 28-foot Donzi *007* that he began to be recognized as a force in the sport. The company and the boat, designed by Wynne and Walters, were inadvertently named by Aronow's attractive secretary who tended to refer to him as "Donzi, baby." So, Donzi it became. And Donzi became the first boat company to build high-performance boats exclusively.

Aronow next sold Donzi to Teleflex and moved next door to create Magnum Marine. With the Magnum 27, Aronow achieved the long and lean shape and flashy style that would eventually distinguish an offshore high-performance boat from any other. Basically, he did this by taking the 23-foot-long Donzi, with an 8-foot beam, and cutting it in half and adding 4 feet to the middle. "He was taking the deep-vees and making them longer—to twenty-seven, then thirty-six and thirty-nine feet, and still with an eight-foot beam," said Wynne. "And the boats got better and better. A long, narrow boat is better for very high speeds, and as power became available, he could get those speeds with a larger, longer boat."

With his boats, Aronow "took basic designs and modified them and did so very effectively," said Wynne. "He was not a designer but rather an innovator with tremendous promotional ability and a very astute businessman. He had a great ability to grasp things quickly whether technically, socially, or financially. He was very quick-witted."

From 1967 until his retirement from racing in 1969, Aronow broke course or world records in each of his sixteen victories, driving a series of deep vee hulls to fame in races in the United States, Europe, and Sweden. During this campaign, he used a variety of single and twin inboard rigs as well as multiple outboards to prove he could win using any kind of power. He was gaining recognition not only as a top builder but as the foremost driver as well.

Aronow, who wore his reputation as a ladies' man with a twinkle in his eyes and a big grin, was the source of more stories than Agatha Christie. He had a cavalier approach at times, a certain nonchalance; but in business he was tough, very tough, a man who prided himself on his ability to cut the better deal. With friends, he was warm and open. And unquestionably, he was not dull.

One time a young man who had just started building high-performance boats with jet drives, pleaded with Aronow, his hero, to take a ride in one of his boats. Finally, Aronow agreed. "Coming back, Don roars up to the dock and cuts the engine," chuckled John Crouse. "He didn't know anything about jet drives. He didn't know that if you cut the engine you lose all your steering. Aronow slams into a piling, the boat splits in two and starts filling up with water. The kid looks up at his hero in disbelief and Don turns to him and says, 'See, kid, you could have got killed in this boat.'"

Another incident occurred when Aronow was on board the 115-foot yacht of a fellow racer in the Mediterranean. The other driver was aboard with his mistress when his wife unexpectedly arrived on a motor launch. The wife pulled out a Beretta intent on killing her husband and then herself, said Crouse. "Aronow

The checkered flag was no stranger to Betty Cook, shown here with throttleman John Conner (left), and navigator Dick Clark. Within eight years after she started racing in 1974, Cook had become the sport's premier driver, winning two world and three national titles.

steps in and throws the gun overboard. Then she decides she's going to get the gun or commit suicide and she jumps overboard. Don jumps in after her and saves her," he recalled.

After the Magnum 27, which is still being produced today by Magnum Marine, Aronow sold the company to Apeco and went on to build a boat for himself called *The Cigarette*, with lines similar to the Magnum 27's. Aronow's racing career peaked in 1969 with the 32-foot Cigarette. His first Cigarette was built with Elton Cary, but when his noncompetitive clause expired with Apeco, Aronow returned to Fleet Street to start his next company called Cigarette Racing Team. With one Cary Cigarette hull in Europe and another in the United States, Aronow won a record eight races in a season, a feat no one would equal for eight years, and captured his second world and third national titles. At the Viareggio race that year he set the Offshore speed record of 74.3 statute mph.

"The Magnum 35 was the first big runabout," explained Allan Brown, who helped Aronow launch his first boat and then worked with him at Donzi. "The Cary 49 was the predecessor of all the big Magnums and it was a forty-nine-foot runabout. That had never been done by anybody before Don. The Cigarette was the same way. The power available in those days was basically fat and heavy and not very powerful. The power wasn't around to push a Cigarette. When the power became available from Kiekhaefer, Don built that *Cigarette*, which was the first in the class, and he created the market," continued Brown, founder of Nova Marine which was later sold to Wellcraft. Now a consultant, Brown also has been general manager of Cary, chief engineer of Magnum, president of Cougar's American division, and director of product development for Cigarette.

"The Cigarettes were longer, higher, and wider than previous boats in that class had been," explained Brown. "For instance, the Donzi 28 looked pregnant because it had accommodations down below. The accommodations were required by the international Offshore rules then. There wasn't anything else around that size except the Magnum 27, which was a low-slung, good little boat. *The Cigarette* was the first boat big enough to have a good-size bunk and galley down below and still look like a raceboat and go fast."

Aronow's success was such that others measured theirs against his. Looking back on his Offshore racing years, Wynne points with pride to his two favorite designs. One was the 32-foot *Thunderbird*. This boat, the first gas turbine as well as one of the first alumimum racing hulls, won the treacherous 1966 Sam Griffith Memorial Race in which thirty-three started and only two finished. This was the boat's only race, since gas turbines were disallowed shortly afterward. The second and last boat Wynne raced, called *Ghost Rider*, won every race in 1966 in which it was entered. "That was where I was competing head-to-head with Don," said Wynne. "He had won the Miami–Nassau in 1965. With *Ghost Rider* I was able to come back and beat him in the Miami–Nassau Race that year."

After his stellar season in 1969, Aronow decided to call it quits. Despite the smiles, he had been wracked by countless internal injuries from a collection of crashes of boats, motorcycles, and cars. The final blow was when his tall, handsome son Michael suffered paralysis from the waist down in an automobile accident. Although he retired from racing, Aronow continued building and selling boats and boat companies. He sold Cigarette to Harold Halter and started Squadron XII which, in turn, was sold. With his sixth and final company, USA Racing Team, Aronow shifted gears, building catamarans as well as deep vee monohulls.

While Aronow was creating his companies, the sport of offshore powerboat racing was growing around the world, but not without some friction as well as some humor. Promoter Crise had gone on to establish the Bahamas 500 and the Around Nassau races. Some racers, however, unhappy with Crise's dictatorial ways, formed a rival organization, Offshore Power Boat Racing Association of Miami, to run races off South Florida. Allan Brown, a veteran of the 1960s racing circuit, recalled the start of the 1967 Around Nassau Race when Crise waved a giant flag to signal the start and none of the forty racers paid any attention. Then, as prearranged with the racers, Aronow pulled a white lace handkerchief from his life jacket, waved it once, and the fleet roared away, leaving a stunned Crise in their wake.

In 1961, the first modern European race, the English Cowes–Torquay event, was started by Sir Max Aitken, a British publisher and famed twenty-two-plane ace in the Battle of Britain. He and his wife Lady Aitken raced in offshore competition for years. Sir Max's aim was to have the race promote the development of a fast, stable seagoing cruiser. The first contest marked the arrival of the American deep vee hulls in Europe with Dick Bertram and Jim Wynne competing. From Italy came *Speranziella*, a new deep vee craft built at the Cantiere Navaltecnica and designed by Renato "Sonny" Levi, whose influence on high-speed design would be felt in Europe for years to come.

Of the thirty-eight entrants, one of the most colorful was Tommy Sopwith, whose family owned the British aircraft firm of the same name and whose father, Sir Thomas Sopwith, nearly fifty years earlier had regained the Harmsworth Trophy for England with *Maple Leaf IV*. In his 25-foot boat *Thunderbolt*, which was powered by two 325-hp American-made Crusader engines, Sopwith topped the thirty-eight-boat fleet to win. Said Sopwith later, "After the race, my father pulled my leg by saying he couldn't understand what had happened to development because he was driving *Maple Leaf IV* twice as fast as my *Thunderbolt*, but before the First World War." Sopwith agreed, but pointed out that *Maple Leaf IV* had much more power and much calmer conditions in the Solent.

The first American to win the Cowes–Torquay race was Dick Bertram in 1965 with his 38-foot *Brave Moppie*, powered by twin 550-hp Detroit Diesel engines. Jim Wynne collected the victory the following year in *Ghost Rider*.

The first Italian Viareggio–Bastia–Viareggio race was started in 1964 and was also won by Bertram, this time with *Lucky Moppie*, a 31-foot fiberglass boat built by his new Miami company. The victory, though, was dulled by the absence of Sam Griffith, Bertram's sidekick for years, who had died the previous summer of cancer. The Sam Griffith Trophy was founded that fall by John Crouse to be awarded to the world champion, based on points accumulated in the three races that existed at the time: Miami–Nassau, Cowes–Torquay, and Viareggio. By 1977, there were thirty-five races being staged around the world.

The game, meanwhile, had been changing. The boats by now had adopted the Aronow style, becoming longer and faster; the engines were more powerful and the equipment more reliable. Wealthy individuals were buying stock ocean racers and few builders were in the game anymore. The Aronow-built deep vee hulls were replacing the Bertrams as the dominating craft in the sport, and the search for speed was heading in a new direction, toward the twin-hulled catamarans.

While ungainly and fragile at first, the potential of the twin-hulled craft was too great to be ignored. Francesco Cosentino, then Secretary General of the Italian Parliament, became the first to win a major offshore race in an inboard-powered catamaran, capturing the 1971 race from Bellaria, Italy, to Patia, Yugoslavia. Three years later, Californian Paul Cook won the

San Francisco race with *Kudu II*, created by Unlimited designer Ron Jones. His victory was considered a fluke, however.

In fact, catamarans were regarded with healthy skepticism until Englishman Ken Cassir astounded the boating fraternity in 1977 by winning the tough Cowes–Torquay race in the 38-foot catamaran *Yellowdrama III*. In the process, Cassir's cat, built by Cougar Marine and rigged with a secondhand pair of 625-hp Kiekhaefer Aeromarine engines picked up from world champion Carlo Bonomi, set a course record of 75.1 mph. In time, England's Cougar Marine would prove Cassir wasn't luckier than most, he was just plain faster. Cassir captured two more races the next season with his wooden cat, and set a new Offshore straightaway mark of 92.167 mph.

As it turned out, 1977 was a banner year for the English. In addition to Cassir's victory at Cowes, an English commodities broker named Michael Doxford surged to the forefront in international competition. Running a pair of 35- and 40-foot Cigarettes, Doxford topped Aronow's eight-year-old record for the most wins in a season by winning nine. Unfortunately, the rules shifted that year. The format for the prestigious Sam Griffith Trophy was changed from a circuit concept to a single-race event, and Doxford was deprived of the award.

Almost as an afterthought, the venerable Harmsworth Trophy, which had been collecting dust for sixteen years, was given to Doxford to mollify him. The Harmsworth Trophy had fallen out of contention after being won by Canada. The rules required the defender's boat to be constructed in the defending country and the Canadians simply didn't have the equipment. After its award to Doxford, the trophy was given to the driver having the most points collected in certain races. The confusion increased when the British decided that smaller, flat-water tunnel boats, rather than offshore powerboats, should race for the trophy in 1984. They also decided that the racing should have a team format. This continued for three years, with interest dwindling. There was no Harmsworth race in 1987 or 1988, although there were indications that the offshore racing fraternity was seeking to claim this international challenge race once again as their own.

While Cassir and Doxford were making headlines in England in 1977, a petite California grandmother shattered the tough-guy image of offshore racing by winning the world championship in Key West, Florida. Betty Cook had done some racing with her husband, *Kudu*'s Paul Cook. After they were divorced, Betty Cook decided to be the best. Within eight years after she started in 1974, Cook had been transformed from a suburban California housewife into the dominant driver in one of the world's roughest sports. In 1977, at the age of fifty-six, the 5-foot 4-inch Cook of Newport Beach, California, earned her first brush with fame by winning the Bushmills Grand Prix off Newport Beach in *Kaama*, her 38-foot Scarab. This marked the first major Offshore race won by a woman driver as well as the first Offshore race for a boat constructed with Kevlar, a strong but light fiber that was then relatively new from Du Pont. Cook also won the final race on the United States circuit. But it wasn't until the world championship in Key West that fall that Betty Cook proved she was as tough, maybe tougher, than her male counterparts. In an event shortened from 183 miles to 127 miles because of storm-tossed seas that were wrecking boats and bodies, Cook—her face bloodied—hung on to win.

She returned the following year to win three races, including the Cowes–Torquay. Cook, her throttleman John Connor, and navigator Bill Vogel, Jr., were stronger in 1979. Using two boats, the deep vee Scarab for rough-water races and a new 38-foot British Cougar catamaran for calm seas, Cook won three American races and picked up her second world title in Venice, Italy. At the Detroit race, her Kaama cat set a new United States record of 83.9 mph. Ultimately, Cook would accumulate a record to rival that of Aronow: two world and three national titles.

In the early days of her racing, Cook once jokingly explained the difficulties in trying to see over the bow: "When you are catapulted out of the water for thirty feet and land another fifty yards down the course, all you can do is keep the bow aimed at a cloud, hang on, lower your center of gravity and speculate as to where the next set of black and blue marks is to be."

In not so light a vein, Cook said that when she started, "to race at all became the challenge. Each time, I thought I'd give in to fatigue, I'd try to hold on for the next twenty minutes, then the next." As she became increasingly successful, winning alone no longer was enough. The greater challenge, she contended, was the equipment—taming the two engines that turned out 1,300 hp, holding them together during the race, and studying ways to improve them in between. This led to her forming Kaama Marine Enginering, Inc., to build her own engines. Kaama, the name of her raceboats also, is an African antelope known for speed and strength.

The English-designed and -built Cougar cats started to make solid impact on the racecourse in 1979 and 1980. Then they started to overtake the deep vee hulls. On August 14, 1982, Tony Garcia won the Coral Gables Challenge race in Michigan in his Cougar cat, marking the first time surface drives had been used to win a major race. Garcia had won a ninety-two-mile club race in San Francisco the year before using a set of Howard Arneson's surface drives.

The combination of surface drives with the catamaran hull pushed speeds higher. As speeds rose, so did the risks. Moments before the start of the first race in the 1981 season, Al Copeland's *Popeyes* ran into *Michelob Light*, a new catamaran driven by two-time national champion Joel Halpern, killing Halpern. Minutes later, another boat rolled at 90 mph, seriously injuring Vince Fasano, the driver, and Sammy James, the throttleman.

"We have run out of boat, in terms of speed, for the existing known boat configurations," said Cook in 1981. "The boats are going about as fast as they can go safely. Some are going faster than they can go safely. The next step in this technological evolution has to be in the engineering of the structure."

In the 1980s, boats would become stronger, but they also would become lighter and the engines would become more efficient. Consequently, speeds continued to edge upward, with top speeds approaching 150 mph by 1987, and, as in Unlimited racing, crew safety became an ongoing concern. The other crucial concern was image.

The popular perception that the offshore powerboat was the tool of drug runners was becoming a sad reality on the racecourse. For years there had been suspicions, rumors, and facts regarding those who purchased in cash equipment costing

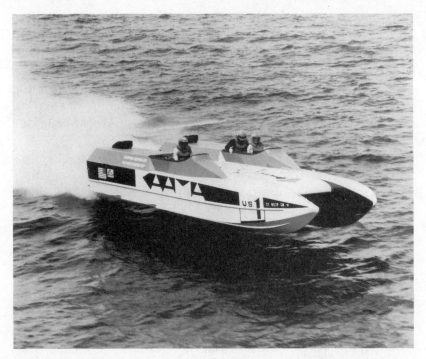

Betty Cook raced a 38-foot Cougar catamaran (above) in calm seas, and a 38-foot deep-vee Scarab in rough water. All her boats were named *Kaama* after an African antelope known for strength and speed.

hundreds of thousands of dollars. There were drivers who wouldn't risk being interviewed on the telephone because they were afraid of wiretaps. Then, like some *Miami Vice* rerun, the sport woke up one morning in August of 1986 to find Ben Kramer, thirty-two, reigning Open Class Offshore racing champion, led away in handcuffs and chains, charged under the Federal Government's so-called Drug Kingpin Statute, the strongest antidrug weapon in its legal arsenal, which is used only against those engaged in continuing criminal enterprises. Kramer's boat company, Apache Boat, Inc., and Fort Apache Marina on Aronow's famed Fleet Street in North Miami Beach were taken over by Federal agents.

Boats in storage were impounded and drilled for secret compartments. Kramer meanwhile was charged with distributing 550,000 pounds of marijuana worth $12 million ($666 million on the street) over the past several years. Kramer, who had a prior marijuana-smuggling conviction, was not allowed out on bail on the grounds that he might be a threat to persons in witness-protection programs.

Kramer was convicted in October of 1988 on charges of operating a criminal enterprise and of conspiracy to distribute more than 1,000 pounds of marijuana. Two months later, U.S. District Court Judge James Foreman sentenced Kramer to life in prison without parole.

The 1985 Superboat champion, George Morales, thirty-seven, was not faring well during this period, either. Morales was jailed for two concurrent sixteen-year terms after pleading guilty to three charges that his airplane-leasing company, Aviation Activities of Fort Lauderdale, had smuggled cocaine and marijuana into the United States for years. One count, from a 1984 indictment for marijuana and Quaalude smuggling, fell under the "continuing criminal enterprise" category. This required three things to be proved: that three or more drug felonies were committed; that the person was a manager or organizer of a drug-smuggling operation employing more than five people; and that great monetary gain was derived by the activities. The second count against Morales was on a 1986 indictment for conspiracy to import 2,640 pounds of cocaine. The third was for a $900,000 tax-evasion charge. Morales was sentenced to serve two concurrent sixteen-year terms for the first two counts, while a five-year sentence on the tax charge was suspended.

In trying to plea-bargain his case, Morales explained that he was flying arms and supplies to the Nicaraguan rebels. Once Morales's planes dropped their cargo for the Nicaraguan rebels, they continued on to Colombia and then back to the United States, possibly loaded with cocaine while still under a CIA-protected flight plan, according to Jonathan Kwitney, author of a book on the CIA's drug connections.

There had been others in the sport connected to drugs. By 1983, "a grand total of 15 American Power Boat Association

91

racers had either been indicted or convicted on smuggling-related charges," reported *Motor Boating & Sailing* magazine.

"People with no visible means of support would show up at Offshore races with three boats—one for rough water, one for flat water, one for normal water—rent suites in the finest hotels, and pay their entry fees in hundred-dollar bills. You have to figure something's going on," said Ed Nabb, Offshore racing's chief referee from 1981 to 1983 and a member of the Offshore Hall of Fame.

The sport's officials started to work with Federal authorities to break the link with laundered money by altering the rules so that boats of record, rather than the drivers, garnered points for the season. As a result, said Nabb, "all hell broke loose when we let it be known we were going to cooperate with authorities to spot boats that hadn't been in the race the month before."

Another rule, suspending a racer who was under indictment or charged with the commission of a felony, was used to oust a dozen or more smugglers in the early 1980s, but it didn't hold up before Morales's high-powered attorney. As bad as it was having Morales and Kramer, two national Open Class champions, behind bars, the worst was yet to come.

On February 3, 1987, Don Aronow drove his Mercedes out of the USA Racing Team parking lot and onto N.E. 188th Street. He passed Cigarette Racing Team and headed toward Magnum Marine on the corner, stopping to visit Fort Apache Marina. Moments after leaving the marina, a stranger in a dark Lincoln Town Car calmly shot Aronow in the chest, blasting his way down to the groin as he emptied a clipful of .45-caliber bullets. Donzi, baby, was gunned down on his street, in the shadows of the companies he created.

Despite the $100,000 reward offered by Aronow's widow Lillian, a composite drawing of the murderer, and a description of his car circulated across the country, the police had no leads and no motive eighteen months later.

The dynamic, wealthy Aronow sold high-tech boats to the world: to the Israeli government, "Baby Doc" Duvalier, Jordan's King Hussein, Vice-President George Bush. For the U.S. Customs Service, he designed and built a line of offshore catamarans called Blue Thunder which were to outrun the smugglers' boats. And he sold boats to those who walked in off the street and paid him in cash.

Mike DeCora, a Miami Metro-Dade homicide detective, followed more than a thousand leads, without luck. There were various theories, though. Aronow was, as one acquaintance phrased it, "a high-performance ladies' man." Did a jealous husband get revenge? "That's ridiculous," said Dr. Bob Magoon, the Miami eye surgeon and three-time national champion who was Aronow's friend for twenty years.

Was it a mob hit, tied perhaps to connections with organized crime during Aronow's years in the New Jersey construction business? After checking, DeCora didn't think so, saying, "He didn't owe anybody anything. He really was a self-made man."

Then there's the Ben Kramer theory. Kramer, the owner of the marina Aronow was visiting moments before he was gunned down, denied through his attorney that he was involved. However, the Kramer-Aronow link bothered DeCora. "Kramer was the big one we looked at on the street. Because of his background and because of his dealings with the victim, there maybe was some animosity between the two."

Kramer had purchased USA Racing Team from Aronow in 1985 for $600,000. Its main customer was the U.S. Customs Service, which told Aronow that Customs would cancel its contract with USA Racing if Kramer kept the company. Aronow then bought it back, although DeCora noted that Kramer apparently "lost on the deal."

With Aronow's death, the wild and crazy days of Offshore came to an abrupt end. To be wild and crazy in the new breed of Superboat meant you were either stupid or had a death wish. As the smugglers were exiting, the entrepreneurs were arriving seeking to inject the shaky, and torn sport with a healthy dose of professionalism.

"The bad element in the sport will be warded off," predicted John Antonelli, Open Class driver and Washington, D.C., real estate developer. "People with shady backgrounds don't like spending a lot of time on national television."

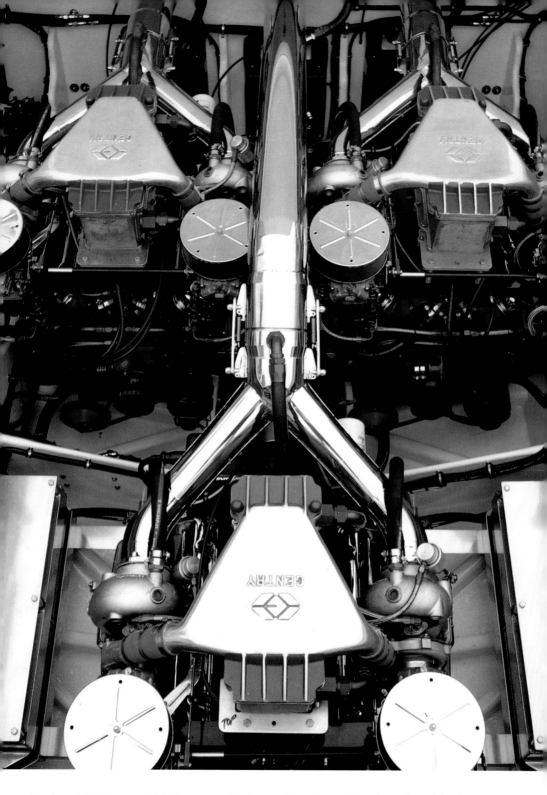

A trio of 850 hp variable-boost turbocharged engines, developed and built by Tom Gentry, powered the 46-foot *Gentry Eagle* to the 1988 Superboat world title. *(Forest Johnson photo)*

Magnum Marine's Ted Theodoli won the first two 362-mile Searaces from Miami to Nassau and back with 60-foot Magnums. *Maltese Magnum*, winner of the 1987 Searace, was equipped with a pair of 18-cylinder 1,840 hp Italian CRM turbocharged diesel engines connected to Arneson surface drives. *(Forest Johnson photo)*

The six-man crew on *Maltese Magnum* set the pace for the 1987 bluewater Searace across the Gulfstream. *(Forest Johnson photo)*

A jubilant Don Johnson, who started driving in 1986, is *numero uno* on the docks after winning the 1988 Superboat World Championship at the Key West World Cup. *(John Crouse photo)*

Gentry Eagle, driven by *Miami Vice* TV star Don Johnson, races to victory in the 1988 Key West World Cup series. The 46-foot Scarab deep vee hull, powered by three Gentry 850 hp engines connected to Kiekhaefer surface drives, averaged 90 mph to win the world Superboat title. *(Forest Johnson photo)*

Miss Budweiser is lowered into the Ohio River for the fateful 1988 Gold Cup. *(Paul Kemiel photo)*

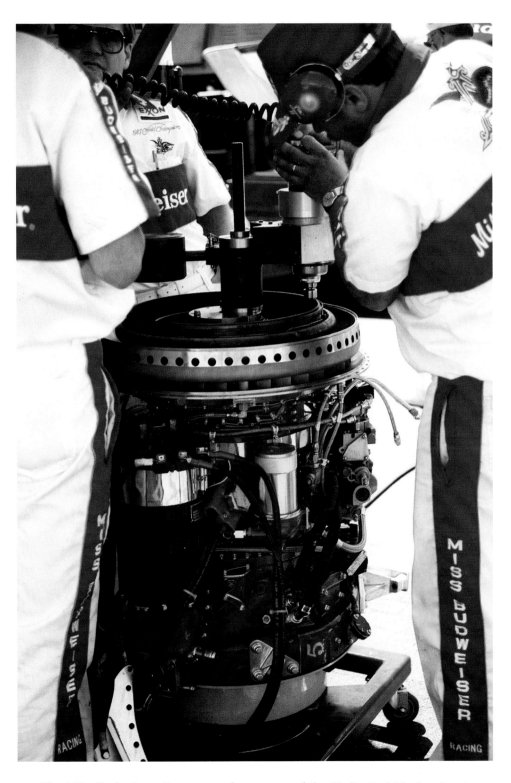

The *Miss Budweiser* pit crew works on one of the Unlimited Hydroplane's Lycoming T-55 L-7 turbine engines. *(Paul Kemiel photo)*

Miss Budweiser, a turbine-driven Unlimited hydroplane driven by Tom D'Eath, "blew its nose" while setting a competitive lap record speed of 193.968 mph in the third heat of the 1988 Gold Cup race on the Ohio River in Evansville, Indiana. This remarkable series by photographer Paul Kemiel shows *Miss Budweiser* becoming airborne, flipping up . . . and over, taking a nosedive, and coming to rest upside down. D'Eath escaped serious injury and went on to win the 1988 national high points championship with *Miss Budweiser*. *(Paul Kemiel photos)*

Unlimited driver Chip Hanauer raises the APBA Gold Cup over his head in joy after winning the famed trophy for the seventh consecutive year in 1988 at Evansville, Indiana. After a collision in the first heat with his *Miller High Life*, Hanauer switched boats to win the cup with *Circus Circus*. *(Paul Kemiel photo)*

Part 2

Racing Today

There always have been men who are fond of doing things in a hurry. This applies to sport as well as to other things; and these men soon had boats built just to have fun with and to be able to go out and pass everything afloat.

—*Motor Boat* magazine, 1904

Chapter 5

The Role of the American Power Boat Association

In 1986, brothers Chris and Mark Lavin raced in a new, high-tech Open Class boat, the 35-foot *Jesse James*. (*Courtesy of Chris Lavin*)

From the mighty, raw power of the unlimited hydroplane to the 10-foot runabout, boat racing is unlike any other form of motor sport, because it takes place on a constantly changing surface—the water. With the ever-shifting wind and water, no two races are ever quite the same. And depending on the power and speed of the boat and on the sea conditions, the sport can be a brutalizing, bone-crushing test on the edge of endurance.

Traveling across heavy seas in the open ocean, the racers must have stamina and must be in top physical condition to sustain the repeated shock of the boat pounding from crest to crest. To this add lightning-fast reflexes and the ability to remain calm and in control as the "edge of the envelope" approaches. In a big offshore catamaran traveling somewhere over 100 mph, the envelope is reached when the tunnel hull lifts and starts to work, creating an acceleration all its own.

A boat running at design speed can seemingly get up on a track and slice across the wave tops, dancing across the crests. In racing a small runabout inshore, a driver feels the slight slapping of the stern as the outboard rhythmically scoots across the wavelets, stepping lightly across the chop. "Once she's dancing," explained one driver, "you know the boat is totally aired out and you've done everything you can do to get speed."

Aside from the aphrodisiac of speed, boat racing offers competitors a chance to pit their skills and equipment against those of others and to test themselves against the oceans, rivers, and lakes. Boat racing combines the elemental challenge of man against the sea, and there is the added pragmatic challenge of holding oneself and one's equipment together longer than the next participant. A boat race also is a mental game, one of strategic moves and, at times, psychological warfare demanding inner toughness. Superb concentration is needed to read every ruffle of wind on the water and sight any debris which might be a hazard—no easy task when one is pummeling across the surface.

Don Aronow was a master of mind games. "He was a tough guy out there, a real psycher," recalled Miami publicist John Crouse. "He loved to run by a guy who was dying in a boat. He'd be laughing and give him a big grin and wave. The other guy would be hurting and here's this guy grinning at him even though Don would be hurting like hell inside. And it worked, too. It was totally demoralizing."

Powerboat racing in the United States is sanctioned by the American Power Boat Association, the sport's national authority. The APBA sanctions races in established classes or categories of boats as well as races among two or more of any special or unusual watercraft propelled by a motor.

The power to sanction international events is granted to the APBA by the Union of International Motorboating (UIM), the recognized world authority for the sport, which is headquartered in Belgium. Because the UIM recognizes the APBA as the United States authority, records set at APBA-sanctioned regattas are eligible to receive world titles.

The modern APBA was shaped over the years by several key developments. In 1913 the association established the first racing commission, whose duties were to "cooperate with race committees of individual clubs in racing matters, issue interpretations of racing rules when disputes arose, and grant sanctions for races." While created to settle disputes in the early years, the powers delegated to this first commission comprise the essence of today's APBA.

Although racing today covers a wide variety of powerboats, some sixty or so years ago APBA racing consisted only of six recognized divisions of craft: Cruisers, Express Cruisers, Speed Cruisers, Open Boats, Displacement Racers, and Hydroplanes. Rating formulas classified the Cruisers and Open Boats, while

Displacement Racers was a category for boats that did not fit into the other divisions.

In 1923, the APBA established the concept of limited classes by adopting in entirety the rules of the Mississippi Valley Power Boat Association, which limited the displacement for the hydroplane classes: 1½ liter, 151, 215, 340, 510, 610, 725, 1,100, and all runabouts up to 625 cubic inches. With the emergence of outboard motors efficient enough to stimulate racing, the APBA established a set of rules for boats propelled by "outboard detachable motors" in 1924. Classes were established for motors under 12 cubic inches (Class A); 12 to 17 ci (Class B); 17 to 30 ci (Class C); and over 30 ci (Class D). During the next two decades additional classes were added and by 1948 regattas were being held for stock as well as racing outboards.

Another significant shift in direction in the APBA occurred in 1949 at a special meeting in Philadelphia when the association delegated equal voting power to individual members as well as clubs. This change was in response to the need for a rules-making system that would allow the drivers and the owners to participate in creating the rules by which they would play the game. Those eligible for membership in the APBA currently are (1) any permanently organized club or association in North America having a regular membership of fifteen or more, devoting its attention in whole or in part to the development of powerboats or to the promotion of the sport of racing boats or yachts of that character, and (2) certain individuals. A competition member may be an individual or a corporation owning a raceboat, and must be a member of an APBA member club. Individuals, regardless of whether they belong to a member club, may join the association, as may businesses. Officiating members are those recommended by the regional chairman for service as regatta workers.

An individual who is interested in the sport but not an owner of raceboats, nor a participant in the sport, nor a member of an APBA member club may become an associate member. An associate member, however, cannot vote, officiate, or hold office. Membership information is available by writing the APBA at 17640 East Nine Mile Road, P.O. Box 377, East Detroit, MI 48021.

Today the APBA conducts races for all types of powerboats, from the Unlimiteds to the family runabouts that can compete in an outboard-performance-craft competition. Nearly four hundred regattas are sanctioned each year in the United States and Canada. More than four thousand raceboats are registered with the APBA by racing members, and clubs, officials, and the various memberships bring the total membership to nearly eight thousand.

The core of organized racing is centered on the more than two hundred affiliated boating clubs of the APBA whose members actually conduct the races that the APBA sanctions. The most visible of these are the Unlimited Hydroplane and Offshore Powerboat national circuits and world championships. With flashy, exotic equipment, high-risk speeds, and daring drivers and crews, these two classes attract the biggest crowds and greatest media coverage. In fact, in 1988 Unlimited races alone were expected to draw some two million spectators onshore and more than 150 million television viewers. Offshore, with a national circuit and an increasing number of sponsored teams and events, today seems a quantum leap away from the Red Crise era.

The APBA sanctions racing in nine different categories. Each category is based on the inboard or outboard placement of the boat's engine and the shape of its hull. Each category is further broken down into specific classes. For each category there is a racing commission which essentially has the authority to supervise racing within that category, including matters involving discipline, new classes, rule changes, race sanctions, and the forming of committees pertaining to running the races.

The categories are:

1. Unlimited Hydroplane. The "thunderboats" are 24- to 28-foot hydroplanes powered by massive aircraft piston or turbine engines. Piloted by highly skilled drivers, the boats compete at speeds reaching 200 mph on oval smooth water courses for such prestigious trophies as the APBA Gold Cup.

2. Offshore. This is the ultimate test of endurance. Catamaran or deep vee hulls up to 50 feet long, and powered

101

by multiple inboard, sterndrive, or outboard engines, carry a driver, throttleman, and navigator across 200 miles or more of open water.

3. Inboard. Automotive-powered craft with classes for hydroplanes and flatbottoms ranging from 11 to 20 feet long and reaching speeds from 70 to 150 mph in circle competition. This includes the Unlimited and Grand Prix Hydroplanes as well as the Jersey Speed Skiffs and racing runabouts.

4. Inboard Endurance. Endurance races are run on a closed course under various formats, including a distance of 100 miles or more, a one-hour time duration, or a series of specific heats.

5. Drag. They are the fastest boats afloat. This one-on-one competition is comprised of blown and unblown hydroplanes and flatbottoms that drag the classic quarter-mile at speeds up to 220 mph. Weekend racers can compete in the Sportsman category for family-rigged ski boats.

6. Outboard Performance Craft. These are the high-speed tunnel boats (modified hydroplanes) and vee-bottoms from 12 to 18 feet long that can turn on a dime at 140 mph. Entry-level classes are offered for a variety of mini-boats having outboard engines from 25 to 40 hp.

7. Stock Outboard. This is grass-roots racing with style. From beginner to advanced classes, only box-stock engines are allowed, placing the emphasis on fine tuning and driving ability. Many notable drivers began their racing careers in these 9- to 15-foot hydros and runabouts which reach speeds of 40 to 80 mph.

8. Modified Outboard. Performance-oriented basics are the key here as stock engines undergo changes inside and out to compete in this category. Exhaust pipes and internal tuning are common on the hydros and runabouts that reach speeds of 60 to 90 mph.

9. Professional Outboard. In this innovative category, sophisticated engines burning alcohol and castor oil power

these hydros and runabouts to speeds greater than 120 mph.

There is an additional category called Special Events which is designed to accommodate the needs of other types of power craft. These include boats such as inflatables, Hovercrafts, and even radio-controlled model boats, as well as what have come to be known as "personal watercraft," the WetBikes and Jet Skis. The APBA gives nearly any motorized water craft the opportunity to race in organized competition for sanctioned national and world championships and records.

The Special Events category also includes the record distance races and record runs for offshore powerboats that have become increasingly popular in recent years, attracting entrepreneurs such as Tom Gentry and Al Copeland, and actors Don Johnson and Chuck Norris. In establishing a record run for a specific distance, a competitor must receive a sanction from the APBA. An APBA representative then oversees the start and finish to log the official times.

Chapter 6

Unlimiteds Today

The Unlimited hydroplane *Miller High Life*, driven by Chip
Hanauer, streaked to a world record lap of 155.979 mph at
the 1987 Gold Cup regatta.

Race Format and Procedures

An Unlimited hydroplane carries one person, the driver, who rides in an enclosed cockpit located ahead of the engine. A crew in the pits, the area at the race site where the boats are moored and repaired, maintains the boat in racing condition.

The Unlimiteds, which run 24 to 28 feet in length, race on oval courses of 1.66, 2, 2.5, or 3 miles in circumference. The 2.5-mile course, however, is preferred. The two turns are to be as nearly similar as possible, and it is recommended that there be 1,200 feet between the side parallels of each racecourse. In addition, there must be an escape route on the entrance to each turn, which must be kept clear of spectator boats.

The starting line is approximately at the center of the racecourse and is marked by a starting buoy having red and white horizontal stripes.

At least two days before the start of a race, the course must be made available for testing and qualification. To qualify for an event, a boat must record one lap at the minimum speed of 100 mph on all racecourses, with the exception of 95 mph on the Miami 1.66-mile course. A *lap* is a completed legal circuit of the racecourse that can be part of a heat, section, qualification, or testing lap. A *heat*, meanwhile, is a completed racing event that is one portion of an entire racing program. A *race* consists of three heats having a minimum of five laps each. The maximum number of boats that may start in one heat or section is six. If more than six boats qualify, the boats will be divided into sections by lot. Drawings for placement in the sections are made at the drivers' meeting prior to racing. For instance, the first boat drawn would be placed in Section 1A; the second boat in Section 1B. Drawings for positions in subsequent heats are made in the same manner.

The boats accumulating the highest point totals during the first two heats are eligible to continue and compete in the final heat. The remaining boats then compete in a "semi-feature" race in which national points are awarded.

Each heat or section is started by sounding a five-minute warning gun and a one-minute warning gun. When the five-minute gun is fired, a yellow flag is raised and the 10-foot-diameter starting clock and four signboards are raised into position. Each of the four signboards marks off the minutes remaining before the start. The clock, a black-out type, has one face painted fluorescent orange and another face painted black. At the one-minute gun, the yellow flag is lowered, a white one is raised, and the clock starts. The fluorescent orange face shows prior to one minute before the start. In the one-minute count-down, the face turns from orange to black. At the race start, the starting gun is fired and the white flag is lowered. A boat that jumps the gun and starts too early is penalized by having to run an extra lap.

Flags, displayed from a visible position on the judges' stand, are used during the race to communicate to the drivers. The flags are:

RED—which means the race has been stopped or postponed. If the race is stopped, the red flag will be accompanied by the discharge of red or orange flares from the judges' stand and from patrol or stake boats.

YELLOW—which indicates there is a hazardous condition on the racecourse, such as a disabled boat.

GREEN—which indicates to a boat that it is starting its final lap.

CHECKERED—which is displayed at the finish of the race to indicate to the boat passing the judges' stand that it has finished. This signal may be accompanied by the firing of a gun to signal the winner of the race.

BLACK—which tells the drivers to leave the course and immediately pull into the infield.

Boats are awarded points in each heat or section based on the order of finish: first place receives 400 points; second, 300; third, 225; fourth 169, fifth, 127; and sixth, 95. The winner of the contest is determined by the order of finish of the final heat. The points awarded at the regattas accumulate throughout the season, forming the basis of the national high-points championship.

Driver requirements include passing a physical examination and an oral examination, as well as showing proof that one has driven in recent Unlimited competition. A new Unlimited driver must prove he has had the required amount of experience in other APBA classes. Then, before a new driver is permitted to drive in Unlimited competition, he must run fifteen laps equal to or better than the course qualifying speed. In addition, effective in 1988 all drivers are required to take an open-water scuba diving course, another in the sport's ongoing safety efforts.

The Thunderboats' New Direction

While driver safety has been the primary consideration of those in Unlimited racing since the shattering deaths of Muncey and Chenoweth, the sport currently is undergoing another sort of revolution. Indeed, the thunder is being taken out of the thunderboats. And 1988 marked the year that the blasting roar of the high-revving piston engine was at times silenced altogether in some heats.

The culprit was the turbine engine with its high-pitched whine. The new hulls entering the circuit in 1988 featured turbine, in which power is generated by simple rotation, rather than piston power, in which power is derived from a solid cylinder that fits into a larger cylinder and moves back and

uid pressure. In fact, most of the major teams
with turbines, with only Jim Harvey's piston-
Boy! Oberto threatening the turbine boats. In 1987,
won every race; in 1988 they won all but two of
these were taken by *Oberto*.

The ...mited boats are organized informally as teams. A team generally is comprised of the owner, driver, sponsor, crew chief, and pit crew. A team also may include a designer and builder.

The relative quiet produced by the turbine engines has had a distinct effect on the spectators, who now can actually hear the slap-slap-slap of the boat running on the water. Without the extreme noise of the aircraft engines, spectators "were picking up a different sound, the sound of the boat reacting to the water," remarked Mike Jones, 1988 president of the APBA and a member of the Unlimited Commission, who was interviewed on the dramatic new directions in his sport. "Now they could see and hear the boats running on the water."

The turn toward the turbine engines is simply a matter of evolution. "It's strictly a power-to-weight situation," said Jones, "and it favors the smaller turbine motors. They are quite powerful and very light."

Power is not the key difference; weight is. The turbines, many of which are Lycoming military helicopter engines, provide 2,650 hp in a 5,250-pound boat, compared with piston-driven hydroplane engines, which provide 2,500 hp in a 6,000-pound boat. Because the turbine engines weigh less, the boats can weigh less. The turbine engine also is the more efficient engine because it has a rotating type of motion, whereas the piston engine first must convert vertical motion into linear motion. The turbine also has constant combustion, but in a typical four-stroke piston engine only one stroke produces power and the other three are users of power. With the turbine, all engine motion produces power.

Following World War II, the Unlimiteds relied on aircraft engines, and by the time the 1980s arrived, each Unlimited team had ten engines that it constantly rebuilt, using them at the rate of one a race. Of course, often they only lasted for one heat and pit crews would have to switch engines for the next.

"It was inevitable they were going to go to some other form of power just because of the lack of availability of aircraft motors in general and parts," Mike Jones explained. The turbine proved the first solution. Some teams have been experimenting with automotive power, although they face an uphill battle to equal the speed potential and the power-to-weight ratio that are already available with the turbines.

"If you look at the smaller classes of boats, and the speeds being attained, you still have a feeling there is a place for automotive power in Unlimiteds. But you now have single-engine turbine boats running laps on a mile-and-two-thirds course at 120 to 125 miles per hour and Unlimiteds on a two-mile course going in the 140s," said Jones, a Seattle accountant who has raced in stock outboard and limited inboard divisions and officiated in all divisions of the sport. "In theory it would be attainable [with automotive power], but again it is a power-to-weight situation and Unlimiteds require a bigger boat because the water they race on is typically rougher."

Designer Jim Lucero was the first to install a turbine in *Pay 'n Pak* in 1982. Two years later, two major teams—Atlas Van Lines and Miller Brewing—sensing a breakthrough, announced they were building turbine craft. In looking back on his experience with *Pay 'n Pak*, Lucero noted that he learned the engines "never let us down. Whenever we had motor problems, it was because of our own mistakes."

According to Jones, the sport is at the crossroads now in deciding whether to continue with turbine power. In the past few years the boats designed around the turbine engine have dominated, such as Bernie Little's *Miss Budweiser*, which won the national title again in 1988. Little, who has been one of the driving forces in Unlimited competition as owner of the Budweiser Racing Team, does nothing halfway. After twenty-seven seasons in the sport, the Little team has won an unprecedented ten national titles. His team has been in the forefront of the sport in terms of innovation and financing as well as victories. When the Florida beer distributor felt it was time to switch from piston to turbine power, he simply bought out an existing turbine team and devoted a year to testing before fielding a winning turbine boat.

"If the sport continues with turbine power," said Jones, "I think we'll see all teams go to something similar to the new *Miss Madison*." Designed by Ron Jones, the 30-foot Holset/*Miss Madison*, the only community-owned racing boat in the world, is unique in that it is able to take several different combinations of power plants, including a turbine. During the 1988 season, however, the boat ran with an older turbocharged Allison engine and finished fifth in the national standings behind three turbine boats and the piston-powered *Oberto*.

Certainly, Little sees a healthy future for turbines, since he has invested heavily in them. He has stocked up on turbines and, as one member of his team noted, he probably has the best supply of the Lycoming T-55 L-7 engines in the United States today with the possible exception of the U.S. Army, which uses them in the Chinook helicopters.

As Mike Jones notes, the turbine is a reliable engine. "It would not be used in today's applications unless it was," he continued. "Aircraft technology has come a long way, and those old piston motors aren't run in many airplanes anymore. Most are jets or turbines. So I think what we're seeing here is a natural evolution."

Unlike the Unlimiteds of the 1950s and 1960s, with their rounded bows and three-point design, today's turbine craft are pickle-forked hulls with stabilizer wings and skid fins for better turning, and they tend to be wider and flatter than their predecessors. Where the old hydroplanes were constructed of plywood, today's boats have leaped into the space age with composite construction using Kevlar, carbon fiber, and rigid foam.

When Chip Hanauer was asked to replace the legendary Muncey as the driver for Atlas Van Lines for the 1982 season, he succeeded beyond his expectations, winning the national title. But shaken by Muncey's death, he had his doubts as to whether he should continue racing. He decided he would continue driving only if he could work to reduce the risks. During the off-season, Hanauer, who has been racing powerboats since the age of nine, and Lucero, the boat's designer and builder, redesigned *Atlas Van Lines*.

Lucero and Hanauer studied the recent fatalities before making their changes. In Muncey's case, Hanauer said, the boat flipped, landing on top of him with his body absorbing the impact. The force of the water then pushed him through the dashboard and cockpit cowling. Chenoweth was thrown from the boat and then "got tangled up with his boat as it tumbled across the water," said Hanauer, a former schoolteacher in his mid-thirties. He and Lucero lowered the cockpit in *Atlas Van Lines* below deck so that the engine and the deck, rather than the driver, would absorb impact. They also installed a five-point seat-belt system, similar to the one used by racecar drivers. Two other drivers had been killed in recent years when they were thrown from their boats. In the 1982 season John Walters was critically injured when he was thrown out of a cockpit. In every case, with the exception of Muncey's, the cockpit remained intact.

"That led us to believe if the driver stays in the cockpit, he stands a good chance of surviving an accident," Hanauer explained. Hanauer and Lucero hence developed the first enclosed cockpit. These enclosures employ the same canopies used to cover the F-16 fighter plane cockpits.

The cabover design, in which the driver rides ahead of rather than behind the engine, soon followed and became the standard. There was some initial discomfort with the cabover concept; drivers felt exposed without the big Rolls-Royce engine in front of them. As Muncey once remarked, "It's sure to make the driver the first one to the scene of the accident."

Nonetheless, the modern Unlimiteds with forward, fully enclosed cockpits are safer boats. Being flatter and wider, they corner better and ride more smoothly. Lucero adds, "There also is greater visibility for the driver. He can sit lower for a better feel for the boat. It's much cooler, gives a softer ride, and decreases aerodynamic drag."

Two drivers, *Cellular One*'s Steve Reynolds and *Miss Budweiser*'s Jim Kropfeld, were each in two accidents in 1987 and 1988 and they lived through all four. Reynolds survived a 1987 crash on the Ohio River, although he required months of rehabilitation, and he was not seriously injured in the second mishap. Kropfeld basically walked away from his accidents. The last came in the first race of the 1988 season in Miami when

Jim Kropfeld, a veteran of more than twenty years of driving, has piloted the *Miss Budweiser* since the end of the 1983 season, winning three national titles. *(Courtesy of Hydroplanes, Inc.)*

Miss Budweiser hooked and *Mr. Pringles* ran over the top of Kropfeld's canopy.

"There is no question in my mind that neither of those drivers would be with us today if they had had the same accidents four years ago," said Hanauer, whose remarkable career was capped by his seventh straight Gold Cup victory in 1988.

The APBA's Mike Jones agrees, adding, "Safety is an ongoing thing . . . but there is no question the boats today are a hundred times safer than they were ten years ago."

The success of the enclosed cockpit is evidenced by the fact that the Unlimited racing commission required all boats built after November 15, 1986, to have them and to meet minimum standards set by its safety committee. Starting with the 1989 season, all Unlimiteds entering competition were required to have enclosed cockpits. Drivers also are required to be dressed from head to toe in fire-retardant materials. And drivers receive special training in the Dilbert Dunker, a crash simulator developed to train helicopter pilots. A driver is strapped in the simulator, plunged headfirst underwater, spun around, disoriented, and instructed in rescue procedures.

Safety efforts currently are concentrated on building a safety cell within the hull to encompass the canopy. And these efforts are no longer limited to the Unlimited hydroplanes but are moving up to the big offshore Superboats and down to the smaller tunnel hulls.

With the advent of turbines and exotic construction, speeds continue to nudge upward. The final race of the 1988 season on Las Vegas's Lake Mead perhaps indicates what is ahead as drivers and support crews learn to wring the most out of new boats and new technology. In Heat 2-A, Larry Lauterbach in *Vantage-Ultra* set a new 2-mile lap record of 131 mph in the first lap only to have Hanauer, driving *Miller High Life*, top it in the second lap as he went 133.630 mph to set a new Lake Mead course record. This was 12.55 mph faster than the previous record set by Hanauer the year before. But there was more to come. In Heat 2-B, Tom D'Eath, who had replaced Kropfeld as the driver of *Miss Budweiser*, moved the Lake Mead 2-mile record up to 139.130 mph and clinched the national points title, as well.

"The speed of these turbines is ahead of their design technology," said crew chief Ron Jones, son of *Slo-Mo-Shun*'s driver Ted Jones. He predicted longer boats in the future with rounder bottoms and larger horizontal stabilizers. And as sponsorship grows, teams will have two boats, he added, so that when one goes down, the other continues. The attrition rate of equipment continues to be high in competition.

The costs of competing in a nine-race national circuit run anywhere from $100,000 to $1 million a year, which includes equipment, travel, and maintenance. At the estimated high end is Bernie Little and his *Miss Budweiser*s. His team has a permanent crew of ten and they are continually building new boats. By the end of the 1988 season, Little was close to having three race-ready boats—his original turbine boat, the one that won the 1988 title, and another nearing completion. Teams at the less costly end of the spectrum will have older hulls, older equipment, and largely unpaid crews.

With the numerous changes in Unlimited racing in recent years—the turbines, the cabover, enclosed cockpits, and improved chances of surviving a blowover—there remains another significant development: better competition. The 1988 race on Seattle's Lake Washington had sixteen starters, the largest field ever for a 2-mile racecourse. "The field has gone up and the quality has gone up," said Mike Jones. In an earlier race in Pasco, Washington, the top ten boats averaged over 130 mph to qualify. And as Jones noted, in the Seattle race, "we had four boats on the same lap actually running seconds apart. The competition is picking up substantially."

The edge of control consequently is that more elusive. "We spend more time at critical speeds now," Hanauer explained. "The difference between blowing over and having the boat right on is minuscule. The ride is so good, right up to the point where it goes over."

Despite the precautions, danger is inherent in racing. The addiction to the adrenaline charge, the challenge of driving the perfect race, overcomes the fear. As Hanauer put it: "Racing is living and dying in three-quarter time. You can experience, in the span of one day, defeat, humiliation, joy, excitement, and ecstasy. In ordinary life you might have to live months or even years to really experience maybe one or two of those emotions. Bill Muncey once said that racing is about life, not death. And that life is so good, and so well defined, that it's worth the risk of having life in general ended in doing it."

114

Chapter 7

Offshore Today

Docked on victory lane, Al Copeland and his crew pose for the cameras on the deck of *Popeyes/diet Coke* after winning another checkered flag. *(Forest Johnson photo)*

On the Racecourse

Offshore powerboat racing is a rugged test of stamina, seamanship, and equipment. Because of the increased speeds and the injuries and fatal accidents in recent years, the rules governing this sport also now include stringent safety procedures.

There are either two or three persons on board an Offshore racing boat. The driver is responsible for steering while the throttleman operates the throttles, a sensitive and demanding task since power must be reduced as a boat starts to fly or the engines will overrev. The third person is the navigator, who uses a compass and charts to keep the boat on course. A minimum of two and a maximum of four persons are permitted aboard during a race and all must be eighteen years or older and, in national races, trained in cardiopulmonary resuscitation (CPR).

Frequently, the navigator or throttleman also is a skilled mechanic who can repair equipment if breakdowns occur during a race. When there are only two on board, one is the driver while the other serves as both navigator and throttleman. Crews competing in national races also must have a United States Coast Guard captain's license or have completed an approved small-boat-handling course. A regulation added in 1988 requires all competitors to complete each year a self-extrication training program similar to that of the Unlimiteds.

Before each race, the boats and equipment are inspected. The morning of the race, riding crew members, boat owners, and officials attend a mandatory drivers' meeting. At the meeting the chief referee and competition director may change the courses or amend the instructions. Offshore courses are unlike other courses used in APBA competition. Rather than being ovals that conform to specific forms, Offshore courses are run from point to point around checkpoints. There are specific course lengths for the different classes of Offshore boats. For instance, all National classes, with the exception of Pro-Stock (P) and Stock (S), run a course that is a minimum of 135 statute miles and a maximum of 160 statute miles. The Sportsman's Divisional Classes A, B, C, and D run courses that are 60 to 80 statute miles in length.

Before the race the competitors are given a chart showing the layout of the course. The chart indicates the sequence in which each checkpoint must be passed. A checkpoint can be a buoy, boat, or landmark. And at each checkpoint there is a check boat with race officials on board to note the mark-rounding times. At each turn, raceboats must negotiate these checkpoints at a distance not greater than 300 yards nor less than 50 yards from the check-boat point.

Offshore officials use the same flag signals as the Unlimiteds to instruct the racers, but Offshore is the only powerboat competition in which a starting clock is not used. Instead, a pace boat is used to start each class separately, with the biggest and fastest boats, the Superboats, going first. The start/finish line, defined by a start/finish boat and fixed buoys, marks the beginning and end of the course. Behind the start/finish line is the 1- to 2-mile stretch in which the pace boat operates. Behind this is the picket line, the point where the pace boat picks up the class which is to be started. And behind the picket line is the safe milling area. In this area, boats waiting to be started must be off plane and must turn in the same direction, counterclockwise. In the milling area itself there are distinct areas in which each starting group waits. To start, the pace boat drives a course close to one side of the chute (the distance from the start/finish line to the picket line) and slowly turns and heads toward the start/finish line, running close to the other side of the chute. The starting boats follow the pace boat toward the starting line at a distance of 100 feet. A single orange flare may be used to denote the start of the first class, with the start of each subsequent class determined by the pace boat alone. Approaching the line at high speed, the pace boat determines the actual start by dropping the yellow flag and raising the green one. A referee aboard the pace boat uses hand signals to control the starting fleet behind him. When the green flag is raised, the race is on.

Generally, the first boat to finish in each class is the winner. However, penalties may result in a revision in the standings, and as a result race officials wait until all boats have finished and all infractions are reported before announcing the outcome. Participants have the right to appeal the decisions of the referee to a protest jury, which is responsible for resolving disputes.

In Offshore competition, the racers must complete the course within a certain time limit. If a boat develops a mechanical problem, the crew may stop to repair or replace the damaged parts. All navigation must be done by the crew on board the boat, using only a compass and a chart. Those who attempt to use "outside means," such as a radio contact to shore or aircraft, are subject to disqualification.

In keeping with its belief that safety takes precedence over racing, the Offshore commission has its own Racing Rules of the Road.

Racing Rules of the Road

1.   Any raceboat encountering an accident should notify Race Control on Channel 78A and render all possible assistance to any vessel or person in peril. If two boats are on the scene, the next raceboat to arrive may continue to race without penalty. The first two boats to give assistance, and thereby compromise finishing points, shall be awarded the points accrued at the previous scoring checkpoint. After giving assistance, these boats must continue to race and finish. Should they improve their finish placement from the points awarded at the scoring

checkpoint prior to the accident, they will be awarded the higher of the two.

2. At all times during a race, the applicable U.S. Coast Guard, state, and local Rules of the Road shall apply.

3. When two raceboats are on the same course, the overtaking boat shall keep clear of the boat being overtaken, and in passing shall allow at least 50 feet of clear water between them. The overtaken boat shall not alter course so as to compel an overtaking boat to pass within this 50-foot limit.

4. Should a raceboat fail to round a mark correctly and thus be forced to renegotiate this mark, the driver must return and circle inside the course and pass the mark on the proper side, keeping well clear of the balance of the racing fleet.

5. Should any check boat or turn boat be absent from its proper position during a race, the race committee shall replace it, if possible, otherwise the raceboat shall negotiate that fixed mark according to race instructions.

In addition, the crew must wear specified safety equipment, including a helmet and life jacket, and for each race specific medical personnel must be standing by as well as aircraft and a minimum of fifteen patrol boats.

There are six Offshore hand signals used by racers to communicate with rescue craft as well as with each other: (1) Hands clasped over one's head means everything's OK, no help is needed at this time; (2) hands waved over one's head means immediate medical assistance is needed; (3) one hand waved over one's head means immediate danger of fire or towing assistance is needed; (4) no signal means immediate response needed by nearest personnel; (5) thumbs up means everything is OK and the medical helicopter can return to its post; (6) a clenched fist raised while on plane means caution, debris or accident ahead, or slowing or avoidance maneuver to follow.

Like the Unlimiteds, Offshore also has a scoring system used to determine an annual national points champion for each class.

Comparison of Offshore Racing Classes

Classes	Designation	Boat Length	Estimated Original Equipment Cost	Yearly Cost of National Campaign	Race Length	Calm Water Speed	Approximate Horsepower
Superboat	No letters. Numbers to 3 digits	35'–50'	$300,000 to $600,000	$300,000 to $400,000	135 to 160 miles	To 130 mph	1,400 to 3,000
Open (U.I.M.I.)	No letters. Numbers to 3 digits	35'–50' (30' in U.I.M.)	$100,000 to $300,000	$95,000 to $250,000	135 to 160	To 120 mph	1,400 to 1,800
Modified (U.I.M.II)	Letter 'M'. Numbers to 3 digits	23'–40'	$75,000 to $150,000	$50,000 to $120,000	135 to 160 miles	To 110 mph	900 to 1,400
Pro-Stock	Letter 'P'. Numbers to 3 digits.	23'–40'	$50,000 to $90,000	$30,000 to $80,000	120 to 135 miles	To 90 mph	600 to 900
Stock (U.I.M.IIIe) A any hull B "Vee" hull only	Letter 'S'. Numbers to 3 digits.	21' Up	$25,000 to $60,000	$15,000 to $40,000	100 to 120 miles	To 80 mph	400 to 700

Divisional Sportsman's Classes

Sportsman	Letter 'D'. Numbers to 3 digits.	29' up	$15,000 to $45,000	$6,000 to $10,000	60 to 80 miles	To 95 mph	To 1,100HP
Sportsman	Letter 'C'. Numbers to 3 digits.	26' up	$10,000 to $30,000	$4,000 to $8,000	60 to 80 miles	To 85 mph	To 900 approximate
Sportsman	Letter 'B'. Numbers to 3 digits.	24' up	$7,500 to $20,000	$3,000 to $6,000	60 to 80 miles	To 75 mph	To 700 approximate
Sportsman	Letter 'A'. Numbers to 3 digits.	21' up	$5,000 to $15,000	$2,000 to $4,000	60 to 80 miles	To 65 mph	To 590 hp

(Used with permission of the APBA.)

121

Offshore Class Rules Summary

Classes	Gasoline Cubic Inch Displacement	Diesel CID	Outboard Requirements	Induction System	Other
Superboat	Up to 1,000 (Unlimited CID for boats over 45' thru 1986).	Up to 2,000	Cubic inches to 1,000. Any number of units.	Fuel injection, supercharging & turbocharging.	None
Open (U.I.M.I.)	Up to 1,000	Up to 2,000	Cubic inches to 1,000. Any number with 1.4 penalty.	Fuel injection, supercharging & turbocharging with 1.4 penalty.	None
Modified (U.I.M.II)	Up to 750. 1.4 penalty for Turbo.	Up to 1,500. 1.4 penalty for Turbo.	Cubic inches to 500. Any number of units. EFI allowed.	Single 4 bbl, no fuel injection. Tunnel or Hi Rise manifolds over 500 CID.	None
Pro-Stock	Up to 750 (Mult. inbrds.). Up to 500 (Singl. inbrds.). Up to 500 (Mult. outbrds.). Limit 3.	Up to 1,500 Twin. Up to 1,000 Single.	Cubic inches to 500. Limit 3. Fuel injection allowed.	Single 4 bbl, eight 2 bbl, six 1 bbl. No ram manifolds or fuel injection, turbo or supercharging.	Cast iron intake (stock). Cast iron exhaust (stock).

Stock (U.I.M.IIIe) A any hull B "Vee" hull only	Up to 366	Up to 732	Cubic inches to 366. Limit 2. No fuel injection.	Same as above	As above

Divisional Sportsman's Classes

Sportsman	Up to 1,100	Up to 2,200	1,100 HP max.	Varies	Vee, cat advances one class.
Sportsman	Up to 1,000 (stock)	Up to 2,000	To 500 CID or 700 adv. HP	Varies	Vee, cat advances one class.
Sportsman	Up to 950	Up to 1,900	To 320 CID or 350 adv. HP	Varies	Vee, cat advances one class.
Sportsman	Up to 469	Up to 938	Cubic inches to 160	Aluminum intake. Cast iron exhaust.	Vee, cat advances one class.

A graduated system of points, running from 400 points for first place to 1 point for twentieth place, is used. This is augmented by a 100-point bonus for a legal start, and all finishing drivers are awarded one additional point for every boat defeated in its class.

In addition to races on the national circuit, there are divisional races held within four regions: Northeast, Southeast, Central, and Western. Each division has its own championship.

There are five classes of boat that compete on the national circuit and four divisional Sportsman's Classes. A summary of each class, with its comparable UIM class in parentheses, is shown on the chart on pages 122 to 123.

Despite the Offshore racing commission's increasingly strong safety requirements, the balancing act between speed and safety continues. And controversy, no stranger to Offshore racing, remains.

Controversy and Competition

The year 1988 undoubtedly was a pivotal one for Offshore. The elected Offshore commission vice-president, Jay Smith, was removed for making "inappropriate business decisions." APBA president Mike Jones stepped in as acting head until Stan Fitts was elected vice-president in the fall. The commission's bank account moved from the red to the black. Most of the drug smugglers seemed to be gone and the businessmen were at the helm. Officiating was upgraded and racers were hitting the starting line in growing numbers. An unprecedented ninety-three boats started in the season's final contest in Atlantic City, a record number for a United States race.

Further, the Offshore racing membership surged, increasing 50 percent to nearly one thousand members in 1988, making it now the largest APBA category. And growth was felt across the board, not just in the national events but also in the divisional competitions, some of which now carry $35,000 in prize money.

"The offshore racers are a strange breed," explained Jones. "They are the people who build skyscrapers, climb mountains, fly balloons across the ocean. Most are people who live in the fast lane but look at every day as a challenge and then go the extra ten percent. They have success and money and are looking for a new challenge," he said.

While the sport flourishes, however, there were signs that long-running debates on such subjects as the catamaran versus the deep vee hull, safety versus speed, gasoline versus diesel power, and offshore versus inshore courses were likely to bring future changes.

Ever since Englishman Ken Cassir proved the worth of the catamaran by winning the tough Cowes–Torquay race in 1977 with the 38-foot Cougar called *Yellowdrama*, the days of the deep-vee have been numbered. In the early 1980s, Ted Toleman broke the 100-mph barrier for the Open Class in his 40-foot Cougar cat. Don Aronow, creator of the Cigarette which has become virtually the generic term for the modern deep vee raceboat, contended for years the catamarans were a passing fancy, that they would break apart in heavy seas. But then he abruptly changed his tune, as USA Racing Team, his last company, turned to building only catamarans.

There is another aspect to the hull debate. Dick Genth started racing around 1963, and with each of the various production boatbuilding companies he has run (Formula/Thunderbird, Wellcraft, Chris-Craft, and Donzi), he has used high performance "as a vehicle to promote the bulk of the business, which is the broad scope of the family runabouts and cruisers. So much of our knowledge has come from the performance end."

But many in the industry no longer expect advances made in offshore racing to necessarily transfer down to the production boats. "It's a different breed of boat out there now," says Genth, referring to the 50-foot Superboat catamarans.

Catamarans, after all, have never met with success as pleasure boats. With them, it's go fast or not at all, an inflexibility of design that lacks appeal in the marketplace. The durable deep-vee, at times with modifications, remains the predominantly popular hull shape.

"The majority of people in racing have some tie-in with a

boat manufacturer, and we're all producing vee hulls," notes Gus Anastasi, vice-president of high performance at Wellcraft. A veteran racer, Anastasi also races with *Miami Vice* star Don Johnson, who started racing on the Offshore circuit in 1988 and, incredibly, wound up winning the 1988 Superboat World title. Clearly, the builders have little interest in developing cats, which are becoming the sole property of small custom builders such as Jaguar Marine or wealthy racers such as Al Copeland and Tom Gentry, who support the custom builder or put their own shop together.

For a while, it was fashionable to have two boats, a catamaran for calm waters and a faithful deep-vee for heavy weather. But new construction methods allowed catamaran hulls to became stronger, lighter, and more durable. At the same time, courses were shifted to run largely in the calmer waters close to shore rather than far offshore. The rationale was to create greater spectator interest, which in turn would develop greater sponsor interest. However, it was a development that also favored the catamarans.

While some have suggested that a long offshore leg be incorporated, Fitts does not believe this is necessary. "We don't need a longer leg; we need a leg that requires navigation to find the checkpoint because navigation is an integral part of Offshore."

The Europeans, who do race offshore and across some difficult waters such as the English Channel, think this is nonsense. At the 1987 world championships in Key West, the Italians in particular scoffed at the course being rerouted to avoid known treacherous waters by staying close to shore.

"This is not offshore racing. Offshore racing is not inshore racing," asserted Fabio Buzzi, a racer who is the primary engine and transmission builder for many of the Italian teams and who has also designed some of their hulls. "The fact is, all your boats are directionally unstable and can't handle open water," Buzzi said of the American fleet.

Buzzi also criticized the short-distance legs. "Overtaking so many boats is a dangerous situation," he said. "They say it is good for spectators. Offshore racing is not a spectator sport. In Europe there are no spectators in the racing areas." However, in the United States it's another story, with races such as the Atlantic City contest drawing more than 300,000 onlookers.

There is no doubt that the European and American racers are headed in different directions. During the first day of racing at the 1987 Key West worlds, which ultimately were won by Englishman Steve Curtis and his Cougar, less than half the field finished. Eight of those eleven boats were foreign, five from Italy. Three of those four hulls were designed by Buzzi and four of the five were powered by diesels.

Buzzi's dominance continued. His stellar season in 1988 culminated in his winning the UIM World Championship for the Open Class, a tough series held in Guernsey, England. Then he shipped his 44-foot boat to Florida, renamed it *Gancia dei Gancia* for a new sponsor, and swept the three-race series to claim the Open Class title in the Key West World Cup. His diesel-powered craft also posted the fastest speeds of all cup classes, including the Superboats. Indeed, by the time he reached Key West, Buzzi reportedly had had the same diesel engines in his boats for eighteen months. This is amazing longevity considering that some American Superboats, which race with four engines each, have their gasoline engines changed between every race. For some, that meant twelve gasoline engines were needed for the Key West series.

Diesels are central to Buzzi's systematic approach to racing. Many Italian competitors prefer diesel power because of its reliability and lower operating cost, and because of a technical advantage: The rules allow diesel engines to have twice the displacement of their gasoline counterparts. While gasoline engines have had the edge in speed, that edge is being erased by new, lightweight, yet powerful diesels such as those crafted by Buzzi.

As Anastasi sees it, "Diesel is going to be here regardless of what anyone says. But in performance boats it's not going to go big. I don't care how good it is or how big it is. People still want a high-revving gas engine."

"In the last five years speeds have increased twenty-five miles per hour on the average," noted racer Chris Lavin of Westport, Connecticut. "And guys are out there touching a hundred and fifty miles per hour." And they are running catamarans, or tunnel hulls, which with their enclosed cockpits and stabilizer fins look more like Unlimited boats than the traditional offshore deep-vee.

"One of the important things in any competitive sport," points out Stan Fitts, "is that speed is not necessarily the most important ingredient. The issue is not that some boats are going a hundred and fifty miles per hour, but rather the type of competition created to give everyone an equal opportunity to participate. We would like to see more consistent, safe speeds where the competition would be greater." This, he expects, can be achieved through technical limitations such as restricting the carburetor and manifold. "That's what we're looking at now," he added, "and we're looking at it in cooperation with the manufacturers because this is of mutual concern to the sport and the boat and engine manufacturers."

The possible restrictions are in the future. For the present, those in racing are trying to deal with the high speeds they have created. And not all are happy. "There are boats on the drawing boards that can go in excess of a hundred and fifty miles per hour," says Bob Latham, president of Latham Marine of Fort Lauderdale, a leading manufacturer of high-performance accessories. "The scary part is they will be running on the sea, which is an uncontrollable, always changing surface. Everything can be fine and then you can get a hole or rogue wave and fall into a situation where you are hanging on and going for a ride and hoping everything will be all right."

Latham, who has been racing offshore himself since 1976, believes "the boats are going too fast for the crews. Offshore was meant to be a test of men and equipment, not a test of speed."

Catamarans, now running close to 150 mph, are on the razor edge of control. "Their speeds are outrunning the capacity of the hull," said Wellcraft's Anastasi. "They are starting to fly like a hydroplane, barely touching the water." If a boat hits a wave at the wrong angle, the results can be devastating. "A cat that stuffs at ninety miles per hour is going to stop roughly within its own length," said Latham. "This is like slamming into a brick wall at a hundred miles per hour."

Allan "Brownie" Brown, offshore racer and a builder for

After learning to drive a Scarab for his *Miami Vice* TV series, actor Don Johnson won the Mississippi River race in 1987 and the Superboat world title in 1988. *(Courtesy of Wellcraft)*

twenty-seven years, takes the long view of the sport. "The technological breakthroughs have been absolutely phenomenal, primarily in speed but also in size. The boats have gotten bigger and still gone faster under basically the same set of rules. In UIM Class I [equivalent to U.S. Open Class], the standard has been one thousand cubic inches since day one but the top speed has gone from forty to a hundred and forty miles per hour."

However, Brown also believes the boats are going too fast. "We make a big mistake in this country with our so-called offshore racing, which is in fact inshore racing. The boats are so delicately balanced in the interest of top speed they are not capable of running in true offshore waters, which puts us at a hell of a disadvantage. No one wants to build a vee-bottom boat anymore, which really is a sea boat, and go out and finish ninth or tenth." Brown sees American racers losing the advantage to the Europeans. "If we don't race in smooth water, the Europeans will beat us because they race regardless of what the weather is on race day, and they generally run in eight- to twelve-foot seas. We've become so shocked with fatalities over here, that if there is a sea bigger than the height of your bathtub, they flag the race."

A number of safety issues remain unresolved in Offshore competition. While cockpit covers are mandatory on Unlimiteds starting in 1989, there is no agreement to their benefit in the Offshore ranks. "You cannot enclose an Offshore boat safely," asserts Latham. A capsule must have a trap door that opens out, he points out. "With a boat lying upside down, the water pressure that keeps it afloat also works to keep the trap door closed. And if you have to swim down to get out from under your boat, your life jacket is working against you. . . . If you have a hole above your head or off to one side where you can squiggle out, you have a chance."

In April 1988, two racers died when their catamaran, with fully enclosed canopies, overturned in Florida waters. Reportedly, they were unable to get out of the cockpits.

Jaguar Marine's Jack Clark won't race without canopies ever since his boat flipped at 115 mph during the 1987 worlds. He believes the canopies saved his life and that of his crew. Racers Chris Lavin and Don Roberts rolled their canopied cat *Jesse James* during the first race of the 1988 season. Both emerged unscathed, which Lavin attributed to the canopy. Before the race, they were the first Offshore racers to go through the dunker test, similar to the one used by Unlimited racers, which teaches racers to extricate themselves from crashes.

The soft-spoken Lavin is one of the sport's most courageous drivers. Lavin, in his mid-thirties, started racing with his brother Mark. Mark essentially ran the team while Chris managed the family's real estate interests in Connecticut. In 1985 the brothers' 30-foot Conquest cat named *Jesse James* won almost every race on the national circuit that they entered, collecting the U.S. title as well as the world. The next year, the Lavins returned with a new 35-foot *Jesse James* Conquest cat which featured the first serious attempt in Offshore to protect the crews. Both brothers wore restraining harnesses and were surrounded by a cockpit safety cocoon, but they did not yet have a cockpit canopy. During the 1986 worlds in Key West, after easily winning the first of three races in their fleet, *Jesse James* stuffed and submarined at 90 mph. Tons of water rushing over the windshield and into the cockpit struck Mark Lavin a mortal blow to the forehead. Since then Chris Lavin has become a leader in an Offshore safety program that is developing protective crew capsules, or cocoons, and improved restraining harnesses and enclosed canopies. He and his father formed the Mark Lavin Safety Foundation to underwrite research leading to greater safety for all competitors.

Chris Lavin returned to the sport, now to head the *Jesse James* team. He was determined to build the ultimate Superboat, the most technologically advanced as well as the safest. This new 48-foot *Jesse James* was expected to begin racing during the 1989 circuit. Designed by George Linder, who also designed the Conquest and Shadow cats, the new boat was built in a custom South Carolina race shop for Rich Luhrs's Conquest Marine of Westwood, New Jersey. For Lavin, the appeal of the Superboat Class is that it allows for unbridled innovation and speed. Every system on the boat, from the enclosed four-person cockpit to the motors, drives, and 22-inch-diameter propellers, has been custom-designed and built. Linder anticipated the boat would cruise in the 130- to 150-mph range.

"I think this should be the best rough-water Superboat in the world," the designer said. The power to propel the wood and axial fiberglass Superboat comes from four 900-hp motors prepared by Batten Engineering of Romulus, Michigan. The engines feature all-aluminum Donovan blocks with four-valve-per-cylinder heads, a first in Offshore racing. "Four-valve technology allows a twenty-percent increase in horsepower just through better breathing," said Linder, who believes four-valve heads will be the next major power-plant innovation in Offshore. "Speeds are going up," he says confidently.

The main safety feature of the boat is its completely enclosed cockpit cover, a single cover that encapsulates the crew. The canopy is constructed from two double-width F-16 canopies fasted back-to-back with a fiberglass roll bar. The safety cockpit was built into the boat and contains an emergency breathing system for the crew. *Jesse James* also carries computers and accelerometers mounted in the tunnel, on the deck, and in the cockpit. These devices monitor everything from the engines and propeller-shaft torque to the air pressure in the tunnel and the G forces on the racers.

Jesse James is one of several exotic new Superboats taking aim at dethroning Al Copeland's team from its pinnacle atop the class. The first blow to Copeland's dominance was made by Charles Marks, a newcomer to the sport, in the last race of the 1988 season when Marks drove his new Superboat, *Eric's Reality*, to victory. Copeland still emerged the points champion in the Superboat Class for the fifth year in a row.

A native of New Orleans, Copeland is the founder and chairman of the 700-unit Popeyes Famous Fried Chicken and Biscuits and seven-unit Copeland's Cajun American Cafes. A high school dropout who has wheeled and dealed his way to a seven-figure annual income, Copeland spends $1.7 million a season to race Offshore. He was the innovator of the first Superboat in 1983 when the class was added to Offshore. He won the national Open Class title in 1984 and the world championship in 1986 and has dominated the Superboat Class since its inception.

His latest Superboat, *Popeyes/diet Coke*, was completed in time to be tuned up by Copeland's son toward the end of the 1987 season and then went on to dominate a sparse field in 1988. While Copeland was working to build the Superboat Class, the heart and soul of Offshore remained in the Open Class. With the arrival a number of new boats, such as *Jesse James*, Charles Marks's *Eric's Reality*, and John Antonelli's new craft, the Superboat Class shows promise of becoming not just a technological showcase but also competitively exciting.

The interior of Copeland's new boat is like the interior of a Rolls-Royce—quiet, air-conditioned, and lushly padded. Thirty percent lighter than his first Superboat, the new 50-footer is made of carbon-fiber composite construction and powered by four 585-cubic-inch fuel-injected engines, each developing 850 hp. The engines were built by Kinetic, a Michigan engine-building firm, based on Ford blocks. They are attached to surfacing drives developed by Copeland and his former throttleman Bill Sirois. Because the engines are so powerful, the Copeland team designed the drives to use chain boxes to transfer the power from the motor into the drive shafts, and consequently the gear ratios are not changed in the drive but rather in the chain box.

The exotic-looking craft, designed by Englishman Peter Birkett, features a canopy with a carbon-fiber top and front and side windows made of the same material used in the F-16 cockpit cover.

The fin on the stern functions like a stabilizer on an airplane. As Bob Idoni, Copeland's crew chief, explained, "When we get the boat going over a hundred and twenty miles an hour, it helps keep it going straight."

The boat, said Idoni, doesn't get up and run until it's traveling over 110 mph. And it hasn't begun to reach its potential. Copeland set a course record in the 1988 Sarasota race by averaging 109.69 mph. "We were coasting," said Idoni.

Just because he has one of the fastest boats in Offshore doesn't mean Copeland isn't aware of the risk. "In the last two years, eight guys have lost their lives and two have been crippled that I know of," Copeland says, adding that it scares him. Copeland, in his mid-forties, races with three diving paramedics of his own who ride in a helicopter over his boat during every race. "It's not because we're not comfortable with the boat, but you never know," Idoni explains.

Copeland says he started as "a Sunday racer." Then he bought "a little pleasure boat and went out and beat everybody. When somebody beat me, I would buy a bigger boat. Finally I got so big I put together the first Superboat." While his competitive drive has taken him to the top in business and racing, Copeland is also philosophic. "You keep safety first and be prepared for anything as well as you can. And then you go for it. You don't overextend yourself."

The attention on Offshore racing was magnified during the 1988 Key West Offshore World Cup, the final competition of the season, because of rookie Don Johnson's remarkable victory in the Superboat Class. The matinee idol, who became addicted to high-performance boats during the shooting of the TV series *Miami Vice*, no longer can be considered just another pretty face on the Offshore circuit. Moby Griffin, the TV series' marine coordinator, taught the actor to drive a Wellcraft Scarab 38 for the show, and Wellcraft gave him a second Scarab for his personal use. Johnson next started doing his own speedboat stunts. And then Wellcraft's Anastasi became his coach.

At one point Johnson told Anastasi "in a joking way" that he wanted to race with him. "I told him whenever he had time, we'd race. Don wanted to run the Mississippi [in 1987] and then before we knew it, we were running races on the circuit to qualify the boat [for the Superboat world title race]," said Anastasi.

Before the 1988 season, Anastasi described Johnson as a "good, down-to-earth guy. People say he's not one of the easiest people to get along with and he's pretty stubborn at times. But when he started with me, he had no knowledge of racing and he followed instructions well. He wants to race, and once you want something like that, you're going to learn."

He learned, all right. Driving the *Gentry Turbo Eagle,* a 46-foot Wellcraft Scarab with a Kevlar deep vee hull powered by three 850-hp Gentry turbocharged engines and Kiekhaefer sterndrives, Johnson qualified for the Key West event by entering the minimum three races on the regular circuit. The races, respectable finishes of 3-2-3, had to be juggled between Johnson's movie commitments.

Bill Sirois, who ran the *Popeyes* team for five years, joined Wellcraft after quitting *Popeyes* during the summer of 1988. Regarded as one of the finest throttlemen in the world, Sirois teamed up with Johnson and Anastasi for the Key West worlds. Sirois admits at first he had his doubts about racing with Johnson but soon realized the actor was a serious racer. "I could see the guy was a natural," he related. "He has tremendous powers of concentration, and he's got the want and the will to win."

In the third race of the series, Johnson finished second to defending world champion Tom Gentry of Honolulu, averaging 87.149 mph over the 149-mile course, but it was enough to edge out Gentry in the title series. Johnson, whose series record was 2-1-2, won world title in the boat Gentry had loaned him for the 1988 season.

"A lot of salty dogs wondered what I was doing here, but by God, I'm world champion," said Johnson after the race. He then threw his arms around throttleman Sirois and navigator Anastasi, saying, with genuine humility: "I get all the attention, but the real credit goes to the crew. What mattered wasn't how well I drove, but how damned good my throttleman was. Bill kept it together and kept us close in every race, and Gus kept me from driving to Bimini. We weren't the fastest boat out there, but it isn't how fast you go that counts, it's whether you're still running at the finish."

After the traditional victory toss into the water, Johnson stood on the deck of his Scarab, arms joyfully thrust overhead, while the crowd chanted, "Don, Don."

Donzi, baby, would be proud of him.

Distance Runs

As a publicity stunt in the 1920s, the legendary Gar Wood raced a train, the Twentieth Century Limited, down the Hudson River from Albany to New York. Two *Baby Gars*, boats *IV* and *V*, started against the train, which roared down the tracks alongside the river. Wood started out driving *V* but when it became apparent that *IV* was faster and was going to outrun the train, he switched boats. Gar Wood knew how to draw national attention, and his remarkable distance races established the idea of running powerboats long distances from point to point.

With powerboats today running across distances as vast as the cold, dark North Atlantic Ocean, this type of endurance racing has acquired a magical appeal. The ocean is one of the last frontiers of adventure and the challenge is elemental, humans pitting their skills against the forces of nature.

Wood began running long distances in Florida in early 1921 to promote his line of express cruisers. Later that year he and his friend Charles F. Chapman drove his cruiser *Gar II Jr.* in a race against the Havana Special train from Miami to New York, beating the train by 23 minutes. His time of 47 hours 23 minutes was held for forty-one years. Now called the Chapman run, this is perhaps the best-known of the distance runs.

There also were distance marathons such as the one on May 28, 1950, when some three hundred intrepid outboard racers started from Albany for the finish line off Manhattan. Of these, 115 managed to finish on that cloudy, cold run down the choppy Hudson; the winning time was 3 hours 18 minutes for an average speed of 39 mph.

The distance runs are truly endurance tests for man and machine. The longer the distance and the rougher the water, the greater the test of physical as well as mental endurance. In recent years, distance runs have come back into vogue. While the Miami–New York run probably has been the most-traveled stretch of water, endurance tests are popular also on the West Coast, with runs such as Seattle to Los Angeles and Ketchikan, Alaska, to Seattle.

Distance runs serve as a laboratory for boats and engines,

a proving ground that has become increasingly important as new technology has entered the marine industry. Wellcraft Marine has used this laboratory effectively. After passing migrating whales, dolphins, and sea lions and encountering 8-foot seas and 20-foot Pacific rollers, a 46-foot Wellcraft Scarab driven by movie star Chuck Norris set a new speed and endurance record on August 3, 1988. The karate ace and his crew of four completed the 440-mile run from San Francisco to Los Angeles with a running time of 6 hours 53 minutes 19 seconds, which eclipsed the previous record set by a gasoline-powered boat by nearly 10 minutes. Norris's elapsed time was 7:41.19, a new diesel record. The time difference was the result of propeller problems midway. While he was at it, Norris also set a new San Francisco-to-Ventura endurance record of 6:30.30.

The Scarab is the same design as Wellcraft's 5000 Scarab Meteor. Built for racing by Team Scarab, it features a single-skin construction using Kevlar and vinyl ester resins. Its foam-packed urethane fuel cells have a 780-gallon capacity. Norris's craft was powered by twin turbocharged 420-hp Caterpillar 3208 diesels connected to Arneson surface drives.

"This is a state-of-the-art production boat and power setup," said J. Robert Long, Wellcraft president, after the run. He acknowledged that the race was run to demonstrate the capabilities and performance of the boat and its engines in the open ocean. "While it is not designed to run the very high speeds of many of today's Offshore raceboats, it is designed to run for long periods of time at high average speeds," explained Long.

In 1987, Team Scarab also took on the Mississippi River, this time with actor and Offshore racer Don Johnson at the helm. Johnson and his crew—Wellcraft's Gus Anastasi and river pilot Thomas George—knew that speed alone would not be enough to beat the original record run set in 1982 by Michael Reagan, President Reagan's son. The strategy during the 1,039-mile run from New Orleans to St. Louis over the Labor Day weekend was dictated in part by the river itself, with hazards such as floating debris and hidden sandbars as well as river traffic that at times created conditions similar to the 6- to 8-foot seas usually found in offshore races.

The two-day competition, called the Budweiser Challenge

Cup, took its toll on the boats and only five of those who started finished. Johnson's course record was 19 hours 51 minutes 9 seconds with an average speed of 52.34 mph. His 43-foot Scarab was powered by twin MerCruiser/Lamborghini engines and MerCruiser outdrives.

As the Offshore racing courses were moved inshore in the 1980s—along the coasts and into the Great Lakes to benefit sponsor and spectator interests—there were those who lamented the passing of the true-blue, rough-and-tumble days of Offshore when men would jump in a boat and roar off to Bimini on a bet. After all, where was the challenge of the elements, the navigational skill, the romance in closed-course racing inshore? As the Offshore circuit has emerged into a more marketable commodity, those who lamented the loss of races across the open ocean found other outlets, such as promoter John Crouse's new race from Miami to Nassau and back to Miami nonstop, and that granddaddy of distance runs—the treacherous North Atlantic Ocean.

Crouse started the 362.3-mile Searace, the longest Offshore race, in 1986 to revive blue-water, point-to-point, no-holds-barred racing. There are no official checkpoints and only one required turn off Nassau's Paradise Island. During the first two years of the Searace, Miami boatbuilder Filippo "Ted" Theodoli was not only the first to finish in his 63-foot diesel-powered Magnum express cruisers, but also the only one to survive the course. With Offshore innovator Jim Wynne aboard, the gracious Italian marquis who owns Magnum Marine and insists he doesn't build "raceboats," outlasted six other racers the first year and five the next. A shrewd businessman who once raced cars and ran a New York advertising agency, Theodoli's upset victories in 8- to 12-foot seas in 1986 and placid waters the next received considerable attention, in large measure because his Magnums are not stripped-out racing machines but rather luxurious high-performance cruisers.

"We don't build raceboats. But when invited to participate in a challenge, we will," said Theodoli. The finish time for his first victory in 1986 was 6 hours 40 minutes. The following year he shaved 30 minutes off his time. "We could have done it faster," he related, "but we didn't because the others either

Former world champion Tom Gentry, one of the most talented and
innovative competitors on the offshore circuit, challenged the
North Atlantic with the remarkable 110-foot *Gentry Eagle*.

broke down or dropped out. We proved that you can win a race with a regular motor yacht."

Well, not exactly "regular." His Magnum that year was equipped with a pair of eighteen-cylinder 1,840-hp Italian CRM turbocharged diesel engines connected to Arneson surface drives. Magnum in fact was one of the first builders to adopt the surface drive.

"Originally the famous Miami–Nassau race was run in little bitty production boats with a couple of men on board. They had to go through the Gulf Stream and over the Tongue of the Ocean," said Theodoli. "Now they race near land, in lakes. It's not the same thing. In the old days you went on your own. There was no Coast Guard to follow you. If anything happened, you were on your own."

Ted Theodoli's Miami–Nassau–Miami record was snapped up on June 3, 1988, by Hawaiian real estate developer Tom Gentry, who used the course to tune up his huge new 110-foot *Gentry Eagle* for an assault on the transatlantic record and in the process beat Theodoli's record by 50 minutes. Gentry next took aim at the New York–Miami record set by George Morales two years earlier. Gentry, a former world Offshore powerboat champion, claimed that title June 19. His time for the 1,093-mile course from Miami to New York was 19 hours 17 minutes 23 seconds, a scant 13 minutes 57 seconds faster than Morales.

The North Atlantic proved to be another story. This ocean is completely unpredictable, majestic one moment, mad the next. To cross it is the ultimate challenge, the supreme test of crew and equipment. But with recent developments in propulsion, there is a new breed of high-speed powerboat capable of traveling greater distances and competing for records once held by ocean liners. In 1986 a 72-foot British powerboat, *Virgin Atlantic II*, made three refueling stops with supply ships en route in setting the record of 3 days 10 hours 31 minutes, beating the record held for thirty-four years by the liner S. S. *United States* by 2 hours and 9 minutes.

In the summer of 1988, two boats and their crews, Gentry's *Eagle* and an Italian boat, *Azimut Atlantic Challenger*, attempted to set the record for the fastest crossing from Ambrose Light off New York Harbor to Bishop Rock off England's Scilly Isles, some 3,400 miles away.

The 88-foot-long aluminum Italian boat was designed to run nonstop while Gentry's boat intended to make one stop, because its crew believed that refueling would take less time than running with the extra weight. The hazards involved in racing across the Atlantic include Nantucket Shoals, the treacherous area of shifting sandbars off Nantucket Island, and Iceberg Alley, the stretch where the Labrador Current brings icebergs down into the ocean along the east coast of Newfoundland and produces banks of fog. After that it's a straight run across 2,000 miles of open ocean to Bishop Rock.

The greatest enemy, though, is the pounding of the waves, which leaves the crew punch-drunk, working at 50 percent capacity at best, and struggling against vertigo and hallucinations. Large waves, 10-footers or so, are potential killers. Unless one maintains the correct speed and attitude, the boat will "fly," soar off one wave crest and into the next wave with such a force that the boat may be destroyed and the crew injured, possibly fatally.

The natural question is why would anyone want to do this? The tangible rewards are meager, disproportionate to the risk. There is no monetary remuneration. Instead, the record holder is given the Blue Riband, a historic award, and a silver trophy. For that, though, a person like Tom Gentry would spend six million dollars on his boat and equipment.

"It's a whole new challenge to come up with a technique that will work," said Englishman Dag Pike. Pike had been navigator on the British record holder as well as navigator on the *Azimut Atlantic Challenger*. "It's like we've done the easy south face of Everest, now we've got to go up the hard north face. We're breaking new ground."

Richard Branson, a British entertainment magnate, was the first to apply raceboat technology to an ocean crossing with his *Virgin Atlantic I* and *II*. Since his success, the technology has changed rapidly. But it was Branson's record that prompted the 1988 attempts. Dr. Paolo Vitelli, president of Azimut, the Italian boatbuilding firm, bet an English friend he could do better and build a boat to go nonstop. Gentry, meanwhile, was intent on "getting the Blue Riband back for the United States."

Gentry's 110-foot aluminum deep vee hull, more than double the size of a raceboat, was built at Vosper Thornycroft, Ltd., in England and designed by Peter Birkett, an English raceboat designer. However, the basic hull shape and unique engine and drive combinations were strictly Gentry's. Gentry, in fact, is an innovator who started his own marine engine company. "He went for turbocharging rather than stick with what everyone else was using, the fuel-injected style of racing motor," said John Connor, Gentry's throttleman. "He built his own engines with turbochargers, won the world championship, and now is marketing them."

The 110-foot *Gentry Eagle* is powered by two German-built MTU sequentially turbocharged marine diesels, each generating 3,480 hp at 2,100 rpm. The diesels are connected to Swedish-built KaMeWa water-jet propulsion systems. For added thrust, Gentry installed a lightweight Avco Lycoming diesel turbine, producing 4,500 hp, between the diesels and connected it to an Arneson surface drive. This was the first time a surface drive had been connected to a turbine. In all, the engines provide 11,360 hp, enough to drive the 50-ton craft at a lightweight speed of nearly 80 mph. Fully loaded with fuel, the boat weighs another 50 tons and runs 65 mph on all three engines.

Azimut's Vitelli, meanwhile, sought to find the best balance between displacement and seakeeping. The boat was to weigh 125 tons at the start and 40 tons at the finish. Because of the substantial change in freeboard, water jets were the only means of propulsion capable of using the full power of the engines throughout. To the two Riva Calzoni water-jet drives, Vitelli connected four turbo supercharged Italian CRM diesel engines, each generating 1,850 hp maximum at 2,075 rpm. The engines work in pairs, linked to the drives by means of dual port reduction gears. The craft has an average speed of 48 mph, running 35 mph fully loaded and 70 mph lightweight.

These two state-of-the-art craft were in New York ready to go by late June. Neither had a specific time for starting. The crews were looking for a calm period on the ocean, waiting for a high-pressure system to go by so they could run behind it.

"The whole secret," said the veteran Pike before leaving, "is to leave nothing to chance. And then you've got to push hard and keep on going. You mustn't stop for anything."

Despite the sophisticated equipment, the computer models, and all the planning, the moment of truth for both crews came in midocean. They had waited weeks for a high-pressure system, but the weather didn't cooperate. Finally both set out from New York Harbor on the same day, July 24, hours apart and running independent of each other. Both attempts ended in disappointment amid heavy seas reaching 15 to 20 feet. Gentry's problems began when the spray rail loosened and was sucked into a water jet. Connor heroically dove into the tumultous icy water to try to pull it out. Next it was discovered that a fuel bladder had split and water had leaked into the tank contaminating the diesel. More than one third of the way, Gentry, who at one point had been knocked unconscious while moving about the boat, had enough. He withdrew and put into St. John's, Newfoundland.

Soon after, the Azimut boat arrived at the same dock. A broken rocker arm had shut down one of the engines, forcing the crew to abandon the race. The Italian boat had traveled halfway to England and was on schedule to break the record when the rocker arm broke.

Gentry's problems still were not over. After his boat left Newfoundland en route to New York, it struck an island off the southwestern tip of Nova Scotia at 43 mph and ran onto a rocky beach before grinding to a halt, its hull severely damaged. Gentry was not on board at the time and none of the crew was injured. The boat had been some twenty miles off course when it hit the island.

Neither Gentry nor Vitelli has given up. Both vowed to continue their challenge to conquer the Atlantic. As Gentry put it before leaving New York, "Now that's a real race."

How to Get into Racing

When one watches *Popeyes/diet Coke* blast across the television screen, one isn't likely to think that it is a simple task to be another Al Copeland and get behind the wheel of a Superboat. And that would be true. Copeland's racing team is a highly sophisticated, megabuck enterprise. However, it is possible for almost anyone who wants to race powerboats to do so.

Perhaps the easiest entry-level craft are the mini-boats, which are inexpensive, fun, and gaining in popularity. A mini-boat is a scaled-down pleasure boat, a small runabout or even a tunnel hull, that can run from 30 to 60 mph. Generally 10 to 14 feet in length and equipped with an outboard from 25 to 60 hp, a mini-boat gives one a chance to try out the sport, play the high-performance game, and see if one enjoys competing. Mini-boats can be purchased through marine dealers and the mini-boat races are run either under the APBA Special Events category or in a specific Outboard Performance Craft Class.

The Mini Gran Prix Class was started four years ago, based on the design of the full-size Cougar catamaran and called the Cougar Cub. The Cubs are 12 feet long, use 25-hp outboards, and run at 40 to 50 mph. Outboard Marine Corp. helped establish the class and encouraged manufacturers to build hulls conforming to the rules. Mini Gran Prix boats must be factory-built fiberglass stock boats with stock outboards, and they must be equipped with a kill switch, which stops the engine if the driver is ejected. With these stock boats the only changes that can be made are to the timing, propeller, or carburetor jets, a factor aimed at holding costs down. A Mini Gran Prix racer—boat, motor, and trailer—costs about $3,500.

In the Sport C Class, mini-boats use 30- to 40-hp outboards, custom props with optional engine tilt, and trim controls. A Sport C mini-boat, motor, and trailer runs about $5,500.

After testing the waters in the minis, one can move up to any one of the APBA classes such as the stock outboard ranks or Offshore competition. One can even set one's sights on dethroning Copeland.

"It's not a great mystery to participate in Offshore today,"

144

said Stan Fitts, vice-president of the Offshore commission. "Offshore is not only for those who can afford to play with expensive toys. Offshore is a business for a number of individuals. Offshore also is a way for others to try out some ideas with the technology available now. You can make an investment from fifteen thousand to fifteen million. Offshore runs the whole gamut.

"In the past," he continued, "when one thought about the racers of the Sixties and Seventies such as Sandy Satullo, Doc Magoon, and Don Aronow, the situation in the marketplace was one where everyone could read about it but not participate. Today everyone can be a participant."

To this end both the Offshore and Unlimited commission offices have developed marketing programs that include television packages, race sponsorships, and supportive materials to help race teams secure sponsors for their boats. Regardless of whether one elects to seek sponsorship, and regardless of the size of one's wallet, experts caution not to enter Offshore competition without doing some homework.

For $15,000, however, one can go to a marine dealer who handles high-performance equipment and buy a good boat, outboard motor, and racing equipment and go out and race. One can start this way with a production boat in the Sportsman Classes and, noted Fitts, "when you get your feet wet and get into it, you can go right up the ladder."

Even if your budget is in the Superboat range, this might not be the place to start. Says Chris Lavin, driver of the Superboat *Jesse James*, "You can get into the sport fairly cheaply and have a lot of fun." If one's budget allows, Lavin recommends starting "with outboards and a small tunnel boat, spending initially fifty thousand dollars for the boat, engine, and parts. You could probably go with a first-year racing budget of seventy-five thousand dollars [which includes travel and maintenance] and possibly cheaper if you buy used equipment and maintain it yourself."

Not only is the competition fun and exciting at this level, Lavin points out, "it may be more fun than what *we're* doing, where the frustration factor is right up there." Lavin made this comment when his frustration factor was evident due to the delay in the construction of his new *Jesse James*. Chris and his brother, Mark, bought their first raceboat in 1981 for $20,000. They raced in the Northeast, competing in five races, which cost another $30,000.

At the other end of the spectrum is Copeland, who has a $250,000 boat and $500,000 in engines and who takes a crew of twenty to ten or twelve different races on the circuit. His annual budget was reported to reach $1.7 million.

Once one has determined the level at which one intends to compete, one should go to the races, see the boats, and talk to the crews. "Talk to the pros, the guys like Richie Powers and Bob Idoni, talk to the team managers, the throttlemen and setup men. These are the aces. Find out exactly what to do," said John Crouse.

"So many people get into racing, putting in tens of thousands of dollars, without researching it," he observed.

The first criterion is to make sure one obtains a good, solid sea boat. The best combinations of engines, drives, and propellers can be fairly complicated, with the technology rarely static for long. And be sure to research safety procedures and techniques.

"Even getting into the production and modified class boats is like stepping into a racecar in the Indianapolis 500—and more things can happen to you in a boat. You don't sink or get lost in a racecar. People who have raced cars and raced offshore say offshore is much more exciting, but you can't go into it as a lark. . . . Every major race in the last two years has had a big boat crash," Crouse noted.

Remember, speed alone is not enough. Those who are consistently successful, from Gar Wood to Fabio Buzzi, are drivers whose boats experience the fewest mishaps, those who came to the starting line with their quality equipment in the best condition.

Part 3

High-Performance Boats Today

I have always liked speed—efficient speed, that is; speed with a minimum of lost motion.

—Lindsay Lord, *Boating* magazine, 1988

Chapter 8

Designing for Speed

The luxurious 110-foot megayacht *Thunderball* streaks across the seas at 50-plus mph, illustrating high performance on a grand scale. *(Courtesy of Denison Marine)*

In Italy, explains Magnum's Filippo Theodoli, the part of the boat that touches the water is called the *opera viva*, or "living part," while the portion of the boat above the water is called the *opera morta*, the "dead part." "What's important is what you have on the water," says the Italian marquis.

And when it comes to the *opera viva* in powerboats, there are two distinct classifications: displacement hulls and planing hulls. A boat with a displacement hull occupies, or displaces, an amount of water equal to its own weight. It sits down in the water and travels slowly through, not over, the water. The laws of hydrodynamics limit displacement boats to a maximum speed that is close to 1.5 times the square root of their waterline length. Thus, a boat that is 36 feet long on the waterline can reach a maximum speed of 9 knots. If you add more power in an attempt to outgun the hydrodynamic limits, the hull only begins to push down in the stern, creating such a large bow wave that the boat cannot climb over it. Displacement hulls are generally long and narrow with clean, fine entries and often with rounded bottoms. Fuel consumption tends to be low, especially with diesel power, and range long. Displacement hulls come in all sizes and shapes, from canoes to trawlers.

Planing hulls are designed with bottom sections that provide lift. When properly powered, they rise up out of the water to skim on the surface, riding on a portion of the aft underbody. A boat rises on a plane when its displacement is fully or primarily supported by hydrodynamic lift. A planing boat's forward speed creates lift, reducing wetted surface and thus increasing speed. The Unlimited hydroplanes, for instance, ride on the tips of the two sponsons and the lower half of the propeller with the hull airborne. And the design of the Offshore tunnel hulls is headed in much the same direction.

Before a boat gets on plane, it passes through two modes. It starts in a displacement mode, either at a standstill or traveling slowly, in which its weight or displacement is fully supported by the water. The second mode is in semi-planing or hump speed, in which the boat is trimmed up in the bow and dragging a large wake. Once through the hump, the boat levels off on plane, supported by hydrodynamic lift.

The term *hydroplane* was given acceptance by W. H. Fauber, one of the powerboat pioneers. In a 1911 article Fauber defined the hydroplane as "a craft equipped with planes or surfaces presenting an upward angle to the direction of movement, and designed to act on the water in a manner to lessen the *displacement* and *skin friction* of the boat, for the purpose of accelerating the speed, or securing desired speeds with a lesser expenditure of power." (Fauber's italics)

From the beginning, the planing hull was regarded as an entirely new type of watercraft. In pointing out what he believed was the difference between displacement boats and the hydroplane, Fauber said: "In the displacement boat, one deals with static buoyancy, wave resistance, stream lines, and friction, whereas in the hydroplane, the element of *dynamic force* predominates to such an extent that a new order of things exists."

At that time, some felt that the term *hydroplane* was not appropriate because sometimes the surfaces on which the boat rides when speeding are not always planes. Other names were used to describe this new type of boat, such as "skimmer," "glider," "bateau planeur," and "ricochet." But Fauber determined that "hydroplane" was just as appropriate as "aeroplane" since planes "are not generally made with surfaces that are true planes. . . . Even though the surfaces of the boat may not be planes, a pathway is planed through the water, and a

that does this comes near being a hydroplane; there-
til some more appropriate name can be suggested, we
oceed with this one."

In the 1930s, Lindsay Lord pioneered a new branch in naval
architecture—the development of planing-hull design. A leader
in the design of fast commercial craft, Lord was one of the first
to approach the subject on a scientific basis and his book, *The
Naval Architecture of Planing Hulls*, became the bible of planing-
boat design.

Lord became intrigued by hull design during his late teens,
while a student at Boston University. He had a canoe and put
a two-cylinder Johnson engine in it through a well in the bottom. The next year Johnson came out with a new 5-hp motor.
"I put that one in the canoe and to my disgust and bafflement,
the speed remained the same," Lord observed. "The stern of

A rugged competitor, Don Aronow takes one of his early deep vee
hulls through some choppy seas. *(Courtesy of Donzi Marine Corp.)*

the canoe just settled down to make waves under the push of a bigger engine. I was really baffled and decided that the only solution was to go to MIT."

At the Massachusetts Institute of Technology the professors were divided between the specialties of either sailboat or ship design and none would stoop to designing powerboats. The arrival of Prohibition changed that. When the rumrunners "got the idea that they could well afford fast boats, they went right to the head of the School of Naval Architecture at MIT, Professor George Owen," he said. Owen wouldn't be openly connected with the rumrunners. Nonetheless, Lord was assigned the design of a rumrunners' boat, "for experience." "That's how I started designing fast boats," said the naval architect.

During this period, boatbuilder Frank Huckins also called on Professor Owen and again Lord got the job "for the experience." He worked out hull bottom lines, using the elements of two adjoining cones per side to make a developed surface. Huckins watched Lord illustrate this conic method and then remarked, "Four cones. . . . Do you realize we have the Quadraconic hull?" Huckins went on to make the name famous. Later Huckins expanded the lines to 78 feet and won a Navy contract for PT boats. All of the early PT boats were notorious for pounding apart. As Lord observed, "The sailors said the Higgins PTs would drown you, the ELCOs would break your legs, and with the Huckins, you weren't sure which would happen first."

Lord spent World War II in a Hawaiian yard involved in PT-boat repairs and research. The rebuilding work allowed him to try experimental forms which gave him extensive experience with fast boats, ultimately leading to his book. Because of his PT experience, he said, he saw the need for greater beam than had been the standard, and of reducing the pounding by using convex sections forward. The convex forefoot in planing boats, conceived by John L. Hacker, is stronger and also disperses the water, he explained.

The performance of planing hulls is a magnification of every characteristic represented in the lines. As Lord explained in his classic text, it is the shape of the plane that determines speed potential and seakeeping qualities as well as lift. In the planing hull, the plane's major function is to give the boat lift. And each part of the plane must not only perform its own function but also be modified so as to contribute toward lift without endangering the boat's seaworthiness. For example, as Lord notes, the forefoot must smooth the way, allowing the boat to enter easily, without jarring; the forward chines must maintain the hull in a buoyant planing position so that it rides over rather than through steep waves; the after chines and total deadrise must allow the plane to take a positive bank while steering; the keel and lateral plane must give directional stability, and all of these must be accomplished in a manner consistent with obtaining the greatest useful lift from the maximum plane area.

The idea of steps goes back at least to 1872 when the Rev. C. M. Ramus suggested their use to the British Admiralty. Steps are athwartship (crosswise) breaks in the planing surface intended to reduce the skin friction. Like the transom, a step ends a planing surface and the purpose of this is to cause the water to miss contact with the plane and thus reduce wetted surface and increase speed. Steps are "ventilated" by having the sides open to the atmosphere above the waterline. In the 1920s and 1930s, the steps used in the Gold Cup boats were "ventilated" by means of a pipe bringing air into the step area. This eliminated the tremendous suction the step induced. Steps also can be ventilated by exposure to the atmosphere. Steps are common today except on some tunnel boats. Because these hulls are so narrow the steps are ventilated by the air rushing in from the sides.

The longitudinal strips on the planing surface are known as *strakes*. Strakes run more or less parallel to the chine of the keel and are often used to help in increasing lift. The extent to which strakes are effective is sometimes debatable. Jim Wynne, the Miami designer, recalled that when he and Ray Hunt were testing some of the early Bertrams, "we were placing strakes in different places to see how the boats performed. On one test we knocked the strakes off a boat and we didn't know it until we got back. The boat ran just fine." This led Wynne to believe "there's some black art in offshore racing. And strakes are not an essential part of the boat."

In the case of the catamaran, or tunnel hull, a tunnel is

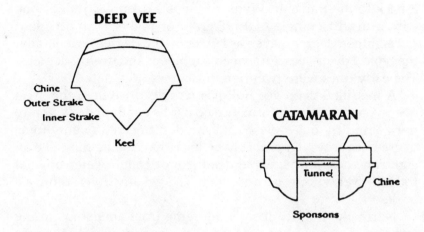

DEEP VEE

Chine
Outer Strake
Inner Strake
Keel

CATAMARAN

Tunnel
Chine
Sponsons

Two types of high-performance hulls: the durable deep vee, the best performer in rough water; and the catamaran, which performs best on calm seas.

formed between the hulls which makes use of aerodynamic lift. Boats such as the Hickman Sea Sled and the Apel three-point hydroplanes, which used aerodynamic lift nearly fifty years ago, have evolved into today's Unlimited pickle-fork hulls and Offshore tunnel hulls. The drawback, of course, is the difficulty of controlling the lift and preventing a blowover.

As for the deep-vee, Lord contends, it "has been around a long time as a desperate solution to the self-destruction of fast boats leaping off one wave to crash back down on the next."

Nonetheless, the dominant form in recreational boating to-day is the deep-vee. The term *deep-vee* is used generally to refer to anything that has a constant deadrise from roughly amid-ships back to the transom. The *deadrise* is the angle formed by the centerline between the bottom panel and the ground. Thus a hull with a 25-degree deadrise would have a much sharper vee than a boat with a 15-degree deadrise. The dihedral angle is that obtained by measuring the angle formed by the centerline and the two bottom panels inside the boat. Thus, a boat with a 25-degree deadrise would have a 130-degree dihedral angle.

A deep vee hull will have a fairly high deadrise and carry

it back to the transom. Wynne defines a deep vee hull as one with a deadrise angle of 16 degrees or higher. "Some might say eighteen degrees, even as low as fifteen degrees. Generally, the typical deep-vees are sixteen, eighteen, and twenty degrees. The early ones were twenty-four degrees," he noted.

A modified deep vee hull has less deadrise than the "real deep-vee of a high-performance boat," he continued. "If you're not going fifty miles per hour, you don't need a twenty-four-degree deadrise. It's probably better to have something like an eighteen- or twenty-degree deadrise for rough water but not the full twenty-four, because there is a penalty. Everything's a trade-off."

Normally, the deadrise is the same from amidships to the transom. On some boats, though, the deadrise angle changes in this area, a development known as variable deadrise. The purpose of the variable deadrise is to improve the hull's sea-keeping ability at the cost of reduced speed.

Indeed, there is no single perfect boat design. Every boat represents a compromise of design factors. Traditionally, a deep vee hull has meant poor fuel economy and short range, although the new breed of diesel engines, such as those used in the Gentry and Azimut boats, is starting to change this. Also, a boat with a high deadrise may be fast but it is not stable. It is a vee-shape, after all, and the sharper the point of that vee, the harder it is to keep the boat balanced. A boat with a high deadrise also will not carry a load well. "It's good for certain applications—going very fast. But if you're not going fast and have a heavily loaded big boat, it's better to have less deadrise," Wynne explained. The best compromise, said Wynne, is the boat that is most successful for its purpose.

Trends: From Microwaves to Megayachts

After nearly thirty years of study by naval architects and racers, the deep vee hull probably has been developed to its maximum potential. Meanwhile, the catamarans or tunnel hulls used in Offshore racing still have to find acceptance as pleasure craft. Yet, basic elements of high-performance boating are changing.

The high-performance vee-hulled boats being produced today are evidence of four distinct trends: (1) greater styling and packaging, (2) the use of exotic new materials to produce ever-lighter craft, (3) more powerful propulsion systems, and (4) bigger, faster boats. High performance is moving up from sport boats to cruisers, creating a new breed of megayacht.

Not long ago, it was enough that high-performance boats were the fastest craft afloat. Lean and mean meant the razzmatazz of raceboat lines, possibly standup racing bolsters, and big, unmuffled engines. No one noticed if the interior was frequently an unfinished shell; no one went down below anyway. No more. It's now fashionable to go fast in both style and comfort.

"They were rough-and-ready products a few years ago, hot motors with fiberglass wrapped around them with little concern for creature comforts or elegant styling," explained Bob Gowens, president of Cigarette Racing Team.

As the boats continue to evolve, Gowens believes, the move toward styling parallels the rise of styling in the automotive industry. "The sports cars of the 1960s were basically sheet metal wrapped around a hot engine. They were fast but not very refined," he noted. "Today, a Porsche 928 has all the creature comforts of any major luxury car—sumptuous leather seats, fabulous air conditioning, great sound systems, all wrapped around a lot of performance. Cars have preceded boats, but boats are becoming more refined. Customers are going to demand that from their boats."

How far will refinement go? As far as the customer wants —or the boat can take. From plush leather interiors to coordinated exterior and interior colors and splashy hull graphics, a boat's overall look has become as important as what's under the sunpad. The amenities, though, must be appropriate to the boat. Gowens does not expect, for instance, to be adding a galley fit for Julia Child on the Cigarette 35. However, he is considering adding a microwave.

Reggie Fountain, the former racer who heads Fountain Powerboats in Washington, North Carolina, said that in the past buyers "didn't care if the cabin was empty. The cabin wasn't important to them. And to put anything in there it had to be designed to keep from breaking apart when you ran the boat."

This has changed. According to Fountain, who has hired a Detroit automotive stylist to improve interiors, an increasing number of families are buying high-performance boats for cruising. The idea is to travel on the boat, in much the same way one would travel by car, and eat and sleep ashore. "You can buy a yacht that you can fire up in Washington, North Carolina, from my ramp and casually run up to New York City that afternoon. This is a whole new way to use a boat. People are traveling more on the water and they want to be visible. What better way than in some rocket sled that looks like it came from outer space?"

The concept of packaging also has hit the marine industry and it is becoming the way people buy boats, particularly the smaller sport boats and runabouts. In approximately three years, it is anticipated that 75 percent of all outboard engines above 25 hp will be sold in packages through boat manufacturers. Packaging involves selling the boat, engine, and often the trailer, too, as one unit, and a color-coordinated unit, at that. As Tom Dugall of U.S. Marine Power, part of the Brunswick marine group, notes, at the height of the season, most marine dealers cannot rig enough boats. Obviously, packaging cuts rigging time substantially. Packaging appeals particularly to an entry-level, first-time buyer rather than one seeking higher-end equipment. The boat is essentially turnkey ready—much like a car—and one can just drive away with it. With conglomerates buying boat and engine companies and packaging the two products, a buyer can also expect good pricing because of the economics of scale.

During the 1980s, high performance has been moving into bigger boats. It began with the Aga Khan and the King of Spain. In 1979, English designer Don Shead was introduced to both, separately, and was commissioned by both to design a luxury yacht. For King Juan Carlos, Shead designed *Fortuna*, a 90-foot yacht built by Palmer Johnson in Sturgeon Bay, Wisconsin.

Reflecting the trend toward bigger performance yachts, Tempest
Marine in 1988 introduced a line of fast yachts from 60 to 85 feet.
The *Tempest 60* (above), is designed to be owner operated. *(Courtesy
of Tempest Marine)*

Fortuna, with its sweeping lines, can hit 60 mph thanks to a
pioneering power system. Shead used two MTU diesels and a
Lycoming gas turbine with water-jet propulsion.

The Aga Khan commissioned *Shabaz*, a 56-footer built by
Souters in England. A revolutionary, costly, cold-molded composite of wood and carbon fiber, *Shabaz*, a semidisplacement
boat, was regarded as the fastest boat in the Mediterranean
when it was launched, reaching just under 60 mph.

The custom builders followed. Magnum moved up to 63-
footers that run 60 mph. And as Ted Theodoli noted, "When
you get to wherever you want to go fast, you have all your
comforts, your kitchens and baths. This is the epitome of high
performance, one that can do all the jobs; go fifty miles per
hour in heavy seas and not rock and roll and do crazy things
. . . because it comes basically from the deep-vee-oriented boat."

Some are giving a new spin to the trend to bigger, faster

boats. In 1988, Tempest, which had made 42-foot sport boats, went into production on a line of high-performance yachts ranging from 60 to 85 feet. The new Tempest 60, though, was designed to be owner-operated rather than run by a captain.

As Jerry Berton, who is overseeing Tempest's move into big boats, explained it, "Seven years ago only a relatively few people were involved in high performance. Now everyone is high-performance oriented. Customers with these high-performance boats will move into bigger boats, because the trend is always up. At a certain size, though, usually sixty feet, they can't be owner-operated. You can't just jump in and go have lunch because they are physically too big for you to handle the lines by yourself."

Tempest's new 60-footer does have space for crew quarters in the stern, he continued, "but it's really designed for the owner-operator. And that's really the limit in size for people who want a speedboat without dealing with a captain."

At the pinnacle of high performance, in terms of size, power, and cost, is the new breed of megayachts. They are similar to the *Gentry Eagle* and Azimut transatlantic boats in the sense that they have both range and speed, two factors that used to be incompatible. Because of the weight of the engines and the amount of fuel required to reach high speeds, it simply was not possible in the past to build powerboats that could go both far and fast. The high-performance megayachts are now considered to be such craft: 100 feet long or more and capable of a top speed of 30 knots or close to 35 mph fully outfitted.

"Everything that can possibly be done inside yachts has been done—from Jacuzzis to swimming pools to waterfalls. The thing that will always be unique is more speed, boats that go faster. That's where we're headed," notes designer Tom Fexas, whose 126-foot Atwood yacht *Time* tops 35 mph.

Three years ago, according to *Boating* magazine, yachts capable of 25 knots plus (nearly 29 mph) comprised 10 to 15 percent of the world market for 100-foot-plus yachts. Today these yachts comprise greater than 40 percent of that market.

The first high-speed megayacht in the United States was *For Your Eyes Only*, built in 1985 for John Staluppi of West Islip,

New York, by Denison Marine of Dania, Florida. Staluppi, a multimillionaire car dealer in his early forties, is not one to travel slowly for long. As Staluppi says, he was happy traveling along at a normal speed "until another guy got alongside who thought he could pass us." He'd then accelerate and be gone in a rush of power.

The 105-foot *For Your Eyes Only*, designed by Joe Langlois, Denison's chief designer, ran just over 30 knots, or 35 mph, with two turbocharged MTU diesels developing 1,960 hp each and KaMeWa water-jet drives, making it the fastest large American yacht when it was launched. After he decided it was too small for lengthy Caribbean cruising, Staluppi sold the boat and in 1988 took delivery of the bigger and faster *Octopussy*. Built by Hessen Shipyards in Europe, the 130-foot boat has three 3,500-hp MTU engines, each driving a water jet. Top speed: about 55 knots or 63 mph.

Reportedly Staluppi was so determined to have the fastest megayacht, one topping 50 knots, that his contract with the builder stipulated that if a certain speed wasn't reached, he would not have to accept the boat. As a result, everything that went into the boat, from the engines to the towels and silverware, was weighed to ensure the designed weight would not be exceeded.

Staluppi took delivery but ran into competition for the fastest megayacht title from 110-foot *Thunderball*, the latest from the Denison yard, which was built for Staluppi's friend and neighbor John Rosatti, who at age forty-four owned fifteen New York car dealerships. *Thunderball* is equipped with a pair of 3,480-hp MTU turbocharged diesels and KaMeWa water-jet drives. It also runs in the 50-plus mph range, and in early sea trials went from 0 to 50 mph in an amazing 10 seconds and from 50 mph to zero in 8 seconds.

The Denison hulls have flat planing bottoms with a sharp stem and forefoot, widening slowly going aft and ending with a constant-deadrise, shallow-vee planing surface. The result, says Langlois, "is an efficient planing hull that also can be run at semidisplacement speed without losing anything."

Such yachts, as long as an eleven-story building is tall and traveling at 60 mph, require careful handling. "A normal every-day captain just can't hack it," Langlois noted. Looking ahead, he sees megayachts in the 70 to 80-mph range not being un-common, with greater use of the gas turbine. Currently, there are some twenty megayachts under construction around the world. "They are here to stay," Langlois concludes.

Chapter 9

Construction

A worker puts the finishing touches on a boat in U.S. Marine's production line. *(Courtesy of U.S. Marine)*

The signs and portents were there on the Pacific Ocean on February 12, 1977. On that day Rocky Aoki, the restaurateur, won the Mission Bay offshore race in California with his 38-foot Bertram deep vee boat named *Benihana* after his chain of Japanese restaurants. Aoki became the first driver to win a major powerboat race using a hull made of Kevlar. The use of Kevlar, a Du Pont aramid fiber lighter and five times stronger than steel, resulted in the saving of hundreds of pounds on Aoki's boat. The revolution in boatbuilding materials and methods was beginning.

The vocabulary of the modern era also now includes such terms as axial fiberglass, S-glass, E-glass, carbon fiber, Nomex, vinyl ester resins, Klegecell, balsa core, modified epoxies, Airex, and vacuum-bagging. In the 1980s, the new construction materials and resulting new applications for marine use started to move in earnest from the laboratories of major chemical and plastics companies into the shops of the custom and production boatbuilders. And many believe major breakthroughs in boat construction are still to come as the development of new families of chemicals becomes feasible.

Indeed, construction techniques today have come a long way from the good old days of offshore racing, the late 1950s and early 1960s, when the raceboats were built of wood. As fiberglass construction emerged in the 1960s, builders used the successful raceboats as molds. A builder would turn a winning wooden boat upside down, coat it so the fiberglass wouldn't

164

adhere, and make a mold from it. The basic materials were woven fiberglass matting and polyester resin, which in many cases today still form the basic product.

The ease with which builders could crank out low-maintenance fiberglass boats led to a tremendous expansion in the numbers of recreational pleasure craft. At first the quality was less than sterling and boats did delaminate, the glass separating from the matting sometimes with alarming frequency. Today, for the most part, the quality of boats being produced in the United States is high and the engineering is solid, as evidenced by the growing number of manufacturers who provide hull warranties.

The quality of construction, however, is likely to show up first on a high-performance boat before it does on a slower displacement boat. When an offshore powerboat "crashes through the water, it's like crashing through a wall. Think about what the boat has to take," remarked Craig Barrie, racer and marketing director of Cigarette. Offshore racing still is the proving ground for construction and design. The boat that holds together on the course, running at 100 mph or so, stands an excellent chance of retaining its hull integrity when used as a pleasure craft with a cruising speed of 50 or 60 mph.

"There is a definite trend toward performance, not racing performance, but being able to cruise at fifty miles an hour safely and not break down. People want to be able to go out and cruise fast," noted Reggie Fountain, former racer and now head of Fountain Powerboats.

In recent years, some of the big production builders have catered to the surging interest in offshore-style craft by adding high-performance models. These boats may be constructed in a simpler manner than the custom offshore boats, but before a big boat company invests in molds and marketing, it has usually done a thorough job of engineering.

The elusive leading edge is never static, however. On the racecourse and in the dealer showrooms, there is a continual push for greater speed. More-powerful engines require hulls that are stronger yet still light. As a result, new materials and methods evolve as fast as builders and their customers are willing to pay the premium.

The range of construction methods used in building high-performance boats today is seen in three methods used by three different companies: Cigarette Racing Team, the famed Don Aronow–created company which builds high-quality custom deep vee race and pleasure boats; Jaguar Marine, a custom builder of tunnel-hull offshore raceboats and probably one of the country's smallest boatbuilders; and U.S. Marine, the world's largest boatbuilder. The cost of a high-performance boat is related to the cost of the materials, the amount of labor involved, as well as the size and type of engine. A boat that is intended to travel at great speeds, such as 125 mph, will cost far more than a boat intended to travel at a moderate 50 mph. The boat designed for slower speeds does not require the use of exotic materials to hold its hull together, and because it tends to be a production, rather than custom, the boat also benefits from the economics of scale. A step-by-step look at how three diverse boats are built illustrates the craftsmanship and materials that go into a modern high-performance boat as well as demonstrates why the prices of boats can vary radically.

Three Different Methods: Cigarette Racing Team

Cigarette entered the world of high-tech composites in 1986 when it switched from using the traditional woven fiberglass mat to the new axial fibers and Kevlar, a material used in bulletproof vests and in tires as reinforcement. Generally it takes thirty-five days to turn the raw materials into a sleek 35-foot pleasure boat capable of reaching 90 mph. Each boat essentially starts as a series of kits comprising the parts needed for particular phases, such as the hull, electrical, mechanical, carpentry, and rigging.

The first step is to make the mold from which the fiberglass hull will be made. The mold is built from a plug, usually made by a company specializing in plug construction. Val Jenkins,

Cigarette's general manager, explains that a plug maker uses some fiberglass, wood, and various kinds of filler material in making a plug, "anything he feels is suitable to make it hold its shape, but in the end he's going to throw it away.

"Most new boats today tend to be based on an existing boat," Jenkins continued. "You take one of last year's models and modify it. In some cases, though, such as our thirty-one-footer, a boat is built totally from the ground up from plans and with a wooden plug. That plug was built similarly to a boat but marine-grade wood was not used. In some cases a plug maker will use furniture-grade plywood, which falls apart when it hits the water but has a real good surface finish on it. It only has to last through one molding process."

To make the mold, a builder basically coats the plug with a gel coat and then builds up successive layers of fiberglass on top of the gel coat until he has a structure that is rigid enough to support its own weight and the weight of the boat that is going to be built inside of it. At Cigarette, said Jenkins, the mold is made of fiberglass but of a higher-temperature material than the boats to enable it to "stand more abuse."

The aim is to obtain a form strong enough to support the boat without distorting itself as the boat is loaded into it. "The mold is a big empty shell that is going to gain twenty-five hundred to three thousand pounds as the boat is layered into it. You keep piling the layers in and when it's over you've got a lot of weight in the boat," Jenkins explained.

The hull lay-up is relatively straightforward. First the mold receives one layer of gel coat, which will form the outermost surface of the hull. Next follows a skin coat, or check mat. This is a high-grade, lightweight mat that will conform closely to the twists and turns of the outside of the boat. The purpose of the skin coat, said Jenkins, is twofold. First, it eliminates air bubbles because it conforms so closely to the mold form. Second, it provides a barrier between the outside gel coat and the material that will be layered behind it, material that otherwise might "print" or show through the gel coat. Next follow successive layers of axial fiberglass fabrics which are laid in by hand according to a precise pattern.

The original fiberglass mat was a woven material with individual strands interlocked at a 90-degree orientation. The axial materials are not woven. Instead, piles of material are laid one on top of the other and stitched through and through; they can then be stitched to a mat. This means one can install multiple layers at one time and the direction of the fibers can be closely controlled. "You can have some running the long way, some running forty-five degrees one way, forty-five degrees another, and then stitch that whole mess together," Jenkins said. The ability to control the direction of the fiber means a hull can be built stronger with less weight. This is bread-and-butter development in offshore since it translates directly to better performance.

Jenkins compares the directional use of fibers in a boat to that in a fishing pole in which the fibers run the length of the rod. "If the fiber runs across the pole, that obviously is a place where the rod will break or at least not bend. It's the same in a boat."

. A woven mat, with its fibers crossing at 90-degree angles, also "is nothing but a succession of little holes in which the resin collects and forms a well. The axial fibers, in addition to allowing us to control direction, have no holes to hold the resin," he noted. Consequently, less resin is used which results in approximately a 25 percent savings in weight. The savings in resin, however, doesn't offset the added expense of using axial fabrics. These generally are twice as expensive as woven fiberglass, pound for pound. The value lies in having a stronger, lighter hull. And the change in materials is fairly dramatic. Prior to using axial fibers, a Cigarette hull was comprised generally of 70 percent resin and 30 percent fiberglass. Today the proportion is 50–50.

Cigarette builds between two hundred and three hundred boats a year (exact figures are not divulged by this privately held company), and of these 10 to 12 percent are constructed of Kevlar. Kevlar replaces the axial fiberglass in the structure. Because Kevlar is somewhat stiffer and stronger than the axial fabrics, less of it is used.

"You don't gain a lot of strength, because you've taken material out of the boat," Jenkins went on to say. "One thing you do increase is toughness. Kevlar boats are pretty rugged, but the ultimate failure point is not radically different than in boats with axial fibers; they just stand up better."

Several different kinds of resins are used in the construction process, depending on the fibers used and the area of the boat. All the boats are skin-coated with AME 4000, a modified epoxy resin made by Ashland Chemical that has a higher heat-distortion value, Jenkins said. With Kevlar boats, Cigarette uses AME 4000 throughout. "It's a very elastic resin and can take a terrible pounding," he continued. "Overall, you are looking for toughness, strength, and resilience."

With axial-fiber construction, Cigarette uses a general-purpose polyester resin as well as the AME 4000. Cigarette does not use carbon fiber, although it is used on a number of raceboats. "It's such an expensive fix," Jenkins noted. "It costs a lot of dollars to save a few ounces." However, Cigarette is looking into the use of carbon fiber to reinforce some areas that have to support a lot of weight, for example, in bonding the stringers to the hull.

The workmen laying down the pieces of fabric follow a "cut list." Each area of the boat requires a specific number of layers, and part of the control of a hull's strength involves the manner in which these pieces of fabric overlap. The fabric pieces overlap down the center of the hull, and in some places on the transom there are triple layers because of the areas of double overlap in the center. Workmen alternate the lay-up around the boat, doing one section at a time, overlapping sections to provide increased strength where needed.

Next, the stringers, the longitudinal hull supports, are set in jigs and fixtures to make sure they are in the correct positions. They are "tabbed down" with 6-inch-square pieces of fiberglass. The jigs are pulled out, leaving the stringer system in place. The stringers are covered up with material matching that used on the bottom of the hull—axial fabric or Kevlar. However, the axial fibers may be used in different orientations, Jenkins explained, to place more fiber for holding the stringer to the boat or to add more fiber on top of the stringer and thus make it stiffer.

In an analogous process, the cabin liner has been made on another set of molds, has been trimmed and cleaned up, and now is ready to be installed. This is placed inside the hull with a big jig, a steel fixture to which the liner is clamped. The alignment pins on the jig line up with holes welded into the framework of the mold, so the liner and hull are fit together within a minuscule one-eighth-inch tolerance.

"Now it's time to pull this mess out of the mold," chuckled Jenkins. A hoist is used to pull out the hull which then is trimmed. It is now five days into the construction process.

Each boatbuilder has his own sequence of installing fuel tanks, plumbing, and wiring. At Cigarette some of these installations are done before the hull and deck are put together. The fuel tanks are made of welded 3/16-inch aluminum and bolted to the stringer system with stainless-steel bolts. Then the space surrounding them is filled with two-part polyurethane foam.

Seven and a half days into the construction process, the deck is set on the hull and screwed down. The metal guardrail is screwed to the deck and sealed with silicone. Then workmen bond the hull and deck on the inside with fiberglass.

The engine room is painted red, a tradition with Cigarette boats, and the mechanic now begins the engine installation, which takes about twelve days. Until recently, the most popular engine was the MerCruiser 420 (TRS drive); now, Jenkins said, it's MerCruiser's 454 Magnum with the Bravo drive. "The sky's the limit in this place," he continued. Jenkins recently built two boats that had pairs of 850-hp engines—a total of 1,700 hp on boats 35 and 38 feet long. "You're talking about going nearly ninety miles per hour. That's fast enough to undress you, literally blow your clothes off, and make your face change shape." Of course, this isn't necessarily everyone's idea of a good time.

Some subassembly and fabrication has been in process since the hull construction began. At the same time the carpenters and electricians begin work on the inside of the boat. Cigarette builds its own wiring harness. The harness contains the wiring for all the power requirements, and the wiring conduit is bonded into the hull.

Bob Gowens, Cigarette president, also noted that the company manufactures all the mounting brackets for the hydraulic pumps, which are through-bolted. "The trim and drive-angle setting in rough water at high speed is critical," he said. "The last thing you want is for the pump to be ripped off the engine-room bulkhead."

Fourteen days after the deck was put on, the boat is approaching the time for its sea trial. Jenkins then decides whether the boat is to be painted before having its sea trials, an ongoing juggling process that often varies with the space available in the paint shop.

Every boat is given an extensive sea trial that lasts anywhere from five to six hours to three to four days, depending on the complexity of the equipment. One function is to document what has been built into the boat. One section deals with the boat itself and here the chief mechanic, who generally conducts the sea trial, lists the boat's weight and what was on the boat when he weighed it. Another section describes the engines, the manufacturer, model, horsepower, and serial numbers; another gives the same information about the drives as well as noting their reduction and the propellers they are equipped with.

Then the boat is run through some speed tests. While each boat usually has a speedometer, a radar gun also is used to check speed. "There are tolerances inside of which the boat has got to operate. If it doesn't, that tells you there is something wrong with the engine or boat," said Jenkins.

Then the boat heads back down the creek into the test area, which is the open ocean unless adverse weather conditions require the runs to be made in the Intracoastal Waterway. "Here we're trying to shake the boat up a little, bounce it around and see if anything rattles loose," the general manager went on to say. He or the chief mechanic will make quick turns at high speed and purposefully mistreat the boat, all the time checking the fuel system. Then the boat makes a run with a specified setup of trim and flaps. On a second run the driver tries for all-out speed. Both results are recorded.

Another series of tests follows back at the dock which involves making sure the water pressure works and checking to see if anything shook loose during the sea trial.

From here the boat heads for the paint shop. Cigarette uses Du Pont Imron, a paint used on many cars. It is a multicoat process with little waiting, forty-five minutes or so, between coats. In some cases—particularly if there are graphics such as a large screaming eagle—the boat will be given a clear overcoat for durability.

Cigarette makes all its upholstery by hand in its plant on North Miami Beach's Fleet Street. The stand-up bolsters are framed in fiberglass rather than wood and then upholstered over this frame. The cockpits are generally made of Naugahyde, although some have been done in leather. Cloth generally is used in the interiors. "But if the customer wants snakeskin, we can do it. We've done almost everything," Jenkins related. The customer picks the paint scheme that integrates with the upholstery. Once the upholstery is in, it's time to clean the boat up. At this point thirty-five working days have been put into the boat and it's ready to be delivered.

Cigarette tries to do as much work as possible in house to control quality and timing. This tends to add to the cost of the boat but results in a craft of recognized performance. The three basic models, 31-, 35-, and 38-footers, range in price from $100,000 to $300,000, with the cost a function of size and horsepower. Cigarette provides a one-year warranty on the hull and all rigging performed by the company. Certain components, such as the engines and stereos, carry their own warranties from the manufacturer.

Jaguar Marine

A fifteen-minute drive from Cigarette and N.E. 188th Street in an industrial area of Pembroke Park is Jack Clark's Jaguar Marine. Clark started racing in 1984 with a 30-foot Chris-Craft catamaran and won the APBA Pro-Stock championship and APBA Southeast Divisional championship. He also was named 1984 rookie of the year. Clark's success fueled his desire to build his own boat. And the following year he moved up to the Open Class in a boat of his own design and construction, the 35-foot wooden Jaguar tunnel hull. "It was ugly and people laughed, but it was fast," Clark said. It was fast but not particularly successful. The problem was that its wooden construction wasn't tough enough, said Clark, who sank the boat twice in 500 feet of water.

Clark took 1986 off from racing to search for what he felt was the optimum method of construction. The method he developed resulted in his being named Offshore designer of the year and tunnel-boat manufacturer of the year in 1987, based on his 35-footer *Thriller*, which raced in the Open Class in 1988 as *Coors Light Silver Bullet*, the first boat constructed with Clark's new process. Since then Clark has produced John D'Elia's Open Class speedster *Special Edition*, which won the U.S. Open Class title in 1988, and John Antonelli's 46-foot Superboat Class craft.

Clark wasn't far off base in naming his boat *Thriller*. During the Key West world championships in November 1987, Clark, riding as throttleman, and Ed Martinez, the driver, had the

Thriller, built by Jack Clark's Jaguar Marine, represents the leading edge of raceboat construction. The 35-foot tunnel hull is crafted of Kevlar and an Airex foam core, making it exceptionally light and strong. *(Courtesy of Jaguar Marine)*

173

dubious distinction of proving that it is possible to barrel-roll an Offshore raceboat at 115 mph and walk away without a scratch. Clark later said it justified his faith in the fully enclosed canopies. The boat bounced off a wave, rose up on its side and then rolled over upside down, skidding along on its top for several seconds before completing the flip and finishing upright.

"Ed and I had practiced what we would do if this happened, and when the time came, it was amazing how we just did what we were supposed to without thinking," he related. "Each of us grabbed the mouthpiece [from the emergency air supply] and stuck it in his mouth and got hold of the grab rail to brace himself. The safety harnesses worked perfectly and we were just waiting to pop the canopies and get out when the boat stopped. But as she slowed she just went back over on her feet again."

After his two earlier sinkings, safety was a key factor for Clark in building *Thriller*. He set out to build not just a fast boat but one that wouldn't sink. In this he has succeeded. He developed a rotating mold system and a vacuum-bagging technique using an Airex foam core that ensures his boats will float in addition to being exceptionally light and strong.

Clark begins the process by waxing the mold, which initially requires a minimum of six waxings. The plug for *Thriller* was his wooden-hulled prototype. After the mold is waxed and prepared, mold-release valves are set. The air valves are used to blow the section under construction out of the mold and yet they have to be able to withstand the pressure of vacuum-bagging.

Essentially, Clark builds the boat in sections, and these sections are comprised of three layers—the laminate outside skin, the core which in this case is Airex, and the glass inside layer. The sections meet end-to-end in the process, forming one continuous bond. "It's like building three boats instead of one and that's why it takes so long to build them," he noted. He spent seven months building *Thriller*. The process is now down to four months. In 1988 Jaguar delivered three boats, with that number expected to double in 1989.

Once the mold is ready, the gel coat, the exterior color of

the hull, is applied followed by the skin coat. Next the hull fabric is selected. Clark works with two modern forms of fiberglass—S-glass and E-glass—and Kevlar. S-glass generally is loomed with the fibers running in one direction, being held together with cross-stitching or glue. E-glass is a standard, non-woven fiberglass with fibers running in two directions.

The "wet bag" process now begins as the outer layer of the sandwich is constructed. The fabric for the particular section—such as the deck, or side or top of the tunnel—is cut. Then a "tape line" is established. This is done by fitting the clear plastic vacuum-bag film or casing over the fabric. The casing, which has a line of tape on the outer edge, then is rolled back out of the way. Next a layer called the peel ply is cut to fit and placed on top of the fabric. This material allows the resin to pass through it, but it will not stick to the resin. Then the bleeder fabric, similar to felt, is cut to size and placed on top of the peel ply. The bleeder fabric is used to absorb excess resin squeezed out under pressure. On top of the bleeder fabric goes a cut-to-size bubble pack, clear plastic film with bubbles. Finally, on top of all of this goes the plastic casing bag. The vacuum connector, which runs into the bag, is set up and taped off and the vacuum gauge inside the bag is set. This enables the workmen to read the pressure inside the bag. Then the bag is rolled back again and all the pieces are taken out in sequence right down to the E-glass or Kevlar. This was only a dry run.

Now Clark determines the "gel time," or how much time he has until the resin sets into a solid form. He does this by testing the resin at different catalyst rates. Catalyst rates, which are carefully recorded, depend on factors such as the temperature of the air and the humidity. He uses Dow Chemical's Derakane vinyl ester resin for its strong adhesion and ability to flex and retain its strength.

Once the gel time is known, his workmen get into position. The skill here is to get the materials laid, the bag down, and the pressure applied before the resin hardens. The fabric is "wet out," which means the resin is applied to it, first underneath and then on top. This is placed on the skin coat and excess resin is squeezed out. Next the peel ply is pulled down over it followed by the felt bleeder fabric. Over this goes the bubble pack and clear film casing, which is securely closed around the tapeline. The vacuum hose is hooked up and dialed into the predetermined pressure setting. Using atmospheric pressure, by sucking air out of the bag, equal pressure is applied to the laminate which removes excess resin while also minimizing the voids or air pockets between the fabric and the skin coat. This vacuum process requires a minimum of five workers, and the material can be under pressure for up to an hour.

At the end of the vacuum time, the pump is turned off, the bag is stripped off, the bubble pack ripped away, and the peel ply and bleeder fabric containing the excess resin are discarded. "You are left with the finished product, with the glass literally pressed to the skin coat up against the mold," said Clark. The next area, is then cleaned and prepared and the process begins again with a new tapeline being set.

And that's just the first layer. The second layer is the Airex foam core. Clark repeats the procedure, using 1-inch-thick Airex, a rigid PVC foam, instead of the fabric. The peel ply is layed on top of the foam. Bleeder fabric is not used because resin is not being pulled out here. Instead, the vacuum pressure is applied to push the Airex core down. Instead of using the Derakane vinyl ester resin, which is used on the fabric, Clark uses a system developed by the manufacturer in which the Airex is set in a Core-Bond bedding compound.

Airex is unique among rigid plastic foams since it can be compressed up to 50 percent of its thickness without rupture or crumbling of the cell walls. This makes it ideal for use as a core material in construction of boat hulls destined to take high-impact, slamming loads, and heavy pounding in open seas. Because it has memory, Clark noted, the foam core returns to its original shape after taking a hit. The foam core also ensures the craft will not sink.

After the core of foam has been vacuum-bagged into place throughout the entire hull, the first step or layer is repeated to get the "sandwich construction." Clark and his crew start all over again, putting down fabric and establishing a tapeline over the Airex core. The layers of the boat, from outside to inside, then will be: gel coat, skin coat, laminate (choice of a fiberglass or Kevlar), Airex and Core-Bond, and laminate. Clark also uses carbon fiber and Kevlar in various areas of the boat for greater strength. The bulkheads are vacuum-bagged outside the boat. The stringers and bulkheads are installed by the vacuum-bagging process, as is the deck.

Once the bulkheads and stringers are installed, the boat is removed from the mold. Before the hull and deck are joined, the fuel cells are installed; these are flexible fuel tanks, similar to those used in airplanes and racecars. Foam inside the cells prevents fuel from sloshing around. Fuel cells are lightweight and their construction provides an added margin of safety as well. The deck and hull are joined in a double-bonding technique: bonding inside and outside the hull.

Clark's tunnel hulls weigh approximately 100 pounds per foot. Thus, a 35-foot Thriller hull weighs 3,500 pounds and the 46-foot Superboat hull weighs 4,600 pounds. The upper end of high performance does not come cheap. The basic 35-foot hull costs $125,000 while the 46 runs $185,000.

Clark's innovative mind doesn't stop with hull construction, either. With his *Thriller*, he devised a system whereby its two 700-hp MerCruiser engines are mounted on rails and can be moved forward or aft to the optimum position for the sea conditions on race day. Different-sized drive shafts accommodate the various engine placements.

"If this were possible in a pleasure boat," said Temptest's Jerry Berton in admiration, "you'd know exactly where to put the motors on the boat, right to the inch. . . . Now they will know how the boat will handle in every possible condition and it allows them to get that dialed in, optimizing the different gears and the propeller selection. And this should increase performance by ten percent."

U.S. *Marine*

Unlike Cigarette and Jaguar, U.S. Marine is not in the high-performance business as such. U.S. Marine, based in Seattle, is the world's largest builder of pleasure boats. Its affiliate com-

panies include: Bayliner, with its incredibly popular Capri runabouts; Cobra bass boats; Maxum Marine; Quantum Marine;
and U.S. Marine Power with its Force outboard engines. In
1988, U.S. Marine produced 54,000 pleasure boats, an increase
of 14,000 over 1987. Further indications of its rapid growth are
seen in its annual sales, which totaled $612 million for 1988
compared to annual sales of $50 million six years earlier. U.S.
Marine achieved its rapid growth by appealing to the main-
stream, those who desire family-oriented boats. For the 1989
model year, however, U.S. Marine unveiled a new affiliate
group—Ariva. Ariva marked the firm's entrance into the high-
performance field, but at the lower end of the speed spectrum,
in the 50-mph range. The Ariva, if you will, is a go-fast family
boat.

As Jerry Stansfield, a U.S. Marine executive, explained, before the firm launches a new boat the purpose or need for the
craft in the marketplace is identified. The performance criteria,
"whether it is designed to go 50 mph or 25 mph, will determine
the shape of its hull."

U.S. Marine has two different lamination processes that it
uses in construction, one, called Unitized Construction, that it
uses for smaller boats such as the Capri runabouts and the
Ariva 20, and the other, called Marine Core, for larger craft.
Unitized Construction is primarily a function of how the lamination is reinforced. Typically, says Stansfield, U.S. Marine
uses woven roving in boats such as the Capri. First the gel coat
is applied to the mold. This is followed by chopped fiberglass
strands, which provide a bedding for the roving and allows for
greater adhesion between the layers of roving; it also acts as a
skin coat, preventing the woven pattern of the roving from
showing through the gel coat. The chopped strands are sprayed
into the hull with a resin catalyst and then rolled out by hand
to enable complete saturation of the glass material by the resin.
Next, wetted roving, saturated with resin, is hand-rolled onto
the chopped-strand surface. Layers of roving are overlapped
at the keel and chine for added strength. This method of construction is typical throughout the industry.

U.S. Marine, however, has found a unique way to reinforce
the hull with its Unitized system. The internal components are

incorporated into an interlocking structural grid, serving as one integrated stiffening system. This begins with the stringers, strips of Alaskan yellow cedar that are fiberglassed into place and rolled out like part of the lamination. Then the floorboards, seat bases, console frames, engine boxes, and the like are either stapled or screwed into place. These components form an interlocking grid which is then glassed into place as well. As a result of the grid, these interior sections, rather than being screwed on as dead weight, also become an integral part of the stiffening system. "We try to make the boat exceptionally seaworthy and sound without being heavy and requiring extra horsepower," said Stansfield.

The larger boats are built using a process which U.S. Marine calls Marine Core. This involves the use of laminates in addition to fiberglass roving, which helps add bulk and stiffness without adding weight. The laminates include Klegecell, a closed cell foam, and Coremat, a polyester matrix material with Saran microspheres. For additional stiffness in the decks, materials such as end-grain balsa core and marine plywood are used, depending on the particular application.

According to Stansfield, the Marine Core process enables the firm to take out 15 percent of the weight of a typical fiberglass part and add 20 percent more strength. The Klegecell is used as a sandwich with matting or roving on either side. Balsa core and Coremat also are core sandwich materials.

The inside surfaces in areas such as the engine compartment or storage spaces are given an opaque white resin base coat for a finished look. Some interior work is done while the boat is still in the mold, such as the stiffening and basic components to ensure that the boat maintains hull shape when it is removed from the mold. After removal, the boat is placed on a dolly and sent through the assembly process. A number of subassemblies take place before the deck and hull are joined, such as installing the wiring harness, seat bases, cabinetry, engines, and drive systems. Most of the deck hardware and deck wiring also are installed so that once the hull and deck are joined there is little left to assemble. The final step is installing the upholstery.

The deep vee-hulled Ariva, the family boat with "a performance orientation," as Stansfield puts it, carries a 260-hp

MerCruiser sterndrive on the 24-foot model. The cost of boat and motor runs $19,995. And the boat is turnkey ready, just add fuel. Standard equipment includes built-in swim step and ladder, stereo, convertible top, entertainment center, full instrumentation, power trim and tilt, and power steering. As is the trend among major manufacturers today, U.S. Marine also packages its boats with a color-coordinated, tandem-axle trailer. In the case of the Ariva 24, the cost with trailer, runs $23,495.

The top levels of performance will remain the elusive province of the wealthy and the racers. However, the fun of going fast in a seaworthy boat today is within the reach of just about every budget.

Chapter 10

Marine Propulsion

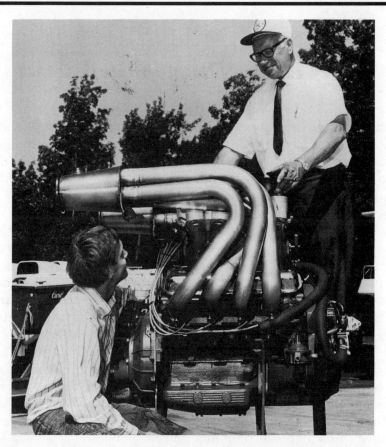

E. C. Kiekhaefer with his son Fred, now president of Kiekhaefer Aeromarine, Inc., examine their "Champion-Maker" 625 hp offshore racing engine. *(Courtesy of Kiekhaefer Aeromarine, Inc.)*

Engine Development

Some of the greatest strides in high-performance boating today are in the area of propulsion. Increasingly powerful sterndrives, mammoth 300-hp outboards, relatively lightweight turbocharged diesels, and gas turbine engines, along with evolving surface drive and water-jet propulsion all are stretching the horizons of performance.

High performance has always meant speed. But today it is not just speed that counts. It is speed plus reliability, speed made good over distance. The racer with the biggest, hottest engines doesn't win if he can't finish the course. And at the recreational level, yes, it's a kick to go fast. It's also an embarrassment, an inconvenience, and at times possibly a threat to one's safety, if one's engines or drive system breaks down.

Ten years ago the offshore raceboats were pushing 80 mph. Today the racers are reaching 150 mph and the recreational boats are running 70 to 90 mph. The beauty of this speed is not that one will be running flat-out but that one can cruise at 50 or 60 mph. This greatly expands the range of the boat, which in turn puts a greater premium on reliability.

Speed always has been the aphrodisiac but the search for speed has taken various directions. In the early 1900s Europeans went to great lengths to see how fast a boat could go under power and began competing on the water, with the enthusiastic participation of some of the burgeoning automobile companies such as Mercedes, Panhard, Delahaye, Peugeot, Renault, and others. However, the development of marine power in America took a different route. Blacksmith shops from New England to Chicago rapidly became equipped to build marine engines.

The growth of the marine-engine business led to the first New York Boat Show in 1905 and to the formation of the National Association of Engine and Boat Manufacturers (now the National Marine Manufacturers Association) two years later. The fifty-two charter members were primarily marine-engine companies—Standard, Rochester, United, Buffalo, American, and others, all of which disappeared long ago.

Today, marine engines are based on automotive engines. But in the beginning, United States automotive engines, with the exception of some such as the Simplex, Lozier, and Kermath, were not good enough for use on the water. In France and Germany, the early marine engines were derived from the automotive engines built for the wealthy. The American automotive engines of 1905, however, were unreliable, and in general the automotive engine was not acceptable for marine use until the 1930s.

The internal-combustion engine was developed for the marine world long before its use in automobiles. The cutting edge of technology was the pioneering path on the water, a fact directly related to the use of the engines. A marine engine generally runs at a constant speed close to full output all the time, requiring quality engineering, while the engine output in a car is less demanding. For instance, at 60 mph, the 200-hp car engine may be developing only 50 hp.

The term "internal combustion" literally means an engine that burns all its fuel internally, inside the cylinder. Conversely, the external-combusion engine burns its fuel outside of the engine, such as under the boiler of a steam engine. The early internal-combustion engines had problems with ignition and carburetion. They had no standard method of mixing fuel with air and no standard system for igniting it, and, while today octane ratings are specified on every gas station pump, in the early 1900s a fuel's volatility and specific gravity varied with the well from which it was pumped.

As the internal-combustion engine developed, replacing the coal-fired steam engine in launches, the idea of hanging it outside the boat over the transom gained in appeal on smaller craft. By 1910 thousands of outboard motors had been produced, but of the original outboard manufacturers the only one remaining today is Evinrude, owned by Outboard Marine Corp.

At the turn of the century Dr. Rudolf Diesel was developing his own variation of the internal-combustion engine. Instead of igniting the fuel with a spark, the customary method, Diesel compressed air until it became hot enough to cause ignition without any additional help. By 1902 one of his engines was propelling a boat around Paris on the Seine. Diesel's compression ignition eliminated the need for the troublesome electrical components required for spark-ignition engines. The competition between the compression and spark-ignition systems, between diesel and gasoline, continues to this day, each with its own advantages and disadvantages.

The primary power choices are between two-cycle outboard engines and four-cycle automotive engines, gasoline or diesel. Outboard engines, generally used on smaller craft, come equipped with propellers designed to fit the horsepower output. The four-cycle engines, meanwhile, are connected to one of four drive systems: (1) the standard propeller and strut below the surface of the water used today mainly in large cruisers and trawlers—that is, in displacement types of boats; (2) stern-drives, the steerable outboard-type drive unit; (3) surface drives, in which the propellers run on the surface of the water; and (4) jet drives, in which water is pumped out at high speed to propel the boat forward.

An outboard is considered a two-cycle or two-stroke engine because it delivers power on every other movement of the piston in the cylinder. When the piston rises in the cylinder, it compresses a fuel charge which ignites, driving the piston down on a power stroke. There are no valves. The fuel-air mixture enters the cylinder through a port in the wall exposed when the piston is down. The exhaust exits through another port, opened in the same manner. Fresh fuel pushes the burned charge out. Outboard engines are relatively simple and durable. Oil is mixed with the gasoline to provide lubrication.

With the four-cycle engine, only one piston stroke out of every four produces power. With one stroke, the piston compresses the fuel-air mixture, which is ignited to produce a downward power stroke, the second stroke. The third stroke pushes the burned gases out an exhaust valve, and the fourth stroke brings a fresh charge of fuel through an intake valve. And the cycle then begins again, with the piston compressing the fuel-air mixture.

Part of the power supplied by the marine engine is consumed by the frictional effect of the hull, which drags water along. Thus, a smooth hull exerts less friction. There also is mechanical friction, which saps engine power as it is transmitted through the transmission, drive, and propeller. This is reflected in the different means of determining horsepower: brake horsepower, indicated horsepower, shaft horsepower, propeller horsepower, and effective horsepower. The engine is rated in brake horsepower, named after the original measurement device. Indicated horsepower is a theoretical measure of engine power, representing the total force exerted by the burning fuel. Shaft horsepower is the power transmitted by the shaft, and propeller horsepower is the power put into the propeller. Effective horsepower is the net result, the power that pushes the boat.

Another term commonly used to describe an engine is *compression ratio*, which is a measure of how much the fuel charge in the cylinder is compressed before it is ignited. Generally, the more a fuel charge can be compressed, the greater power it will produce. The compression ratio of a cylinder is determined by dividing the volume of the cylinder with the piston at the bottom by the volume with the piston at its top position. It is expressed as a ratio such as 8 to 1, which is common for gasoline engines, and 16 to 1, which is about average for diesel engines.

Other key terms used to define an engine are *bore*, *stroke*, and *displacement*. Bore is the diameter of the cylinder in which the piston moves. The distance the piston travels from the top to bottom positions is the stroke. The displacement is the volume of the cylinder between the piston's upper and lower positions; this multiplied by the number of cylinders gives the engine displacement, expressed in terms of cubic inches or liters.

Conceivably, the two most significant developments in propulsion in the last thirty years were Jim Wynne's invention of the sterndrive in 1958 and Carl Kiekhaefer's conviction that Wynne had a good idea. Wynne, whose prototype was based on an 80-hp Volvo engine coupled to a Mercury outboard lower unit, reached an agreement with Volvo for the use of his patent. Kiekhaefer, the stubborn genius who founded Mercury Marine, was gradually persuaded of the merits of the sterndrive, and in 1961 Mercury introduced its first sterndrive, the MerCruiser. Mercury eventually signed a ten-year fixed-fee agreement with Volvo. From raceboats to runabouts, Mercury's MerCruiser sterndrives have dominated the high-performance field for some thirty years.

Kiekhaefer started Mercury in 1939 when he paid $25,000 for a bankrupt Wisconsin company that had in its inventory three hundred outboard motors it had built for Montgomery Ward but couldn't sell because they didn't work. While he hadn't intended to get into the outboard-motor business, Kiekhaefer, an engineer, saw a chance to raise some capital. "We had our backs against the wall," he said in a 1980 interview when he was seventy-three. "We had to satisfy the old orders. Those motors had to start and keep running." His solution was the reed valve, and of all his more than two hundred patents in marine-engine "firsts," Kiekhaefer said he was proudest of this simple steel device the size of a razor blade.

"It made engines start easier and run better and eliminated backfiring through the carburetor," he said. "And as you know, fires are definitely a no-no on a boat. You can't get away from them."

Some of his other inventions include two devices that are now common on automobiles as well as on marine engines: the electronic, or breakerless, ignition, and the alternator-generator. "Carl revolutionized the industry," observed Frank Scalpone, who worked for Kiekhaefer at Mercury and later became executive vice-president of the National Marine Manufacturers Association, the industry trade group. "He dominated powerboat racing from its very beginning. And the ten-horsepower Mercury Lightning he introduced in 1946 devastated the industry. It was a ten-horsepower engine with an eighteen-horsepower thrust.

"And all those stories about him calling up in the middle of the night because he had an idea—they're all true. No labor was too much for him. He's the only guy I know in any industry who would delay a product from the market because it wasn't exactly right," Scalpone said.

"That's just smart," Carl Kiekhaefer explained. "Look at all those automobile recalls. We never had a recall."

Kiekhaefer's Mercury Marine merged with the Brunswick Corporation in 1961. Nine years later he resigned as chief operating officer to revive Kiekhaefer Aeromarine Motors, which then built high-performance engines and accessories. Kiekhaefer Aeromarine, Inc., with Kiekhaefer's son Fred as president, continues to make high-performance accessories and in 1988 introduced new drives.

In the early 1970s the combination of Don Aronow's Cigarette and Kiekhaefer Aeromarine's Champion Maker engines proved unstoppable, elevating high performance to a new level. The Champion Makers were 454- and 468-cubic-inch engines that used mechanical-fuel-injected Chevrolet-based blocks. The success of those engines, recalled Fred Kiekhaefer, was due largely to his father's "incredible attention to detail." The desire to make a perfect product was carried through in the details, "down to the individual componetry used in the heads and rocker system and connecting rods, the crankshafts, vibration dampers, and high-capacity fourteen-quart oil pans," said Fred Kiekhaefer. "He had custom transmissions, hydraulic power takeoffs for the steering systems. He pioneered full hydraulic steering. That was created here and used just on our race engines. There are no belts on the engine, it was all solid gear-driven. We had our own water pickups, our own fuel-injection pumps that were driven mechanically from the gear drive. We made our own headers also, which had greater water-flow volumes and therefore ran a lot cooler."

The biggest advantage by far of those engines, said Fred Kiekhaefer, was their reliability. To this day, Kiekhaefer Aeromarine still makes components for the MerCruiser 3 Speedmaster drives, such as the lower-gear housings, shafts, and gears.

Outboard power today has jumped into the sterndrive range, and there are areas in which outboard power is preferred. For example, a pair of outboard engines may be preferred in an open fishing boat that can be run out to a reef and the props then tilted up.

Outboards are the most popular form of propulsion, with 444,000 units sold in 1987 versus 144,000 sterndrive boats, according to the industry trade association. The outboard figure includes those units under 120 hp where sterndrives don't compete. However, a more revealing picture is seen in sales figures from 1981 to 1987. These show that outboard unit sales have grown 39 percent, while sterndrive sales are up a remarkable 182 percent.

Indeed, the sterndrive is the mainstay in the marketplace. "The basic reason the sterndrives took off in the first place," said Fred Kiekhaefer, "was that the basic automotive power plant, when not overstressed, was just a much more reliable, quiet, and unobtrusive type of propulsion system. Most people don't want to stare at a tower of power—they want to enjoy the boating environment and they are not tech weenies on the hardware."

Despite the advantages of having the four-cycle power plant inboard—protected from the elements, easily accessible, and positioned aft so that it takes up less space than an inboard installation—and despite the advantages of the steerable, trimable outdrive, the sterndrive's progress was often bumpy. The flaws included the need to transmit power through two right angles, an engineering problem that bit into horsepower and made for cranky machinery.

With earlier sterndrives, Outboard Marine Corporation (OMC) ran into difficulties with its ball gears between the engine and the drive. If the trim was set too high under full power, the ball gears tended to melt, causing the engine to separate from the drive. It's no wonder OMC seemed happy to dominate in outboards and to leave the sterndrives to Mercury. MerCruiser and Volvo relied on a universal joint instead of ball gears, which worked well, allowing the engine to be mounted rigidly to the hull and the drive to be trimmed up and down. Volvo owned a patent on the universal joint, while MerCruiser owned a patent on a gimbal ring and they shared each other's devices under a gentlemen's agreement. MerCruiser, already dominant in offshore racing, ran away from the recreational pack.

All sterndrive manufacturers, though, faced the same devil in the form of galvanic corrosion. Electrolysis played havoc with aluminum casings submerged all season in salt water, and when the drives had to be repaired, the casings were often corroded together, making repair even more difficult.

The popularity of the sterndrive today is largely a result of overcoming these faults while increasing the power in the process. The sterndrive is expected to continue as a major force, a fact not lost on engine manufacturers. OMC's attitude toward sterndrives changed dramatically when it entered the ring swinging with its successful OMC Cobra sterndrive in 1985, the same year the Volvo/Wynne patents expired. Volvo Penta introduced its innovative Duoprop outdrive and is working to increase its small share of the market. Yamaha has taken the plunge, coming out with sterndrives for the 1989 model year, three years sooner than originally anticipated. Kiekhaefer Aeromarine unveiled heavy-duty racing drives in 1988. Mercury's MerCruiser Division responded with two strong new products. With such aggressive competition, sterndrive progress should continue its innovative pace.

Sterndrive Roundup

MerCruiser

The original MerCruiser sterndrives were named MerCruiser I and II. These designations have been replaced by Alpha One and Bravo One. The Alpha One sterndrives run from the 2.5-liter, 120-horsepower, four-cylinder engine through the 5.7-liter, 260-hp V8. The new 7.4-liter V8 Bravo One, with its large-diameter shafts and sturdier bearings and gears, is capable of handling nonracing applications of the 454-cubic-inch block. There is no transmission, as the shift is in the drive. This results in less weight, lower cost, no loss of transmission power, and more weight aft, which means less wetted surface. The hot Magnum series, 350- and 454-cid sport-boat packages, has benefited from racing development. The Magnum 454 coupled with the Bravo drive is the current star. The racing packages are those in the Performance Products group and carry an HP designation followed by the horsepower rating: HP320 EFI, HP420, HP575, and the newest entry, HP630 Lamborghini. These use a nose-cone-style Speedmaster gearcase with a Borg-Warner hydraulic transmission.

MerCruiser engines use General Motors blocks, with the exception of the exotic HP630 Lamborghini. The 561-cid, twelve-cylinder Lamborghini is rated at 630 hp at 5,300 rpm and currently is naturally aspirated, without fuel injection. This six-carburetor machine can be connected to the MerCruiser Super Speedmaster II or IV drive.

MerCruiser also has a line of conventional inboard engines and was expected to come out with a line of diesels—both sterndrives and inboards—from the former BMW Marine group, which now is part of MerCruiser.

MerCruiser pioneered two methods of combating corrosion. Its MerCathode II system, which is standard on the Bravo One, draws current from the boat's battery and blocks the stray voltage in the water, stopping corrosion due to the galvanic current. This does away with the need to inspect and replace sacrificial pieces of zinc. The second process, EDP, is a technique in which unpainted parts are given a negative electrical charge and the epoxy paint is given a positive charge. The opposite charges attract and, *wham*, the paint is bonded to the parts, resulting in a protected surface.

Outboard Marine Corp.

Outboard Marine Corp. returned to the fray in earnest with its introduction of the Cobra sterndrives in 1985. OMC began with a goal of making its drives easier and less expensive to repair, and, this time using the universal joint and gimbal housing, they succeeded. The new repair approach of remove-and-replace led to such improvements as positioning the water pump, a component likely to need attention on any engine, on top of the drive instead of burying it in the exhaust housing. The Cobra line includes a four-cylinder 3-liter model rated at 130 hp; two 4.3-liter V6 models, one rated at 175 hp and the other at 205 hp with a four-barrel carburetor. The V8 units run from new 200- and 235-hp units introduced for the 1989 model year, providing ample muscle for smaller boats, up to the high-performance packages—the new King Cobra 350 and King Cobra SE454.

The Cobra 200 is based on the 302-cid V8 block used in Ford's Mustang GT, while the Cobra 235 is based on Ford's 351-cid engine block. The basic engine of the King Cobra 350 is the 5.7-liter, 350-cid Chevrolet V8 with two-bolt main bearings, 4.00-inch bore x 3.48-inch stroke. For this marine use, Chevrolet developed a special high-rise intake manifold. The exhaust manifold outlets are larger, enabling the engine to breath more deeply. At the top of the performance end is the King Cobra SE454, a 370-hp engine based on the Chevrolet 454-cid block. OMC also has been developing a 476-hp Ford V8 based on the 351-cid block with techniques adapted from Ford's NASCAR engine research, such as flow visualization studies to optimize the design of the combustion chamber.

All Cobras are available in counterrotating models for twin-engine applications. This means that one propeller turns clockwise and the other counterclockwise, neutralizing propeller torque and loading, and providing better handling.

To combat corrosion, OMC engineers developed both an external system and internal components. OMC uses an anti-corrosive aluminum alloy, called Deep Guard. Inside, the solid steel-alloy drive shaft and splines are immersed in oil rather than water for longer life. OMC also has a nineteen-step painting process to enable the surface to bond tightly with the paint. Other Cobra features include power steering and power trim.

Volvo Penta

Despite a well-engineered and proven product, Volvo Penta still has had difficulty capturing a significant share of the United States market. Volvo was hit hard when Bayliner, the world's largest boatbuilder, switched from Volvo to OMC Cobra stern-drives for many models in 1986. Volvo has been fighting back with its Duoprop, an advanced concept using twin counter-rotating propellers on a single-axis sterndrive unit. The Swedish company designs and manufactures engines, marine transmissions, and industrial components. The engines range from 120 hp to 307 hp for gasoline engines and from 9 hp to 450 hp for diesels. Volvo currently is the only major manufacturer offering a diesel sterndrive in the United States. In gasoline-fueled stern-drives, Volvo offers its conventional model 290 and the unique Duoprop. Volvo Penta's four-cylinder engines are made in Sweden, while its V8s, based on GM blocks, are made in Chesapeake, Virginia.

Volvo unveiled its patented Duoprop in 1983, mating it to fuel-efficient diesel engines. In 1986 Volvo offered it with gasoline engines as well. Duoprop is more efficient than a single propeller because it delivers more engine power to the propeller and loses less energy through the water. Volvo designed the Duoprop to achieve a 10- to 15-percent efficiency gain over a single outdrive propeller. With a conventional drive having one propeller, the water comes off the blades in a rotating column. The rotating water is regarded as lost power because it doesn't propel the boat forward. The water comes off the Duoprop in an almost straight line, resulting in increased efficiency and neutral tracking. The top range for the Duoprop now is 55 to 60 mph. To compete effectively in the U.S. sterndrive market, Volvo can be expected to come out with a big-block power plant and new propeller designs.

To help prevent corrosion, Volvo relies on a special aluminum alloy with corrosion-resistant qualities. The surface of the drive leg receives a multistep finish consisting of prime, paint, rub, glaze, and bake, and then this is repeated, forming a layered skin. Volvo also relies on sacrificial zinc anodes.

Yamaha

Yamaha, like Volvo, will work to increase sales to small and mid-sized boat manufacturers who are unhappy with the recent mergers of large builders with engine companies. Yamaha decided in 1985 to enter the sterndrive market, with 1991 as the target date. However, that was pushed up to 1989 due to the recent acquisition of boat companies by engine manufacturers. To meet this timetable, Yamaha has had to forgo the idea of entering the market with a completely different product, at least for the short run. Some significant changes have been made, however. The initial line consists of three models: two V8s and a V6, running from 180 hp to 240 hp. Yamaha entered into an agreement with the Crusader Engine Division of Thermo Electron Corp. to marinize General Motors blocks for the sterndrives. Crusader is marinizing the blocks to Yamaha specifications, including Japanese ignition and air-induction components. The engines are fitted to the Japanese-built outdrives at Yamaha's Atlanta facility. All models are available with counterrotation and are rated at the propeller with the result that the familiar 205-hp V6, for instance, is rated by Yamaha at 180 hp. It is expected that by September 1, 1989, all sterndrive manufacturers will propeller-rate their engines.

Yamaha has developed a distributorless ignition, the first for a marine four-cycle engine. And, in an effort to make its sterndrives user-friendly, it has included several features that already were on its line of outboards, for example, a microcomputer management system that monitors timing, fuel quality, and other engine functions. It also protects against overtrim. If the drive is trimmed over 14 degrees, a gauge will flash; beyond 16 degrees, the system automatically reduces the rpm to 2,500. There also is easy access to components that require minor servicing such as the oil filter, which is located on the top front portion of the engine.

Yamaha's research into corrosion has produced anticorrosion features that include a number of grounding straps to ensure galvanic continuity and four large anodes. Also, the drive is painted in a five-stage process to form a corrosive shield.

Kiekhaefer Aeromarine

While Yamaha takes aim at the three major sterndrive manufacturers, MerCruiser, OMC, and Volvo Penta, Kiekhaefer Aeromarine, long noted for its line of competition-quality performance components, is busy carving a niche in the top end of sterndrive performance. Kiekhaefer's throttle/shift levers, K-Plane trim tabs, trim indicators, propellers, and exhaust silencers are standard fare for Offshore raceboats and top-end sport boats. The firm also repairs and upgrades high-performance drives and transmissions for Offshore competition. Kiekhaefer recognized a market among Offshore racers for a more durable outdrive as the capability of racing drive units was being surpassed by ever-increasing engine horsepower. The result is Kiekhaefer's new sterndrive for serious competitors, which made its debut on the Offshore circuit in 1988 on boats such as Charles Marks's new Superboat and Don Johnson's 46-foot Gentry Scarab Superboat.

The sleek drive is designed for gasoline engines up to 1,000 hp for racing and 500 to 750 hp for recreation. Incorporating what Kiekhaefer has learned about offshore performance over the last twenty years, the company's engineers designed a sterndrive that surfaces. A single stainless-steel cylinder trims the drive twice as deep as other drives so the operator can move his propellers between surfacing and submerged. Thus, he retains the sterndrive advantages of maneuverability and trimability while gaining the low drag and high speed associated with surface drives. With its deeper trim range and a large drive plane above the propeller, the drive virtually lifts the boat on plane. For boats equipped with turbocharged engines, the drive can be raised on acceleration to let the prop slip while the engines rev to reach their horsepower curve.

With this drive, the engineers attempted to address the

problems they had observed in rebuilding racing drives, such as twisted splines, broken gear teeth, and universal-joint failures. As a result, gears and shafts are stronger and bearings are bigger and more stable. Like MerCruiser, the Kiekhaefer drive uses a pair of vertical drive shafts, spreading the torque load over two smaller sets of gears rather than one large set. Steering is controlled by a pair of stainless-steel hydraulic cylinders and hydraulic lines are concealed. Trim is controlled by a single hydraulic cylinder located under the gimbal housing for maximum trim range. For protection against corrosion, the entire unit is hard-coat anodized before painting.

Porsche: In the Fast Lane

No sooner did Lamborghini team up with MerCruiser than Porsche got into the act. Actually, Porsche's arrival on the marine scene in 1988 had been in the works for five years. The result is a unique marine gasoline engine at the top end of performance—and cost—which is based on the 928 Porsche engine. To optimize an engine is a difficult, expensive process and only those on the Offshore circuit, such as Buzzi or Gentry or Copeland, are inclined to do it. And even then, they are restricted to trying to pump up the horsepower, using engine blocks that have been around for fifteen or twenty years. Greater power will be wrung out of gasoline engines by brute force— by using bigger blocks, bigger cams, bigger carburetion. And the increased power has to offset the increased weight. Others, such as racer Chris Lavin, are experimenting with four-value engines.

Unlike these efforts, Porsche leapfrogged into the modern era by being able to start with the modern five-year-old Porsche block. Here, the block and heads are cast of aluminum alloy, which alone makes the engine unique in the world of four-cycle marine power. And, as a result, the compact engine is remarkably light: The basic five-liter V8 weighs 616 pounds, an amazing 1.9 pounds per horsepower. Two of these 360-hp en-

The WP 928 S/4 Porsche marine engine, based on the 928 Porsche automobile engine and introduced in 1988, is designed to run both long and fast. The five-liter V-8 engine weighs only 616 pounds. *(Courtesy of Titanium Marine)*

gines, designed to run at 6,000 rpm continuous operation, amount to a savings of some 1,000 pounds from the stern, according to Jerry Berton of Tempest Marine who also is distributing the engines through Titanium Marine Ltd., of Blue Point, New York, the importer.

The WP 928 S/4 Porsche engine is designed to run both long and fast. Porsche repeatedly tested the engine between 70 percent and full throttle for 400 hours without failures, including tests in which the engine was in a simulated marine environment. The importer projects an engine life of 5,000 hours, which is comparable to a diesel. This engine also is easily maintained, with a change of oil, oil filter, and air filter needed every 150 hours.

The marinization of the engine is a joint effort by Porsche and Wizeman GmbH of West Germany. The marinization includes such special components as a three-circuit cooling system—a freshwater circuit for the engine, another freshwater circuit for the exhaust manifolds and heat exchanger, and a seawater circuit for the heat exchanger and the exhaust.

Perhaps the greatest attention was given to making the engine durable. The casting process, for example, produces a block with a surface hardness comparable to that of industrial diamonds. Porsche engineers fabricated both the cylinder liners and the engine block from aluminum alloys selected for their identical thermal-expansion rates. The piston slides on this extremely hard surface with little wear. This lack of friction, combined with the minimal distance between the piston and cylinder, allows the engine to use fuel more efficiently and to run more quietly with exceptional reliability.

The four-valve-per-cylinder design operates with dual overhead camshafts. Proper lubrication is ensured by a force-fed high-pressure oil-pump system with channels cast directly into the engine block, as in racing engines. Valves reset automatically, up to three thousand times each minute, minimizing valve wear with required servicing needed only after every five hundred hours of operation.

Porsche uses a new electronic fuel-injection system that measures and computes air density, humidity, and air pressure to provide the precise fuel/air mixture. The state-of-the-art electronic ignition system is virtually maintenance-free, according to the importer. There are no breaker contacts to burn out and no disruptive capacitor. Further, a comprehensive gaggle of sensors and meters monitors all operating functions. Cockpit instrumentation shows rpm, water temperature, oil temperature, oil pressure, oil level, battery charging, and camshaft drive-belt tension. A separate warning system automatically switches off the fuel supply and gives visual and audible signals when limits are exceeded.

In initial tests, with two engines connected to MerCruiser Bravo One drives, a prototype 32-foot Tempest ran 70 mph. For more muscle, there's the Turbo Offshore, which is the same block turbocharged and rated at 750 hp at 6,700 rpm. This uses the same technology as Porsche's Le Mans race engines. Reportedly the Turbo Offshore puts out one horsepower for every pound.

On the down side, there's the cost, which guarantees these engines will remain in a class of their own. While the price was somewhat of a secret, the engines reportedly run three and a half times the cost of a MerCruiser. The good news, says the importer, is that they are expected to last twenty times longer.

Turbocharging and Supercharging

In the quest for ever-greater horsepower, one turns to supercharging and turbocharging, which, though similar, take different routes to the goal of producing more horsepower. Supercharging forces air or a mixture of air and fuel into a combustion chamber of an engine under pressure. Turbocharging forces air or a mixture of air and fuel into the combustion chamber of an engine by means of the energy in the exhaust.

A conventional, naturally aspirated engine works at a pressure of one atmosphere to move a mixture of air and fuel into its cylinders; in the case of a diesel engine, only air is moved. The engine, for various reasons, does not induce a charge equal to its cylinder volume, thus there is less air inside the cylinder than in the same volume of space outside the engine. Superchargers are driven by gears or belts which absorb a portion of the horsepower they help to make. The turbocharger uses exhaust gases to drive its compressor turbine. While power is not stolen from a turbocharger as it is from a supercharger, one pays for the extra power in the form of back pressure. The restriction of the turbocharger turbine causes a back pressure in the exhaust manifold, requiring greater push from the pistons on the exhaust stroke. Turbocharging is becoming increasingly popular on diesel-powered boats and on the gasoline-powered Offshore raceboats. But because turbochargers present potential lubrication and cooling problems, they are likely to remain limited even within the area of high performance.

Performance Outboards

Place two high-horsepower outboards on the transom of a 24-foot tunnel-hulled production Skater and you have a hot rod ready for Offshore competition. The engines are off the shelf, too. Outboards of 200 hp and up, especially the giant 300-hp V8 powerhouses produced by OMC's Johnson and Evinrude, have added a new level of performance to mid-sized power-boats in the 24- to 34-foot range. High-horsepower outboards also are on the market from Yamaha, Suzuki, and Mercury. These big machines are not used primarily for competition, but for offshore fishing boats, performance runabouts, and day cruisers, giving the recreational boatman speeds approaching 50 to 60 mph.

For the fisherman heading for the offshore canyons, both speed and range are necessary, and the big outboards provide both. Outboard motors weigh considerably less than cast-iron inboards, and because of the weight advantage, an outboard will drive a boat faster on less fuel and not take up as much room in the boat as well. This fuel savings translates into longer range.

A two-cycle engine has no valves, camshaft, or push rods. Intake and exhaust are controlled, in part, by the piston covering and uncovering the ports cut into the cylinder walls. As the piston power head travels down the cylinder, a partial vacuum above it draws the fuel/air mixture into the crankcase through the carburetor and intake port. In the crankcase, the mixture, which also contains the engine lubricating oil, spins around the crankcase and then travels up a passage, entering the cylinder through the transfer ports. As the mixture enters the cylinder, the rising piston compresses it in the cylinder head's combustion chamber. Just before the piston reaches the top of its stroke, the spark plug ignites the fuel/air mixture and expanding superheated gases drive the piston down on the power stroke.

One of the features being touted by the outboard engine manufacturers in recent years is loop-charging as opposed to cross-charging. In a cross-charged engine, the fuel/air mixture enters via transfer ports that are directly opposite the cylinder from the exhaust port. A deflector on top of the piston forces the flow into the combustion chamber. In a loop-charged engine the fuel/air mixture enters the cylinder through transfer ports that angle sharply up. The mixture makes a 180-degree loop in the combustion chamber, burns, and exits through the exhaust port.

Cross-charged engines provide more precise control of the fuel-charge flow at low speeds. The loop-charged engine, on the other hand, generally will rev faster because its piston is lighter and the precise porting and exhaust tuning maximizes power, all helping to provide greater horsepower. On the down side, loop-charged engines tend to be a bit bulkier and heavier than cross-charged engines because their side transfer ports require wider cylinder spacing.

Another recent improvement is oil injection, or automatic oiling. This entails pumping oil from a reservoir outside the engine into the fuel charge at some point. How this is done varies with each manufacturer. Suzuki, which claims to have introduced oil injection to outboards after developing it for its motorcycle engines, places the reservoir beneath the motor hood. A tiny stream of air is forced into the oil flow before it is injected into the engine downstream of the carburetors. This creates minuscule bubbles in the oil and allows it to be more evenly distributed throughout the engine for maximum lubrication. Yamaha injects the oil directly into the manifold behind the carburetor, while Johnson and Evinrude place oil in the system at the fuel pump; the oil pump is connected directly to the fuel pump to consistently deliver the needed ratio of oil to gas.

In another area of advancement, today's powerful outboard engines with dual installations have counterrotation propellers to offset propeller torque.

Also, sophisticated electronics are increasingly finding their way into the engines. Mercury introduced the first production outboards with electronic fuel injection in 1987 on its 220-hp Laser IRi and Mariner 220 Magnum. Here electronic controls monitor engine functions throughout the power range, delivering the correct fuel mixture. All V8 and 200- and 225-hp V6 Evinrude and Johnson models feature SLOW, an acronym for

Speed Limiting Overheat Warning. Sensors monitor the engine temperature and if the outboard becomes too hot, a warning buzzer sounds and the ignition system limits engine rpm until it has cooled down to safe levels. Both Evinrude and Johnson also have an electronic engine-control system, termed QuickStart, on their loop-charged big engines. This increases the idle speed by advancing the spark until the engine temperature reaches the normal operating range on a cold engine, or for some five seconds on a warm engine. Yamaha's ignition system takes commands from a microcomputer that notes throttle position and rpm level while also watching out for power-robbing detonation. If the sensors pick up pings, the microcomputer adjusts the timing. Suzuki's engine-monitoring system keeps track of vital engine functions such as oil level and flow, water flow, and overrev conditions. If a problem occurs, the display on the dash gauge will light up and a caution buzzer will sound. In its top-of-the-line Exante 200, the engine also speaks up if there's a problem. The Exante's voice-communicated engine-monitoring system, the first, provides information about the state of the engine via preprogrammed audio messages.

To the outboard buyer, the question that generally comes to mind is whether it is better to have one or two engines. Is one 300-hp outboard "better" than two 150-hp engines? Each has its own advantages and disadvantages. A single engine costs less, weighs less, is easier to steer, doesn't require throttle synchronization and is slightly more economical on fuel. And one engine is easier to maintain than two. Two engines provide greater security. In the end, it's a matter of preference. However, those who take their big center-console boats to the offshore fishing grounds tend to favor the peace of mind of having two engines.

The Driving Forces

Transmission

The term *transmission* may lead one to believe a marine transmission is similar to an automotive transmission, but this is not the case. The marine transmission is much sturdier for it must be able to transmit the full power of the engine continuously.

The marine engine is a high-speed machine, while a propeller works best at a relatively low speed. This disparity is resolved by the transmission that acts as the variable connection between them. The transmission directs power in a forward or reverse direction and provides a neutral position in which the engine is running but the propeller is not.

Transmissions take different forms, such as being located in the lower unit of an outboard engine or in a large housing at the end of a big diesel-engine's flywheel. The transmission generally used with an inboard engine selects forward, neutral, and reverse by means of clutches, and it reduces engine speed to the desired propeller speed by using gears.

Gears are wheels with teeth that have been machined to a standard size and shape to enable gears of various diameters to mesh and drive each other. When two meshed gears are of equal diameter, their speeds of rotation will be identical. If the gear applying the driving force is twice the diameter, or has twice the number of teeth, of the driven gear, then the smaller, driven gear will turn twice as fast as the larger driver. This would be expressed as a ratio, 2:1.

Many marine transmissions use a planetary form of gearing, so-called because a central gear meshes with a number of surrounding, planetary, gears on a carrier, and these mesh in turn with an outside ring having internal teeth. Relative sizes of the gears determine the drive ratios. And the various relationships between the rotations of the ring gear, the central gear, and the planetary gears determine speed changes.

A clutch is the device used to engage or disengage the driving mechanism and shift from one condition to another. The action of clutches is based on the friction between two surfaces, such as flat plates or drums with encircling bands or mating cones. One drives the other when the two are pressed together and the clutches are then said to be "engaged." When the surfaces are separated, no force is transmitted and the clutches are "disengaged." Some friction surfaces, designed to function without lubrication, are termed dry clutches. Wet clutches, on the other hand, are immersed in a lubricant when running. Because the lubricant reduces the surface friction, wet clutches are less powerful than dry clutches. Clutches must be either completely engaged or disengaged, since partial engagement allows slippage between the friction surfaces which can easily damage them.

Some transmissions provide straight-through drive. In this case, the crankshaft of the driving engine and the propeller shaft exiting the housing are in a straight line. Other transmissions, generally those with reduction gearing, have offset drives in which the driving shaft and the driven shaft are at different levels. The offset drive makes it possible to keep the propeller shaft either lower or higher than the engine crankshaft, as may be necessary. The vee drive is a specialized transmission that allows the drive train from the engine to the propeller to be bent back upon itself, as in a vee. This enables the engine to be set back in the hull.

In a manual transmission there are usually two clutches, or one clutch and a brake band, around a central gear and its surrounding plantary gears, and these are controlled by an external lever with three positions that align the clutch or brake band to produce forward, reverse, and neutral. A cable from the helmsman's console moves this lever. On hydraulic transmissions, the cable positions the lever and hydraulic pressure exerts the force needed to align the clutches and brakes.

Until recently it was fairly simple for designers and builders to select a drive system. A high-performance Offshore-type craft would be rigged with MerCruiser sterndrives. To finish off a large yacht, a couple of holes would be drilled in the bottom for the propeller shafts leading from the transmission. A pair of struts would be bolted on and the job would be finished. While this remains the conventional method for large yachts, today there are several kinds of propulsion combinations for high-performance craft that can be tailored to specific needs, such as maximum speed; speed over distance, as illustrated by the transatlantic boats; and shallow-draft capabilities for cruising the Caribbean. An Offshore-type craft still primarily depends on sterndrive propulsion but there is increasingly greater use of lightweight diesels and surface propellers. Meanwhile, the high-performance megayacht has shed the conventional propeller and strut for either surface drives or water-jet propulsion coupled with massive diesels.

Water-Jet Propulsion

The jet-drive method of propelling a boat does not use a transmission but rather a high-velocity stream of water. The idea behind the water jet is simple. Powerful pumps draw up water through intakes in the bottom. High-speed impellers accelerate the flow and the water is ejected through a discharge in the transom, providing thrust. The stream of water runs out through a nozzle which is used for steering. When the water stream is directed aft, the boat moves forward; when it is directed forward, the boat goes into reverse. This concept of thrust is based on Newton's law, which states that for every action there is an equal and opposite reaction.

The first known water-jet boat dates back to 1787 when an inventor named James Rumsey demonstrated a steam-powered jet boat on the Potomac River. In the first half of this century jet drives were tried, without much success, in Europe, New Zealand, and the United States. The first practical jet drive emerged in 1953 when a New Zealand sheep farmer, having devised a jet pump for a boat to navigate shallow, rocky rivers, began to sell his jet-drive units.

The makers of jet drives stress not just the systems simplicity but its safety as well. The safety factor lies in the lack of a potentially dangerous propeller; the boat can also be used in shallow waters, and beaching and launching are simple. Smaller boats also are easy to trailer, since the boat can be driven right up onto the trailer. The problem of sucking up weeds and debris is solved by grilles over the intakes. And when debris does

The 1989 Evinrude XP 300 is the world's most powerful production outboard engine. The 300 hp V-8 engine is loop charged, as are Evinrude's 225, 200, 140, and 120 hp models. *(Courtesy of Outboard Marine Corp.)*

collect against the grilles, the intake jet stream only needs to be reversed to clear them.

Jet drives have been used successfully in smaller ski boats. It wasn't until King Juan Carlos of Spain installed a trio of KaMeWa jets on his *Fortuna* that the yachting world started to pay attention. Then, in 1986, when the Aga Khan chose the Swedish-built KaMeWa water jets for his 152-foot *Shergar*, jet drives became fashionable as standard equipment on performance yachts. *Shergar* combines high-speed performance, 40 to 45 knots, with economic long-range cruising at moderate speeds. Speed with better fuel economy is attributed to the fact that the drag from conventional propellers has been eliminated. *Shergar*'s jet drives use twin Allison gas turbines on the center of three water jets. This center jet, the world's most powerful in terms of delivered thrust, has a diesel-driven wing water-jet unit on either side.

KaMeWa is the leader in its field, although Italy's Riva Calzoni offers a water-jet system for yachts that have been supplied to the Italian navy and Spanish Customs. The *Azimut Atlantic Challenger* also is equipped with Riva Calzoni drives. KaMeWa has been manufacturing both variable-pitch propellers and water thrusters since the 1930s. In the early 1960s it built a water jet for the Swedish navy, and since then it has built water jets for military and patrol boats, ferryboats, and workboats.

While the principle is the same, the KaMeWa water jets are massive compared to those used on waterski boats. To handle the tremendous flow and thrust, the design and construction of these monstrous units are carefully engineered. A large water inlet on the bottom of the hull leads to an inlet channel where a pump impeller, connected either directly or through a gearbox to the engine, accelerates the water flow. The outlet nozzle, which can be several feet in diameter on the largest yachts, directs the stream of water and provides steering by swinging 30 degrees to port or starboard. A "clamshell" bucket over the outlet nozzle turns under the nozzle, gradually entering the jet and finally giving full reverse thrust. By setting the bucket in an intermediate position, the thrust can be varied continuously from zero to maximum ahead and astern at any power. Mid-closure serves as neutral. Although it is not recommended, a water jet can go from full ahead to full astern without damaging the engine or transmission. Another benefit of the jet drive is its quiet operation, free of the vibration, shaft rumble, and noisy water turbulence associated with propellers.

Surface Drives

Although the surface-drive concept had been around since the early 1900s, it did not become popular until Howard Arneson, inspired by Dan Arena's Surf Drive, made the surface drive feasible in the 1970s. Arneson, a San Francisco inventor who had become enamored of Offshore racing, found that the drag from the lower units was sapping as much as 150 hp at 60 knots on the conventional sterndrive of his race boat. In his attempt to reduce the drag, he zeroed in on surface-piercing propellers.

Arneson initially experimented with fixed surface propellers but ran into steering and control problems. His solution was an articulated surface-piercing propeller that operates 50 percent submerged in the undisturbed water behind the transom at planing speed. The propeller pierces the water on the lower segment of its turning cycle to provide maximum thrust and deliver optimum engine power. A propeller blade does not provide uniform power throughout a 360-degree turn; most of the power comes from the lower half, while the upper half is low on thrust and at times even a drag. Arneson Surface Drives also eliminate cavitation because they ventilate rather than cavitate beneath the hull. This reduces vibration and noise and eliminates hull and propeller erosion.

By placing the propeller at the end of an articulated shaft that can be trimmed up and down, propeller submergence can be adjusted to fit the conditions. This articulation also provides full steering control. A fin on the movable portion of the Arneson Surface Drive unit enables steering control to be maintained in the absence of engine power.

Arneson went on to prove his drives on the racecourse. The system was acquired by Craig Dorsey, and his Arneson Marine, Inc., in Corte Madera, California, was producing the Arneson drive.

Besides lowering the drag, the Arneson system reduces noise by moving the turbulence away from the hull. Steering is accomplished with a patented ball-and-socket connection. This allows hydraulic cylinders to swing the entire propeller shaft, which is linked to the inboard engine by a double U-joint that also dampens vibrations.

Magnum Marine's Filippo Theodoli is a firm believer in the Arneson Surface Drive, which propelled his 63-foot Maltese Magnum. "It's more efficient," said Theodoli. "You have twenty to twenty-five percent better performance with the same rpm and the same engine by using that kind of propulsion. We had a boat here that did forty miles per hour. With the same engines and just changing the drive, that boat is now doing fifty miles per hour." Theodoli, who was one of the first builders to adopt the surface drive, said Magnum uses it regularly although it is not standard equipment. "We suggest people use it instead of going to a bigger engine, because with the same engine you get twenty percent better speed. That's the advantage."

Several other companies offer surface-drive systems, including Betty Cook's Kaama Drive and Tempest Marine's proprietary T-Torque system that has nonsteerable propeller shafts with rudders suspended behind them.

Propellers

Simply put, propellers make or break a high-performance boat.

"We've come a long way from the propellers my father's raceboats were using in the early 1970s," noted Fred Kiekhaefer. "The biggest difference is they are incredibly fine-tuned to their application. And it's not just selecting the right propeller that's important, but getting the right profiles on the blades and getting them very consistent."

Compared to the propellers used fifteen years ago on performance boats, today's performance propellers require an additional two dozen processing steps, he explained.

Any planing boat needs the right propeller for the boat and engine, for without it the engine cannot deliver its rated horsepower. As the throttle is advanced, the rpm increases and the engine produces its maximum horsepower near its maximum rated rpm. A boat will have its own horsepower requirements for various speeds and consequently the engine output needs to be matched to the speed of the boat. Essentially, the propeller controls the full-throttle rpm of the engine. The right propeller allows the engine to run within its rated range at full throttle. For instance, if a boat equipped with a 225-hp engine can go 50 mph, but the engine reaches its maximum-rated rpm at 40 mph, full speed will not be reached. The propeller, the device used to turn the engine's power into thrust, is not correct.

Racers and sport-boat enthusiasts term the process of matching the correct propeller to the boat and engine "dialing in," bringing the equipment up to its optimum performances. This tuning-up process has already been done by manufacturers who sell packages of boats and engines, which is a distinct convenience for the marine dealer and the customer alike. For performance enthusiasts and racers, those who are tweaking and developing their equipment, dialing in is the testing process.

A propeller functions, in part, by throwing water sternward, and as Newton's law of action and reaction illustrates, the result is forward thrust. This is accomplished by the front of the blade, the surface facing away from the transom. The back of the blade, meanwhile, functions like an airplane wing. As the propeller turns, the water flows across this airfoil at an increased velocity, and the back of the blade becomes an area of low pressure of a partial vacuum drawing the water to it. This pull, similar to the lift created by an airplane wing, coupled with the push from the face of the blade forms the total thrust.

A propeller is measured by its diameter and pitch, both expressed in inches. The *diameter* is the width of the circle described by the tips of the blades. *Pitch* is the theoretical distance a propeller moves forward in one revolution. In the water a propeller will move forward about 80 to 90 percent of the theoretical pitch. The difference between actual and theoretical pitch is "slippage," which is necessary to produce thrust. While the use of the word slippage often implies an inherent fault, there can be no thrust without slippage and every propeller has an optimum amount of slippage.

To check whether the propeller is correct, use the tachometer and the rated rpm of the engine given in the engine manual. The right propeller will hold the engine to its rated top speed. If the engine does not reach this speed, the pitch is too great. If the engine exceeds its rated speed, the pitch is too small.

Propellers also experience two maladies called *cavitation* and *ventilation*. Ventilation is the result of air bubbles in the propeller area, created by air from the surface or by exhaust gases being drawn in to the blades. These air pockets make a propeller lose its thrust or bite. Engine rpm may soar, but there will be no corresponding surge of speed. Ventilation can occur when a boat is improperly trimmed with the drives too high, during a sharp turn, or, in the case of an outboard, when it is mounted too high on the transom. Cavitation is caused by a disturbance ahead of the propeller. Here the propeller loses full contact with the water because of the sudden formation and collapse of air-pressure bubbles on the back of the blade caused by the rotating propeller. Air bubbles pummel the blade, resulting in visible wear, a sure sign of lost performance.

With a boat having a single propeller, an unfortunate sideways effect often is created and one has to compensate for this by using the rudder to maintain a straight line. Volvo's Duoprop and the popular counterrotating propellers on twin installations neutralize this problem.

A boat should run without vibration. If vibrations suddenly occur it is likely that the propellers have hit something and have been nicked or bent, throwing the dynamics out of kilter. The higher the speed, the greater the propeller damage will be felt. This should be corrected as soon as possible, since the vibration is not healthy for the shaft, bearings, and engine.

To deliver high horsepower at high speed with a minimum of drag requires specialized propellers such as cleaver propellers in which the blades are not fully rounded but have a straight, cleaver edge. Propellers differ in the shape and angle of their blades, as well as in the number of blades.

The popularity of surface drives has been the major factor influencing propellers in the last decade. "Today propellers are running on the surface with half the propeller exposed almost all the time, which means the loading when the propeller blade slaps the surface of the water is much higher today," said Kiekhaefer. "The propeller we built in the early 1970s probably wouldn't last three minutes today." Today's high-performance propeller blades are thicker, the alloys stronger, and the rate of change of pitch in the rake of the propeller blades is somewhat different.

As propellers moved to the surface, the number of blades was changed from three to four to make the boat run more smoothly. The reason for this is that the more blades there are in the water at any given time, the more resistant the propeller is to the impact of the blades hitting the water and shaking the works. The effect is similar to a multicylinder engine: A twelve-cylinder is smoother than an eight, a six-cylinder smoother than a four, and so on. This is true, also, with a fully submerged propeller, but the fourth blade in that case creates an additional drag that offsets the advantage of smoothness.

In an offshore performance boat that is running with surfacing propellers, the greater number of blades may make running smoother, Kiekhaefer explained, "but you reach a limit where the ability to control the accuracy of each blade is diminished if it doesn't come out of the mold perfectly. Another disadvantage of multiple blades," he continued, "is that you have so much mass out there that any irregularity in either the power output or the load on the propeller tends to really rack the driveline. Once you've got it spinning, like a gyro, it's more difficult to stop and therefore tends to put a lot of extra stress on the drive shaft, propeller shaft, and gear bearings." This leads to shearing the shaft, not an uncommon occurrence with some of the six-bladed propellers when throttle timing on reentry is misjudged. The propeller is moving too fast for the water; it hits and the shaft snaps. Having a multiplicity of blades for smoothness has its tradeoffs: While the greater thrust of multiple blades increases performance, the greater drag tends to reduce performance. The happy medium, Kiekhaefer believes, is to have three blades if the propeller is running submerged and four if surfaced. Some five- and six-blade propellers seem to work in specialized applications, yet Kiekhaefer said the only time he has seen a six-blade work well was in holding on to the torque in some diesel engines.

As the number of blades in surface propellers increases, a phenomenon can occur called transom lift. As the blades slap the surface, they apply a force that reacts by lifting the transom. Some hulls are forgiving of this, some are not. A hull might react by dropping its bow, which increases the drag of the hull and slows the boat down. In other boats, such as the tunnel boats, transom lift can raise the entire boat. As Kiekhaefer explained it, "the trapped air may offset the transom lift and the entire boat kind of lifts out of the water, which happens frequently." This is beneficial since it reduces drag, but dangerous if the boat leaves the water to the point where one no longer has control.

"The boat has to tell you what it likes," Kiekheafer said. "With a tunnel boat, the trapping of air in the tunnel gives it lift. With some boats, when you add the fourth blade on the propeller, the transom lifts higher and then it packs more air in the tunnel. Again, it's the interaction of the hull shape, the wave action, the air entrapment—a whole combination of a lot of complex things."

Diesel vs. Gas

Diesel engines and speed used to be a contradiction in terms. Everyone knew a diesel engine belonged in a trawler-type boat that would chug along at 7 knots for two thousand miles or so. No more. The high-performance diesel has arrived, with small, light, double- and triple-turbocharged diesels powering Offshore raceboats to 100 mph, and with behemoths costing $1.6 million a pair pushing megayachts across the sea at 60 mph.

Just a few of the developments in 1988 illustrate the extent of this transformation:

- Wellcraft, one of the foremost builders of production high-performance boats, introduced a line of diesel per-

212

formance boats, from 32 to 50 feet in length, using surface drives.

- Italian Fabio Buzzi won the World Open Class title in Guernsey, England, and the Open Class in the Key West World Cup using a vee-hull with a stabilizer wing. His 44-foot boat, powered by four of Buzzi's own 500-cid Seatek turbocharged diesels, tops 100 mph. And of the twenty-five boats in the Open Class in Guernsey, eleven ran with diesel engines.

- Harry Schoell, the inventive American designer and builder, emerged late in the year with a daring, new diesel-powered step deep vee raceboat. At 49-feet long, *Varn's Infinity* is the largest Open Class hull in the world, powered by three triple-turbocharged Merlin Marine diesels based on Ford blocks and designed by Bill Lawson.

Traditionally, gasoline engines generally are considered as being capable of high speed, controllable over wide ranges, relatively lightweight, and moderate in cost. Diesel engines, on the other hand, are considered to be heavier, more sluggish, more expensive but cheaper to run, more durable, and safer to operate. Both types of engines are described in much the same terms, such as the number of cylinders and their cubic-inch displacement, and how these cylinders are arranged (in-line, canted, or vee), the rated engine speed, and whether the fuel is naturally aspirated or forced into the cylinders under pressure as in turbocharging or supercharging.

The new role of the lightweight high-performance diesel has both opponents and proponents. The diesel advocates point to the advantage of safety. Indeed, the flashpoint of gasoline is four times that of diesel fuel. Further, gasoline vapors are heavier than air and settle in the bilges and other low, enclosed areas, easily reaching explosive concentrations. This hazard is eliminated with diesel. Diesel will burn, but basically for racers and performance enthusiasts diesel means no explosions—no small consideration. It's also difficult to overrev with a diesel engine because the throttle acts as a governor. Comparatively, a gasoline engine can easily be blown if the boat flies out of the water and the engines overrev, burning up the engine. In raceboats, the throttleman continually adjusts the throttles to keep the engine and propeller synchronized and prevent blowing up the engine. Some boats, including the big diesel trans-atlantic boats, have switches that automatically cut the engine when the propeller spins beyond the tolerance point.

Another inherent advantage of the diesel is that it doesn't need any electrical ignition equipment; it ignites its fuel by compressing air to a combustible level. Electrical ignition equipment can malfunction in the damp, corrosive marine environment. The higher compression ratio of the diesel also makes it harder to start, requiring heavy, powerful batteries.

The durability of the diesel is legendary. After watching Buzzi win the 1988 worlds, Betty Cook observed, "He's gone fourteen races and he's hardly looked at the engines. That is impressive." The hotdogs in Offshore with gasoline power use fresh blocks for every race, which can run up a $200,000 maintenance bill for a ten-race circuit. Those running diesels will use the same blocks all season. Because the diesel engine is 30 to 50 percent more fuel-efficient than a gasoline engine, one often can save more on the weight of the fuel than one has lost due to the increased weight of the diesel.

When it comes to diesels on the racecourse, though, it must be noted that they have enjoyed an advantage in UIM Class One in Europe because diesels carried no penalty for turbo-chargers, giving them a displacement advantage. This has been corrected for the 1989 season when diesels once again will be put to the test.

Diesel power basically came from Caterpillar and General Motors, explained Jerry Berton, who developed Tempest's line of diesel yachts from 60 to 85 feet in length. GM progressively bumped up the horsepower of its diesel engines over the years. "Every year they'd find a way to get twenty or thirty horsepower out of the same old engine," he said. "They were refining the existing blocks." The GM distributors such as Stewart and Stevenson in turn sold the engines to the dealers whose customers wanted even more power. Consequently, GM would sell as a 600-hp-engine its 8V92 model, which the dealer mechanics were then tweaking to 650 hp, then 700 and 780 hp. "General Motors probably woke up one day and wondered why it was letting the dealer tweak its motors. The dealers were getting the money for the tweaking and they [GM] were getting the warranty problems." GM in recent years has been boosting its own engines, Berton added.

Caterpillar, meanwhile, has remained relatively stable with a handful of basic motors. The 3208 engine has been a high-performance workhorse, moving from 355 hp to over 375 hp in a six-year period and heading for 400 hp. "It's not a new technology," said Berton, "but just a matter of getting more out of what they've got in a reliable manner." The newest Caterpillar of note, introduced in 1987, is the hot 3412 which propels Tempest's 60-foot performance cruiser to speeds of 50 mph.

"Diesel is going to be here regardless of what anyone says," asserted racer Gus Anastasi of Wellcraft. "Diesel power has a variety of offerings from the small to the big engines." Wellcraft, he said, developed its diesel performance line primarily to meet the demand in Europe where diesel is the primary fuel. "People there don't know what gasoline is. All the marinas carry diesel because the fishing boats use it," he said. While diesel also is gaining in popularity in the United States, Anastasi doesn't believe it will ever take the place of gasoline in performance boats.

Fred Kiekhaefer agrees with Anastasi. Yet, Kiekhaefer noted, "people become upset with the relative lack of reliability with many of the high-strung gasoline engines that are used in racing and find their way into the recreational community. Enter the perceived value of the diesel because of its historical reliability. However, if you high-string a diesel, you're right back to the same problem. It comes down to this: How can you find the best blend between performance and reliability. The person that finds the best mix in America, regardless of whether it's with a gasoline or diesel engine, is the one that is going to earn his way in."

Meanwhile, the American mindset is toward gasoline engines and the European mindset is toward diesels. As for Kiekhaefer? "Given my choice, I'd rather be in a gas-powered

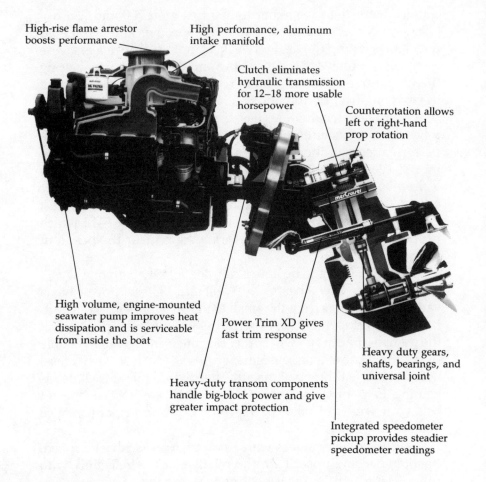

High-rise flame arrestor
boosts performance

High performance, aluminum
intake manifold

Clutch eliminates
hydraulic transmission
for 12–18 more usable
horsepower

Counterrotation allows
left or right-hand
prop rotation

High volume, engine-mounted
seawater pump improves heat
dissipation and is serviceable
from inside the boat

Power Trim XD gives
fast trim response

Heavy duty gears,
shafts, bearings, and
universal joint

Heavy-duty transom components
handle big-block power and give
greater impact protection

Integrated speedometer
pickup provides steadier
speedometer readings

MerCruiser's 454 Magnum combines the power of a 365 hp engine with the strength of the Bravo One drive. *(Courtesy of Mercury Marine)*

boat—unless it breaks," he said laughing. "I've seen incredibly reliable diesels and diesels you can't keep together for three minutes."

The one area where there is no disagreement is with big yachts. The power to push megayachts to high speeds can come only from megadiesels, often working in conjunction with a turbine on the centerline, and connected to KaMeWa water-jet drives or mega Arneson surface drives having 6-foot-diameter propellers. King of the megadiesels is MTU. MTU is an acronym for Motoren und Turbinen-Union of Friedrichshafen GmbH, West Germany. MTU is serious power, power that is not for those faint of heart or lean of wallet. MTU's 396 series diesels, which are used in high-performance megayachts, are essentially handcrafted—machined to scientifically precise tolerances, quality-checked with thoroughness, and priced like an MX missile. The top of the line 396, the sixteen-cylinder monster, costs $800,000 and two are needed. Denison Marine is installing two on the new *Monkey Business*, a 140-foot yacht being built for Donald Soffer, owner of North Miami Beach's Turnbury Isle condominium development around the corner from Fleet Street. Soffer's new 155-ton yacht is expected to top 35 mph fully outfitted.

MTU was formed by competing diesel makers MAN and Daimler-Benz in 1969 to produce quick, lightweight diesels for jet planes, ferries, patrol boats, and the like. The popular 396 series evolved from a lightweight 107-hp-per-cylinder NATO Leopard tank engine that MTU built in the 1970s. MTU, now owned almost totally by Daimler-Benz which bought MAN's share in 1986, has become Europe's largest producer of ultra-high-speed, high-performance diesel engines for special marine and industrial applications. MTU engines have the highest specific power output for their size, making them a logical choice to meet the megayacht's requirements of high horsepower, low weight, and compact design, according to John Moore, sales director for MTU of North America. Power-to-weight ratios are in the 3.28 lbs/hp range. MTU also builds in longevity; the first scheduled overhaul for an engine is six thousand hours or ten years.

Currently MTU has some 95 percent of the high-performance megayacht market. Its European competitors MAN and Deutz MWM are stepping up their marketing efforts, however. And in the United States, Caterpillar has been taking aim at a slice of the megadiesel pie. MTU meanwhile continues its technological push, and a new, more powerful series of engines is on its horizon. The quest for bigger and faster continues.

Part 4

You and Your Boat

I've learned that you go out there and do your best and be happy with the results, not just in boat racing but with every phase of your life.

—Chip Hanauer, 1988

Chapter 11

Buying Your Boat

Wellcraft's Don Johnson Signature model 43-foot Scarab combines performance and pizzazz in a production boat. The streamlined deck eliminates the traditional windshield in favor of recesssed, mechanically operated wind deflectors. *(Forest Johnson photo)*

You are about to embark on the adventure of owning a high-performance powerboat. Because you have chosen high performance, you have already made a statement about yourself. A boat that gets in the groove and tracks at 70 mph cuts an image of power and status, conjuring up visions of Errol Flynn driving a streaking missile. Power is sexy and here it's accented by flashy graphics, mirrored hatch covers, mellow sound systems, and soft leather interiors. But before you buy a high-performance boat, make sure it's really what you want. Be honest in analyzing (1) why you want a high-performance boat, and (2) what you actually plan to do with the boat. The answers may not mesh.

First, make sure you're comfortable with speed. As Magnum's Ted Theodoli explained, "I'm not interested in the Chuck Yeagers. It's no use if I take a client out in a boat and go a hundred and fifty miles an hour. I know my average client is never going to want that sort of thing." And there are some who think they do but find they get nervous going 40 or 50 mph across the water. "I can tell some are terrified, and I'm doing fifty, not a hundred, miles an hour," said the marquis. "But they are not used to it. Fifty miles an hour on the water is a lot of speed. You can imagine what a hundred is like."

Fred Kiekhaefer, the high-performance specialist, recommends being "more conservative than you might otherwise be inclined to be, unless you're an absolute speed junkie. If you have a choice, get something with a little less power than more.

One of the pit areas at the Key West World Cup in 1983. *(Forest Johnson photo)*

The Open Class boats roar across the line in the start of the first race of the 1987 Key West World Cup. *(Paul Kemiel photo)*

Al Copeland's newest Superboat, the 50-foot *Popeyes* with an enclosed canopy, was constructed in 1987 of carbon fiber composite. Capable of speeds in excess of 120 mph, the catamaran is powered by four 585-cubic inch fuel injected engines each developing 850 hp. The stern fin acts as a stabilizer. *(Forest Johnson photo)*

Al Copeland, the high school dropout who is the founder and chairman of Popeyes Famous Fried Chicken and Biscuits, spends $1.7 million a year to race offshore powerboats. *(Paul Kemiel photo)*

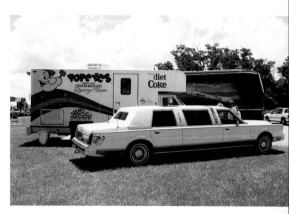

The innovator of the first Superboat, Al Copeland travels to the races on the *Popeyes* plane. *(Forest Johnson photo)*

The *Popeyes* van and limousine round out Al Copeland's modes of travel. *(Forest Johnson photo)*

Streaking to victory, *Popeyes* rides under the watchful eyes of Al Copeland's diving paramedic team aboard the *Popeyes* helicopter. To minimize the risks in a high-risk sport, Copeland always races with the paramedics hovering overhead. *(Forest Johnson photo)*

Fabio Buzzi of Italy proved to be the undisputed king of offshore in 1988, winning three straight races to capture the UIM World Open Class Championship in Guernsey, England, and running away with the Open Class victory at the Key West World Cup. *(Forest Johnson photo)*

Fabio Buzzi's winged *Giancia dei Gancia* proved to be the dominant boat on the European and American continents in 1988. The 44-foot deep vee craft, powered by four of Buzzi's own Seatek turbocharged 620 hp diesel engines connected to surface drives, set a faster pace than even the Superboats at the 1988 Key West World Cup. *(Forest Johnson photo)*

The power behind Buzzi's throne is his 650 hp, six-cylinder Seatek turbocharged diesel engine. *Giancia dei Gancia* races with four Seateks and Buzzi rotated six in all during 1988, while the gas-powered teams used a fresh set with each race. *(Paul Kemiel photo)*

Tom Gentry, a fifty-seven-year-old Hawaiian real estate tycoon, and his wife, Diane, celebrate on the foredeck of *Gentry Eagle* after he broke the Miami-to-New York record. *(Forest Johnson photo)*

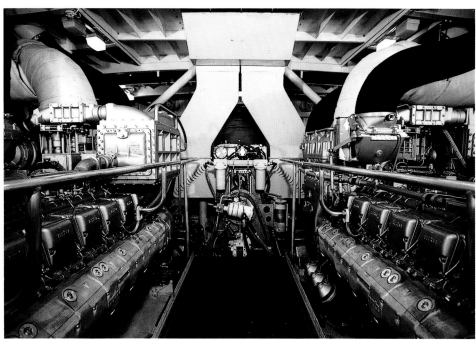

The *Gentry Eagle* is powered by two German-built MTU sequentially turbocharged diesels each generating 3480 hp and connected to KaMeWa water jets. For extra thrust, Gentry placed a Lycoming turbine producing 4,500 hp between the diesels and connected it to an Arneson surface drive. This power mix propells the 50-ton craft, as long as an 11-story building is high, nearly 80 mph. *(Forest Johnson photo)*

With his 110-foot *Gentry Eagle*, former offshore powerboat world champion Tom Gentry set new distance records for Miami–Nassau–Miami and Miami–New York runs in 1988. His attempt for the New York-to-England record failed after water seeped into the fuel tanks, but Gentry aimed to try again. *(Forest Johnson photo)*

Gentry's 110-foot aluminum deep vee hulled yacht features an onboard computer with monitors in front of the navigator; driver and throttleman give a visual display of the boat's position, the intended track, and the trail of where they've been. *(Forest Johnson photo)*

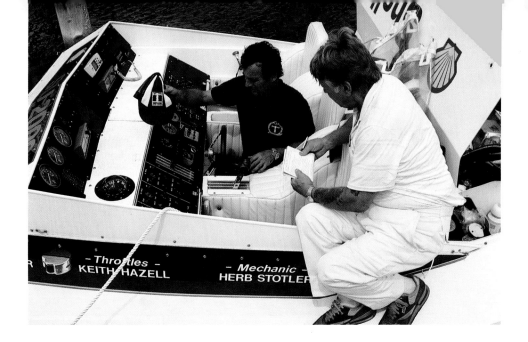

At the pre-race inspection before the 1986 Miami–Nassau–Miami Searace, Knocky House, right, who raced as riding mechanic with Don Aronow in the 1960s, checks out *Spirit of New Orleans* with throttleman Keith Hazell. *(Forest Johnson photo)*

Three time U.S. Superboat champion George Morales soars over calm seas off South Florida in his MerCruiser Special.*(Forest Johnson photo)*

That sounds like heresy coming from me, but that's what I do when I buy my own boat."

Cigarette's Craig Barrie, on the other hand, says he has had customers who say they want to go 55 mph and "then I have seen a little gleam in their eye. They really want to go seventy. Then they're better off with a boat with the capabilities of seventy rather than taking a boat with less power and coming back a year later for different motors and headers."

Once you have determined what level of speed you are comfortable with, determine how you will use the boat, where you will use it, and with whom. There's no use getting a high-performance boat with a large cabin area and sleeping quarters if you're not going to spend time cruising. You might as well get a boat with a large cockpit for outdoor enjoyment if you're not going to use it as a second home. If what you'll really be doing is cruising with your family, then dial down the power a bit more than you might like and get a package that's easily serviced. Also, there's no sense buying a 22-foot-long craft if you intend to take it out in the Atlantic Ocean. Odds are, the conditions will be too rough a good deal of the time and you won't be able to take the boat out. Fast cruising, water skiing, fishing, a second home, even racing: High-performance boats offering all of this with style and luxury are attainable governed by the boat's size and your pocketbook. High-performance boats are on the market ranging from $20,000 for a small sport boat to $6 million for a rocketship such as Tom Gentry's 110-foot *Gentry Eagle*.

Before buying a boat, new or used, try it out, if at all possible. Dealers located on the water should provide a demonstration. The dealer should be anxious to show you how well the boat performs, how easily it handles, how smooth and dry the ride is, how sharply it knifes through the waves.

In trying out a boat, see how quickly the boat gets on a plane. A good sterndrive or outboard should be on plane and running well in five seconds. Bigger boats with cabins will take a bit longer. If the boat has difficulty getting up on plane, it may be underpowered or the engine-drive-propeller configuration may not be the right one for that hull. Also, a boat should turn easily without severe banking. Put the helm in a tight turn at slow speed and slowly raise the throttle to somewhere less than top speed. You should discover whether the stern slips out or the propeller ventilates.

Another good idea is to run the boat on a measured mile and compute its top speed. Compare this with the boat's projected weight-to-horsepower ratio (see page 000). If a boat does not run flat-out within 85 or 90 percent of its computed ratio, there is a problem with the engine or the hull design or perhaps both.

Check to see that the steering wheel doesn't pull to one side or the other. The stability of a smaller boat can be checked just by walking from one side to the other.

New or Used?

There are advantages and disadvantages, whether you buy a boat new or used. Tempest's Jerry Berton advises first-time buyers to select a new boat. A person new to boating has enough to learn, such as navigation, handling, and the local waters, that if equipment problems develop as well, "then boating will become difficult. Trips will become unpleasant experiences." With a new boat, mechanical problems are minimized and the dealer can be expected to teach you how to operate it and support you. Newcomers to boating also should consider buying a package deal—boat and motor together—for boats up to 25 feet or so, Berton feels.

In buying a new boat it also is wise to buy it in the area in which you will be going boating and to check out the dealer thoroughly. "Make sure you buy from a qualified dealer," advises Walter Sullivan, president of BUC International Corp., which publishes the price guides for new and used boats, similar to the "blue book" for automobiles. "How long has he been in business? Whose franchises does he carry? Where does he advertise? Where are his satisfied customers? What is his reputation for service? Does he have a service department? Are his mechanics factory-trained?" In buying high-performance equipment, a dealer's ability to service the propulsion system becomes a significant factor. You also develop a relationship with your dealer. In areas where slips are at a premium, such as the Northeast, your dealer can help you find a slip or arrange for dry stack storage. You may wind up keeping your boat in your dealer's marina. You may want to turn to him for advice. In all, a good dealer can make your boating experience fun and a bad dealer can make it miserable.

As in buying a car, consider depreciation. A boat will depreciate, except in the cases of some large yachts that appreciate, or increase in value, over the years as labor and material costs increase. BUC's Sullivan cautioned that high-performance boats tend to depreciate at a faster rate than more conventional craft. The first-year depreciation of high-performance boats in the range of 24 to 40 feet tends to run 18 to 30 percent. In a conventional runabout the depreciation tends to be 4 or 5 percent less. At the high end, the high-performance cruisers, the lines blur as to what constitutes "high performance." A beamy 45-foot Magnum designed to run to the Bahamas for fishing will be regarded differently and depreciate less than a stripped out, go-fast 40-footer.

There is a slight difference, Sullivan said, in how well particular brand names hold up, but in general, high-performance boats do not hold their value as well as some other types of boats such as family-oriented or fishing-type boats. All boats depreciate more in the first year and then start to level off. Powerboats generally depreciate faster than sailboats, and outboards depreciate at a lesser rate than boats with inboards. The average depreciation rate of all boats runs 3 to 6 percent a year. Add an extra 10 percent for a high-performance boat the first year. Then, if similar craft are depreciating 4 to 8 percent in the third and fourth years, the depreciation of a high-performance boat is likely to run 8 to 12 percent. Sullivan cites factors such as demand and wear-and-tear to account for the faster depreciation of high-performance boats.

Another factor a boat buyer should be aware of is insurance. High-performance boats can be difficult or expensive to insure. Some insurance companies do not insure high-performance boats, while others specialize in them and offer excellent programs, which may cost a premium. Before you make the down payment on your boat, line up the insurance. Your dealer, a marine insurance specialist, or the finance company you may be dealing with all should be able to offer assistance here.

The higher depreciation rate for high-performance boats has a positive side: In theory, the best deal in a used boat is likely to be a high-performance boat, and it might pay to be on the lookout for a clean, used one. A good deal here, says Jerry Berton, depends on time and knowledge. If you buy a used boat for $75,000 that retails new for $100,000, and then spend $5,000 on repairs, you basically save $20,000. But Berton cautions that if those repairs mean you lose the use of the boat for half the season in an area such as the Northeast, where the season is short, and then add in the cost of insurance and maintenance, the overall savings can be negligble.

"Nobody is in boating to save money," he said. "And buying a performance boat is not like buying a sailboat, where you buy a fresh set of sails and you're on your way. You're dealing with machinery and machinery has to work." If buying a used boat, Berton recommends buying it at the end of the season and reconditioning it over the winter so the next boating season will be trouble-free.

In buying a used high-performance boat, one that by nature is run hard, it pays to buy a boat that is built strongly. A strong hull will cost more and last longer. "In the end, you're not going to replace the hull in these boats; you're going to replace the machinery," said Berton. "So if you have a good strong hull and replace the machinery, you will have a better package than if you have a weak hull and now make a big investment to replace the machinery."

A traditional marine survey is the best way to determine if a hull still has its integrity and is not fatigued and weakened. A survey costs anywhere from $200 to $600, but this is a small price to pay to find out the strengths and weaknesses of an expensive piece of equipment that you plan to take offshore. But before you ask for a survey, do some checking of your own. There may be telltale signs of hull fatigue, such as stress marks on the hull, doors down below that are out of line and will not close, and popping screws. Look to see whether there is any separation between the bulkhead structure and the side of the hull; and whether the upholstery is intact or cracked at the corners.

As for the engine, have the compression checked. But realize this will not tell you when the engine is likely to self-destruct. Most high-performance engines need a valve job every 250 hours, said Berton. How long will engines run before they blow? The longest time Berton had heard of was 485 hours. "This was in a boat belonging to a guy who treated the motors like a religion. He never ran the boat hard, changed the oil every fifteen hours, flushed the motors with fresh water every possible time. If he had done a valve job, he might have gotten more."

If you are buying a used boat with a lot of hours on the engines, you should plan to do a valve job, even if it runs perfectly, because the metal is fatigued. "You can do a compression check and metal fatigue will not show up," said Berton. "So do a valve job and get it over with. You don't want the motors to self-destruct July third."

The best way to maintain a boat is not to punish the equipment and to run the engine at a reasonable design speed. "The weakest part of the engines is the valve train," Berton continued. "When you run your motor at four thousand rpms, your valves are going up and down seven times a second. At five thousand rpms, you are taking a chance of reducing engine life. When a boat is fresh, it seems as if you can run it at five thousand rpms forever, but down the road you will pay the price."

It also is important with engines run in salt water to flush the engines with fresh water. The salt water causes serious scaling and corrosion that at the least can ruin the exhaust systems. As BUC's Sullivan points out, beware of someone selling a boat owned by a widow that's been sitting at the dock unused for any period of time. "It's slightly used, ergo, it's supposed to be in good shape. Actually the reverse usually is the case," he related. "A hull used fairly hard involves running the engines often and that's better for an engine than sitting in salt water for any length of time. You can't look inside and tell the condition, whether the gaskets, shafts, or gears are deteriorated. But with the slightest crack, corrosion sets in. If the boat is used, it should be regularly flushed out with fresh water. It might look older on the outside but it may be well kept internally."

Preparing to Sell

Once you buy a boat, start looking ahead to the day when you will be selling it. For the maximum resale value, keep the boat in good condition. Keep the hull waxed and clean. Keep it out of the sun as much as possible, particularly in the Southern Hemisphere, to prevent the ultraviolet rays from bleaching the gel coat. Maintain the engines and other equipment on board according to the manufacturer's schedules and recommendations. High-performance engines are precision equipment operating under high stress. The greater the performance, the more care required. Maintain them properly and keep a log of all work done on the engines as well as on the boat.

It is important to determine the market value of your boat before you put it on the market. This can be found in the annual BUC *Used Boat Price Guide*, which is available through dealers, bankers, and libraries. BUC also offers an evaluation service that costs $25 plus 75 cents a foot. This is available by calling 1-800-327-6929. Boats are sold individually through newspaper classifieds or word-of-mouth, and through dealers and brokers. Sullivan advises selling through a broker or a dealer because they can point out salient features of the boat and create demand. BUC's Yacht Sales Network is a worldwide multiple-listing service for yacht brokers and dealers. "It gives you a great idea of value and what the competition is," said Sullivan. The broker's commission is negotiable, and never greater than 10 percent.

Financing Your Boat

Don Aronow made no bones about it. He had customers who walked in off the street, paid for a $200,000 boat in cash, and drove off with it. That kind of customer still exists in high-performance boating. So do customers who can afford to, and will, buy a boat without financing, paying by check. Most who make such a major purchase, however, will wind up financing it. Fortunately, it is easier to obtain a boat loan today ever before.

As the National Marine Manufacturers' Association notes, there are more lenders today and the competition among them favors the boat buyer. A wide array of loan programs, competitive rates, and terms makes finding a loan as easy, and some time easier, than arranging an automobile loan. In most areas of the country, any new boating purchase that reflects a loan amount of more than $5,000 should be financeable. Obviously, you should shop around for the loan. The dealer who sells the boat often has several sources of financing including local lenders or national firms that offer custom loans through boat manufacturers. Also check your local bank, savings institution, or credit union. Compare rates and terms, which must be spelled out under the Federal truth-in-lending law before any loan contracts are signed. Certain terms in the contracts, such as *points, prepayment penalties,* and *add-on interest,* mean that the boat will cost the borrower more over the long term. The marine manufacturers' association advises shopping for simple-interest loans that have no hidden costs or penalties.

As in real estate mortgages, there are fixed- and variable-rate boat loans. Constant, or fixed, monthly payments through the life of the loan are available in a fixed-rate/fixed-term loan. Variable-rate loans usually offer initial interest rates below comparable fixed rates. Interest rates move up and down with the prime rate. With a boat loan, the length of the loan generally is longer than that for other installment loans, running up to twenty years. And the longer the term of the loan, the less the borrower pays back each month.

Down payments average 20 to 25 percent of the purchase

price. However, down payments and terms vary in different parts of the country. Those buying smaller boats, less than 25 feet in length, should be able to find five- to ten-year financing; buyers of boats 25 feet in length and longer will find ten-, fifteen- and twenty-year terms. For used boats, finance terms tend to be lower and down payments higher. Most lenders require that the boat be insured for the length of the loan.

In figuring your annual operating costs in addition to any finance charges, include estimates for insurance, dockage, fuel, maintenance, and winter storage. The marine industry reports that one of the big misconceptions about powerboating is the cost of fuel. Fuel bills can be high, but in reality engines are not run for a great many hours over the year. On average, powerboat owners use their engines only a hundred hours per year; much of the pleasure of owning a boat is had while at anchor or at a marina.

There also can be tax advantages to owning a boat, and your tax accountant can determine if you and your boat qualify. Basically, if your boat has a sleeping area, a standard kitchen, and a head, it can be considered a second home for tax purposes, providing you are not already taking deductions for a second home. This means you can write off the interest on the loan you take out to finance the boat, as long as the amount of the loan does not exceed one million dollars when combined with the outstanding mortgage on your primary home.

Take a Course

It may be difficult to obtain insurance if you have never owned or operated a boat before. Many insurers require five years' experience or some kind of certification from an organization that offers boating safety courses to the public, such as the United States Power Squadrons or the U.S. Coast Guard Auxiliary. As a matter of safety you must learn the basics of boating. Also, by continuing to learn about the sport through courses and books and magazines, you will increase your enjoyment of it.

For information on the Auxiliary courses, contact any Coast Guard or Auxiliary office. The Auxiliary offers several courses to the public, including one tailored to the needs of power-boatmen. Courses are thirteen lessons, usually held in the evenings or on weekends.

A major activity of the USPS is their work in educating the public about boating. There are two educational programs: one for the general public covering basic boating skills, and another for members that includes advanced courses in piloting, seamanship, and navigation, as well as additional courses in engine maintenance, electronics, and weather. There are some five hundred local courses in boating given to the public nationwide by the Power Squadrons and many Squadrons give the classes two or more times each year. The eleven-lesson course carries a nominal charge to cover the costs of the 150-page student workbook. Call 1-800-336-BOAT (800-254-BOAT in Virginia) for the nearest course. Other sources for boating courses might include your local YMCA, park district, or boat club.

Ship's Papers

Federal law requires that all motorboats be registered and that all motorboats not documented by the Coast Guard display state registration numbers.

Documentation is a process whereby official papers on the craft are issued by the Coast Guard, and this process is the same for large commercial ships as for recreational boats. It is a form of national registration which establishes a vessel's nationality and makes it possible for the owner to obtain a preferred ship's mortgage. For any vessel—commercial or pleasure boat—to be documented it must measure at least five net tons, which roughly corresponds to a boat 30 feet in length. The boat must be owned by a United States citizen, citizens, or corporation. And the captain (but not the crew) must be a U.S. citizen. Documentation is optional for pleasure boats but is required for commercial craft operating in coastal or foreign waters.

There are distinct advantages to having your boat documented. First, you then have the legal authority to fly the yacht ensign. Documentation also makes a boat easier to finance because it establishes clear title through the preferred ship's mortgage. This basically provides that bills of sale, mortgages, and other instruments of title for the boat may be recorded with Federal officials in the boat's home port, giving constructive legal notice. Documentation also may be advantageous when entering foreign waters. A documented boat will have an official number that is marked on the structural part of the hull. With a pleasure boat, the boat's name, hailing port, and state must be indicated on the hull, and this normally is done on the transom.

If a motorboat is not documented, it must be registered with your state. The state will issue you a certificate which must be carried on board when the boat is in use, and the state registration number must be indicated on the boat's hull. Your dealer can provide further information as well as registration forms or tell you where they can be obtained.

Now that you've shopped, purchased a boat, lined up the insurance and financing, had the boat registered, and taken courses, bear in mind that most boat owners trade their boat in every three to five years. Why? Because as you become more skilled, you tend to start looking for a bit more boat.

Chapter 12

Fitting Out Your Boat

The instrument room of the 110-foot transatlantic raceboat *Gentry Eagle* is exceptionally well equipped. *(Forest Johnson photo)*

Fitting out a boat, new or used, can be an enjoyable task, regardless of one's budget. The key is to keep in mind the intended use of the boat and not to load it with unnecessary gear, which adds weight and can hamper performance.

In his fifteen years in the industry, Magnum Marine's Filippo Theodoli has observed that the average client will, with few exceptions, "kill you to take the basic boat price down and immediately after that, he is capable of spending a fortune on accessories, some of which are totally useless." Theodoli, whose top-of-the-line Magnums are owned by royalty, oil sheiks, and the just plain wealthy, recalls one customer who insisted on having a towel-warming machine in the head because after taking a bath he wanted a warm towel. "Do you know what that meant? I had to build a whole new contraption [to provide] hot water."

Another of Theodoli's customers apparently was determined not to get lost at sea. He fitted out his Magnum with five compasses: one magnetic (which is standard), another electric, a gyrocompass, a fourth compass with the loran, and a fifth included "with another instrument," said the Italian marquis. "There were not two that went together. If two were together in one quadrant, they would not be together in another. It's funny, but dangerous, too," Theodoli observed. "I want one I can rely upon. If I want to go to Bimini, I want to find it right away or I may miss Bimini."

In equipping your boat, keep in mind the four keys of fitting out: (1) Identify how you will use your boat—inshore, offshore, fishing, or whatever; (2) determine what you will need to suit the particular use; (3) make sure you know how to use the equipment; and (4) make sure the equipment is in good working order. Remember, it's better to have one good compass that is correctly calibrated than to have five all giving different readings.

Equipment Required by the U.S. Coast Guard

In outfitting, there are two types of gear: that required by the United States Coast Guard, and that which the owner installs on board in keeping with his use of the boat and his personal preferences. The Coast Guard requires boat owners to equip their craft with safety gear that varies according to the class of boat. Class A refers to boats 16 feet in length and under, while Class I is 16 to 26 feet, and Class II is for boats over 26 feet. Other law-enforcement agencies—state, county, and municipal—impose similar equipment requirements on waters that do not fall under Coast Guard jurisdiction, such as some inland lakes and rivers. In some cases, local regulations require the carrying of additional gear. Consequently, owners should obtain copies of their state and local boating laws to be sure they are in compliance.

A boat owner is responsible for making sure his or her boat carries the required gear before leaving the dock. The Coast Guard requires the following:

1. Fire Extinguisher. Class I motorboats must carry at least one U.S. Coast Guard–approved portable fire extinguisher. The approval is indicated on the label. The fire extinguisher can be a 2-pound dry chemical; 4-pound carbon dioxide, or 1¼-gallon foam extinguisher. The Coast Guard currently does not require a fire extinguisher on Class A outboard motorboats of open construction which

do not have built-in fuel tanks, but as the National Marine Manufacturers' Association cautions, this *is* required in some states. Because of the hazard of toxic fumes, vaporizing liquid extinguishers, such as carbon tetrachloride, are not allowed.

2. Personal Flotation Devices. As a general rule, a boat must be equipped with one Coast Guard–approved PFD for each person on board as well as for each person waterskiing.

3. Sound-Signaling Device. Class I motorboats must carry a hand-, mouth-, or power-operated horn or whistle, which is recommended also for Class A boats. The device should be used in safe passing, to warn other vessels in fog or confined quarters, or as a signal to operators of locks or drawbridges.

4. Navigation Lights. Boats operating between sunset and sunrise are required to display appropriate navigation lights. These are intended to keep other vessels informed of one's presence and course.

5. Sight-Signaling Device. Boats 16 feet long and larger operating on coastal waters and the Great Lakes are required to carry approved sight-signaling devices. These would include pyrotechnics such as flares for use at night and international orange flags for daytime distress signals. Requirements depend on the size and use of one's boat; one should check with the Coast Guard or one's marine dealer for the specific requirements.

Recommended Gear

The Coast Guard requirements specify only the essentials of safety gear. There are additional items of equipment that are basic, both for the use of the craft and for increasing the margin of safety and comfort. This gear, depending on the size of your boat, would include an anchor and anchor line, tow line, fenders, mooring lines, first-aid kit, flashlight and/or searchlight, paddle, compass, a chart of the local waters, signal flares, boat hook, marine radio and an EPIRB (emergency position-indicating radio beacon), and a sea anchor for the open ocean. Again, your marine dealer is a good source of advice on what you need for the size of boat you have.

As far as carrying spare engine parts, Jerry Berton advises not to bother with anything except perhaps an extra set of propellers, unless you are planning a long cruise. If an engine problem develops in a twin-engined boat, there is little the average boatman can do about it. "Most people have little mechanical ability," said Berton. "Perhaps you could change a propeller. But for the most part, you're better off getting towed into the harbor. It's very hard work to change a propeller or make any repairs on a boat rolling around on the water."

One item never to be left home, though, is the boat bag. Put the basics in your boat bag: binoculars, a hand-held marine radio and hand-held compass (supplementing those on the boat), sunscreen, and foul-weather gear. Always bring jackets, even if it's 90 degrees and sunny when you leave the dock. On the way home, the fog can set in and with the wind-chill factor at high speeds, you can become cold quickly.

The Marine Radio

For anyone planning to cruise the coastal waters, the greatest safety device to have on board is a marine radio. Before heading for the offshore canyons or the inshore bays, every captain should equip his or her craft with a marine radio and make sure it is in good working order. The captain should also understand how to use it.

The marine radio—also known as a radiotelephone, transceiver, or VHF radio—is the boatman's link to safety as long as he or she is within range of a Coast Guard station that monitors the distress frequency. If you hit a submerged object and are in danger of sinking, if someone on board becomes critically ill, if your motor stops as a storm is bearing down, or if you come across another boatman in distress, quickly reach for the marine radio. Channel 16 is the mandatory channel for distress calls. It also is used for initiating calls to other vessels or shore stations.

Before transmitting on any channel, listen to it for a few seconds to make sure it is not already in use. If this is not an emergency, use Channel 16 to establish contact and switch to any intership or ship-to-shore channel to converse. Be specific and speak clearly. Call the other vessel by its name or call sign. Keep all transmissions brief and all communications under three minutes. Be sure to yield to safety and distress calls.

To call another boat, speak directly into the microphone in a normal tone of voice. Make sure your radio is on. Select Channel 16 (156.8 MHz) and listen for a quiet period to avoid garbling a transmission already in progress. When the air is clear, press the microphone button and call the boat intended. State clearly the name of the boat you wish to contact, followed by the words "This is" and the name and call sign of your boat. End with "Over." End completed communications with "Out" and end transmissions in which you expect a reply with "Over." There is no such thing as "Over and Out." An example of an actual transmission would be: *"Crackerjack*, this is *Stormy Weather*, WA 1478. Over." To avoid confusion, always use this sequence. If necessary, repeat the name of the boat being called three times and then follow with the rest of the transmission. When *Crackerjack* replies, if you are on Channel 16, you must switch to a ship-to-ship channel. When you are through talking to *Crackerjack*, both boats must give their call signs and switch back to Channel 16.

Remember, you can only receive a call if your radio is switched on and tuned to the frequency on which you expect to receive calls. When you are maintaining a watch on Channel 16, you can expect to get calls addressed to you by other boats, and you may receive information that a marine operator has a call for you. But if you are expecting a telephone call from shore, it may be best to call the operator on his or her working channel every so often to "check for traffic." Now, when you hear your boat's name called, put your transmitter on the air and say,

"Crackerjack, this is *Stormy Weather*, WA 1478. Over." Switch to the agreed-on working channel, and when you're finished say, "This is *Stormy Weather*, WA 1478. Out."

By international agreement, there are three emergency signals describing varying degrees of problems at sea. MAYDAY indicates that a boat is threatened by grave and imminent danger and requests immediate assistance. PAN-PAN (pronounced pahn-pahn) indicates that the calling station has a very urgent message to transmit concerning the safety of a boat or persons. The urgent signal is the oral repetition three times of the two-word phrase PAN-PAN. SECURITY is the safety signal used to indicate that a message is about to be transmitted concerning navigation such as a ship backing into a channel, or concerning important weather warnings.

MAYDAY has priority over all other messages and is reserved for a true emergency in which there is real, immediate danger to life and property. Stay on Channel 16, repeating the call if no response is received immediately. Speak slowly and distinctly and use phonetic words for letters when necessary, particularly in giving the letters of your call sign or other important information requested by the Coast Guard.

You may be asked to transmit a "long count" or other suitable signal to allow direction-finding stations to determine your position. If you must abandon ship, try to lock your VHF transmitter on the air by taping down the mike button to provide a signal for homing rescue units. This is done ideally on another channel and after coordination with search craft.

To make a MAYDAY call use the following procedure:

1. Make sure your radio is turned on to Channel 16.

2. Press the microphone button and say, "Mayday, Mayday, Mayday. This is [your boat name, repeated three times, and your call sign]."

3. Again, say: "Mayday [your boat name]."

4. Tell where you are. Give your position: latitude and longitude, a true bearing and distance in miles from a known geographical position, loran coordinates, and description of any nearby navigational aids or landmarks.

5. State the nature of your distress (sinking, fire).

6. Give the number of persons aboard and the condition of any injured.

7. Estimate the present seaworthiness and condition of your boat.

8. Briefly describe your boat: length, color, type, design, or other distinguishing marks.

9. End this message by saying, "This is [your boat name and call sign]. Over."

10. Release microphone button and listen. Someone should answer. If they do not, repeat the call on Channel 16. If there still is no response, try another channel.

If you hear a MAYDAY this is what you should do:

1. Listen. Do not transmit.

2. Determine if your boat is in the best position to render assistance, or if another boat is better located or better equipped.

3. If your boat is in the best position to take action, reply with a call to the distressed vessel in this manner: "*Cracker jack, Crackerjack, Crackerjack*. This is *Stormy Weather* WA 1478. Received Mayday." After the other vessel acknowledges your call, give your position, your speed, and your estimated time of arrival.

4. If your boat is not the logical one to help, maintain radio silence but monitor the frequency for further developments. You may be asked to pass along messages. And make notes so you can include them in your log.

In addition to its safety function, a marine radio can be used for other forms of communication: operational, business, and ship-to-shore. "Operational" means communication with other boats. Business communication is limited to government and commercial boats. For the recreational boatman, the only two areas in which he may use a marine radio to communicate with other boats are for safety and operational purposes. Through shoreside marine operators, a skipper can be connected to the telephone system and from his boat make calls anywhere in the country or the world. Here restrictions of boat-to-boat communication do not apply and the boatman's ship-to-shore telephone conversation can be of a personal nature. But don't forget, others on the marine channel may be listening.

The operation of marine radios comes under the jurisdiction of the Federal Communications Commission. FCC rules require that a listening watch be maintained on Channel 16 if a pleasure-boat radio is turned on but is not being used to communicate with another station. Other vessels are required to have their radios on all the time and to maintain a watch on the distress channel. In short, there are a lot of people both on and off the water who are listening to Channel 16. This means there's a good chance that a MAYDAY will be heard.

A thorough source of information regarding marine radios is the 107-page *Marine Radiotelephone Users' Handbook* published by the Radio Technical Commission for Marine Services in cooperation with the FCC. Copies at $7.25 each are available from RTCMS, P.O. Box 19087, Washington, D.C., 20036. Information on VHF licenses can be obtained by writing the FCC, P.O. Box 1040, Gettysburg, PA 17325, or by calling the FCC at 1-717-337-1212 or 1431.

Electronic Navigation Aids

The basics come first: charts and compass and the knowledge of how to use them. Using dead reckoning, you should be able to figure out where you are at all times. Because of the explosive growth in electronic aids to navigation, you might think such a device relieves you of the chore of learning basic navigation. And, indeed, with loran, satellite navigation, and automatic pilots, you can punch in courses and speeds and needn't lay a hand on the helm to get from one destination to another. But if you rely on these aids, you are courting danger. Electrical systems can go down, and if they do, you will be stuck. If your loran malfunctions and you're ten miles offshore without a clue as to how to find your way home, you're in trouble. Should a thick fog settle in, giving you almost no visibility, you can quickly become disoriented even in the middle of familiar bays and sounds. And if a storm is approaching, you can be in big trouble. And it's unnecessary. In short, you have to be able to function with nothing but a chart.

That said, let's look at the dazzling array of electronic aids to navigation that can provide a tremendous cushion of safety and confidence. These include loran, radio direction finders, satellite navigation systems, radar, and depth sounders.

Depth Sounder. A depth sounder determines depth by measuring the round-trip time for a pulse of ultrasonic energy to travel from the boat to the bottom of the water and be reflected back to the boat. It gives a continuous readout of depth which can be indicated in several ways, such as a digital readout or a video display of bottom contours. Knowing the depth cannot tell you where you are, but it can tell you where you are not. In some instances, a rough estimate of the boat's position can be obtained by matching a series of depth readings, corrected for tidal changes, to depth markings on a chart of the area.

Radio Direction Finder. A radio direction finder (RDF) uses one or more radio transmitters ashore whose signals are picked up by an RDF set on the boat. The shore transmitters have certain frequencies and characteristics that are contained in published Light Lists. In determining the direction of the signals and their characteristics, you can fix your position. While not as accurate as Loran or radar, radio bearings are extremely helpful, particularly for smaller craft operating on the coastal waters and the Great Lakes.

Radar. Radar is used on ships of all sizes down to boats of some 30 feet in length. While space and cost limit the use of radar on smaller and midsized pleasure boats, it is standard on megayachts, functioning as an anticollision device. A radar transmitter on board sends out brief pulses of super-high-frequency radio waves that are reflected by distant objects. The time it takes for the pulse to travel out and the echo to return is a measure of the distance to the reflecting object.

Loran. Loran is an acronym for Long Range Aid to Navigation. Since the late 1970s, loran increasingly has become the standard electronic navigation aid for small craft. Loran is easier to use than an RDF and readings can be accurate to 50 feet or so. A loran receiver on the boat picks up signals sent simultaneously by a pair of stations ashore. The difference in the time of arrival at the receiver of the pulse groups transmitted by the shore station is measured precisely by electronic circuitry, and this information is used to determine a line of position. Two or more signals provide additional lines of position. Where they intersect gives a fix. The on-board receiver displays the time difference, which the skipper uses to plot his position using a chart containing corresponding time-difference lines. Many receivers also display latitude and longitude or range and bearing to the destination. Loran is excellent for use along the coastlines, but does not function far offshore.

Satellite Navigation. The U.S. Navy first used satellite navigation (also known as SatNav or Transit) in 1964 and opened it up to civilian use three years later. Here a set of five or six satellites transmit signals. A boat's receiver picks up a signal, calculates the distance to the satellite and the vessel's direction and speed, and from this gets a fix. Because of the limited number of satellites and their nonuniform coverage of the earth's surface, the time between satellite passes varies from thirty to ninety-five minutes and in the areas of lesser coverage can run four hours. However, for ocean crossings and traveling far offshore, satellite navigation is excellent and improving. The Global Position System (GPS), already partially operational, is scheduled to replace the Transit system entirely. GPS will provide full, twenty-four-hour coverage with four to seven satellites in view from any position on earth. This means a GPS receiver will be able to give you a continuous readout of your position anywhere in the world.

Equipment today can be integrated to gather position, speed, and operations data from various sources. Again, the best source for the electronic navigation aids suitable for your boat and the waters in which you will operate is your dealer.

Once you have completed outfitting your boat, call the Coast Guard Auxiliary and request a Courtesy Motorboat Examination. The CME decal, given to those whose boats pass, is a sign to other boatmen that you are properly equipped. Of course, knowing this yourself is the true value of the Auxiliary examination.

Chapter 13

On the Water

On the crowded waterways in Key Largo, Florida, knowledge of
the rules of the road is particularly important. *(Forest Johnson photo)*

Rules of the Road

The purpose of the Rules of the Road is to prevent collisions at sea, much as the regulations governing the highways are intended to prevent accidents. While the sea may be the last frontier of unfettered freedom, which often is the case, nevertheless you must know the Rules of the Road. When operating at high speed, you need to anticipate potential problems far in advance to be able to have time to correct.

What began as local custom and rules among the early seafarers grew into the Rules of the Road, more formally known today as the 1972 International Regulations for Preventing Collisions at Sea. The Navigation Act of 1977 made these international rules effective in all United States navigable waters "for all vessels." Violations carry fines up to $5,000. The other key rules affecting boatmen are the 1980 Inland Rules, which parallel the international rules, with the language changed to reflect the generally smaller size of vessels and shorter distances involved. Most boatmen operate under the inland rules, which apply to lakes, rivers, and near coastal waters. Enforcement of these rules comes under the jurisdiction of the United States Coast Guard. State or local municipalities also may have specific regulations for operation on certain waterways.

If a boatman is in an accident, he or she can be sure the Coast Guard or the state or local marine police will seek to determine who had the right of way and who was operating in accordance with the Rules of the Road. And it is clear from the inland rules who bears the responsibility: "Nothing in these Rules shall exonerate any vessel, or the owner, master or crew thereof, from the consequences of any neglect to comply with these Rules or the neglect of any precaution which may be required by the ordinary practice of seamen, or by the special circumstances of the case."

The full international and inland rules are available from the Coast Guard in the publication No. CG-169 called *Navigation Rules International—Inland*, which all powerboats 39 feet and longer must carry. Here are the highlights, drawn from the inland rules.

In General

- A boat under way must stay clear of an anchored, stopped, docked, or moored boat.

- In restricted channels, boats smaller than 66 feet, fishing boats, and sailboats must not impede passage of a vessel that can safely navigate only in a narrow channel. Large, relatively unmaneuverable vessels have the right-of-way in narrow channels.

- In traffic separation zones, boats smaller than 66-feet in length, fishing boats, and sailboats also must give way.

- Powerboats almost always give way to sailboats.

- When an auxiliary sailboat is traveling under engine power, it is considered a powerboat under these rules.

- When two sailboats approach on different tacks, the sailboat on the port tack gives way to the one on starboard tack. When they are on the same tack, the windward or upwind boat gives way to the leeward boat.

Except for special restrictions, such as large vessels operating in narrow channels, vessels may be ranked for right-of-way, with those following giving way to the vessels listed ahead of them. The ranking would be: (1) vessels not under command,

(2) vessels restricted in ability to maneuver, (3) vessels engaged in fishing, (4) sailing vessels, (5) power-driven vessels.

Look Out

Every vessel shall at all times maintain a proper lookout by sight and hearing as well as by all available means appropriate in the prevailing circumstances and conditions so as to make a full appraisal of the situation and the risk of collision.

Safe Speed

Every vessel shall at all times proceed at a safe speed so that she can take proper and effective action to avoid collision and be stopped within a distance appropriate to the prevailing circumstances and conditions. The following factors shall be included in determining a safe speed: visibility, traffic density, vessel maneuverability, the sea and wind conditions, the proximity of navigational hazards, and the draft in relation to the available depth of water.

Risk of Collision

Every vessel shall use all available means appropriate to the prevailing circumstances and conditions to determine if risk of collision exists. If there is any doubt, such risk shall be deemed to exist. To determine whether one's boat is on a collision course is to watch the compass bearing of the other vessel. If this bearing does not change appreciably, either forward or astern, a risk of collision exists and the rules for avoiding collision apply. In reduced visibility, one must make proper use of any operational radar equipment on board, including long-range scanning, and of radar plotting or equivalent systematic observation of detected objects.

Actions to Avoid Collision

The rules require that any action taken to avoid collision be made in ample time and with regard to good seamanship. Any change of course or speed should be significant enough to be readily apparent to the other vessel visually or by radar. If necessary, slow down, stop, or go into reverse to avoid collision or allow more time to assess the situation. The effectiveness of one's actions shall be checked until the other vessel is finally past and clear.

Sound Signals

Whistle signals are used only when the vessels are in sight of each other and are meeting or crossing at a distance within half a mile of each other. These signals must not be used in fog or other conditions of reduced visibility as only fog signals may be sounded in this case.

In restricted visibility, a power-driven vessel under way shall sound at intervals of not more than two minutes one prolonged blast. A prolonged blast is one from four to six seconds' duration. A vessel less than 12 meters (39.4 feet) is not required to give a prolonged blast but if it doesn't it shall make some other efficient sound signal at intervals of not more than two minutes.

Danger Signal

When two powerboats are approaching each other and one of them does not understand the intentions of the other, or is not sure that sufficient action is being taken to avoid collision, the vessel in doubt gives the danger signal: five short, rapid blasts on the whistle. This may be supplemented by a light signal of at least five short and rapid flashes. This should alert the other skipper to slow down or stop immediately.

Equipment for Sound Signals

A vessel 12 meters (39.4 feet) or more in length must carry a whistle and a bell; a vessel of 100 meters (328.1 feet) or more in length must also have a gong.

A vessel less than 12 meters (39.4 feet) in length does not need to carry the above sound-signaling equipment but if she does not, she must have some other means of making an efficient sound signal.

For vessels over 12 meters (39.4 feet) in length, there are specifications for sound-signaling equipment such as different whistle tones and ranges of audibility.

Maneuvering Lights

Whistle signals may be supplemented by a light signal synchronized with the whistle. This is an all-round white light, visible for at least two miles regardless of the size of the vessel. If a vessel carries only one masthead light, as is the case for nearly all boats, the maneuvering light can be carried where it can best be seen, but not less than ½ meter, or 19.7 inches, above or below the masthead light.

Actions by Give-way and Stand-on Vessels

The give-way boat, the one which does not have the right of way, is to keep out of the way of another vessel and take early and substantial action to keep well clear.

The stand-on vessel, which does have the right of way, shall keep her course and speed. However if the stand-on vessel finds herself so close that collision cannot be avoided by the action of the give-way vessel alone, she shall take such action as will best help avoid collision.

Rules for Powerboats Under Way

There are types of encounters between approaching boats in which the navigation rules apply: overtaking, crossing, and meeting head-on.

OVERTAKING SITUATION. Any vessel overtaking another shall keep out of the way of the vessel being overtaken. A vessel is considered to be overtaking another when approaching from a direction more than 22.5 degrees abaft the beam of the vessel being overtaken. At night the overtaking vessel would be able to see only the sternlight of the vessel ahead but neither of her sidelights. When a vessel is in doubt whether she is overtaking another, she shall assume this to be the case. Further, any subsequent alteration of the bearing between the two vessels shall not make the overtaking vessel a crossing vessel or relieve her of the duty of keeping clear.

If the overtaking vessel wants to pass on the port side of the vessel ahead, which is the normal procedure if the slower boat is keeping to the right of a channel, it must sound a two-short-blast signal. If the privileged vessel agrees, it immediately responds with the same signal. The faster boat then swings out to port and passes. If the faster boat wants to pass to starboard, which is permissible but not normal, it sounds one short blast, which is returned by the privileged boat if it agrees. Any overtaking vessel receiving a danger signal in reply to its stated intention to pass should immediately halt all attempts to pass and reduce speed.

Any vessels which have reached agreement in a meeting, crossing, or overtaking situation by using the marine radio need not sound whistle signals, but may do so. The international rules do not contain the provision for use of the marine radio in place of whistle signals, but it still could supplement them.

HEAD-ON SITUATION. When two powerboats are meeting on reciprocal or nearly reciprocal courses so as to involve risk of collision, each shall alter her course to starboard so that each shall pass on the port side of the other. This situation will be considered to exist when a vessel sees the other ahead or nearly ahead and by night she could see the masthead lights of the other in a line or nearly in a line and/or both sidelights, and by day she observes the corresponding aspect of the other vessel. If there is any doubt whether such a situation exists, she shall assume it does and act accordingly. When powerboats are within sight of each other and meeting at a distance of a half-mile or less, each vessel must sound whistle signals as follows:

ONE SHORT BLAST means, "I intend to leave you on my port side."

TWO SHORT BLASTS mean, "I intend to leave you on my starboard side."

THREE SHORT BLASTS mean, "My engines are in reverse gear."

The other vessel will, if in agreement, sound the same signal and take any steps necessary for a safe passage. However, if this vessel doesn't think the proposed maneuver is safe, it should sound the danger signal of five or more short, rapid blasts and take appropriate action. At this point, both boats should im-

The U.S. Customs Service has taken to the seas after drug runners in their own Aronow-designed Blue Thunder high performance boats. *(Courtesy of Aronow Powerboats)*

mediately stop or slow down and neither should attempt to pass until agreement is reached. There is no rule as to who should signal first. Both have an equal chance to act first.

Note, the international rules here do not have the half-mile requirement for signaling intent to pass. Instead they require a whistle for each change of course, without reply signals from the other vessel.

CROSSING SITUATION. When two powerboats are crossing so as to involve risk of collision, the vessel that has the other on her own starboard side shall keep out of the way and shall, if the circumstances of the case admit, avoid crossing ahead of the other vessel.

The inland rules require whistle signals in crossing situations also. If the vessels are in sight of each other and will pass within a half-mile of each other, the same whistle signals mentioned above apply with the same meetings. Remember, this applies only if there is risk of collision.

Distress Signals

Distress signals are contained in both the inland and international rules. In an emergency a skipper can use any means possible to attract attention and call for help, including flying the national ensign upside down. Other forms of signaling distress include: calling MAYDAY on the radio, tapping out Morse code SOS, red meteor flares, a person waving his arms, a fog horn sounded continuously, a dye marker, an EPIRB, and a gun fired at one-minute intervals.

Navigation Aids

Navigation aids—buoys and markers—are the signposts of the waterways. Buoys and markers are used to indicate channels, entrances to harbors, obstructions. You should become familiar with the usual Coast Guard buoys and markers as well as any other specialized markers in your area. In entering a harbor, the buoys on the port side of the channel will be green and carry odd numbers. The buoys on the starboard side of the channel will be red and carry even numbers. There also may be a midchannel buoy which has red and white vertical stripes. All three types of buoys may also be lettered.

Etiquette at Sea

We go boating for pleasure, to relax, get away from shore-bound cares and just have fun. Unless you're heading for the high seas, chances are you'll be doing your boating around other boatmen. And often the manner in which you operate your boat will impact others. Keep in mind the speed and noise of a high-performance powerboat can alarm and annoy other boatmen. Revving up at the dock without silencers, for instance, is completely unnecessary.

Fred Kiekhaefer believes that boat manufacturers have an obligation to help owners by building in devices for containing noise and that underwater exhausts and mufflers should become part of every performance boat. "When was the last time you heard a Ferrari without mufflers?" he noted. "You can't sell me on the concept that performance equals noise."

Offshore high-performance boats are intended to run fast offshore where there is no traffic. The operator of a performance boat is responsible for keeping his distance from other boats in narrow and crowded waterways, such as the Intracoastal Waterway and the western end of Long Island Sound. For instance, when you see a person on the foredeck of a sailboat up ahead, you must drop off plane. When you pass a slower boat in a crowded waterway, you should slow down to the point where you do not cause any problems or discomfort to those aboard the boat you're passing. You've got to think ahead, knowing the Rules of the Road and anticipating any difficulties you or the other boats might have. This really comes down to a matter of safe boating and common courtesy.

Zero Tolerance

As part of the escalating war against drugs, the U.S. Coast Guard and the Customs Service have been enforcing the Federal Government's so-called zero-tolerance policy. Under this policy, the authorities can seize, and keep, any yacht on which any amount of illegal drugs is found. Whereas in the past the authorities focused on the drug smugglers, they now are searching for drugs on all "manners of conveyance," which includes cars, boats, and planes. This emphasizes the Government's position that drug possession, regardless of the amount, will not be tolerated.

Most of the vessels seized by Customs and the Coast Guard under this policy have not been taken from the owners. Instead, the owners have been fined.

If you are reluctant to search your guests and crew for drugs before they board, there is an alternative. If the authorities can be convinced that reasonable precautions were taken to ensure a drug-free boat, the chance of the yacht being confiscated decrease. The recommended precautions include posting a zero-tolerance notice in a visible, public area on board, have each salaried crew member sign a statement that he or she will not introduce or use illegal drugs on board, inform guests on board that any illegal drug use will not be tolerated, and cooperate with the Coast Guard and Customs if they board your boat to search for drugs. The Coast Guard has the right to board any U.S.-registered or -flagged vessel inside and outside the twelve-mile limit.

Chapter 14

Boat Handling

Rolando Pieiga shows special handling skills as he "flies" *Miami's Best* from crest to crest in South Florida seas. *(Forest Johnson photo)*

General Principles

To become a good seaman, you must go to sea. It is not possible simply to read about boat handling and then expect to be able to master your boat or even handle it reasonably well. Reading can only point you in the right direction. To learn boat handling is an individual process. You develop the skills by taking the boat out and making small mistakes. At some point you will discover that your reactions will have become intuitive because you've been there many times already. However, one of the great pleasures of boating is that the water and wind conditions never are precisely the same, and in striving to be the best, you will find that the learning process is ongoing. The challenge of pitting oneself and one's craft against the natural forces strikes an elemental chord. And to be able to handle your boat well, to be a good seaman, is a true accomplishment of which you can be proud.

As the owner of a high-powered piece of equipment, your ability to handle the boat correctly is particularly important. Anyone going to sea should know the fundamentals of driving his or her boat. But the problems are greatly magnified when a newcomer to boating steps into a high-performance boat. You must devote time to on-the-water practice.

No two boats handle exactly the same way. Your boat is unique. And just how a boat performs depends on a number

Bernie Gonzalez and his Sportsman D Class entry *The Connection* encounter jarring, lumpy seas in a 1987 race from Miami to Freeport, the Bahamas, across the treacherous Gulf Stream. *(Forest Johnson photo)*

of factors, such as the shape of the hull, the construction, trim, speed, wind direction and strength, current, and the nature of the sea. Once you understand how your boat handles and the forces that affect it, you will develop good judgment. You have to look ahead, be able to foresee situations and react promptly. Good seamanship is based on a combination of common sense and experience.

World Offshore champion Betty Cook started learning to drive an Offshore raceboat when she was a grandmother. In the eleven years she competed on the circuit, garnering a record to equal that of the legendary Don Aronow, she suffered bumps and bruises. But as one of the paramount drivers, Betty Cook never had an accident or any serious injury, a remarkable record. She was tough, but she also was careful; her boats were meticulously rigged and she had a top-notch crew with one of the best throttlemen in John Connor.

"When you think about a recreational boat going eighty miles an hour! Why, that was the top speed for Offshore race-boats fifteen years ago. And in that situation you had a driver, throttleman, and navigator. In the recreational boat, one guy does all three things," said Cook. "That is alarming. It's difficult to convince a person that he or she must have the patience to take things step-by-step, even if he or she has owned a powerboat before."

Cook cautions that experience in other powerboats does not prepare a person to handle a high-performance craft. "There's a fine line in speed above which you can get into trouble very quickly, and I think it happens around forty miles an hour, because really things happen much more rapidly," she related. "The inner reaction between the boat and the water, which is a variable from moment to moment, happens quickly, and before you can think about it you may be in trouble. A boat goes out of the water, for example, and you've got to be off the throttle so you don't overrev the engines. You've got to have a good hand on the wheel because you don't want the water to toss the drives around when they come back in. If that happens, you can have a situation where you spin it out and everyone gets spit out of the boat."

In running at high speed, you must watch the water, learn to read the surface for wave patterns, and you also must watch your gauges. You have to watch the oil pressure and make sure, if you have a twin-engined boat, that the engines are synchronized. This sounds simple. But when you are running at speed over lumpy water you may have an uneven hand on the throttle. And, as Cook noted, if you tilt your hand right or left, you unsync the engines.

The difference between driving a high-performance boat and any other type, Cook observed, "is like driving a car at sixty-five miles an hour and driving it at a hundred."

Some handling principles apply to all powerboats. The handling characteristics for a boat with a rudder and a single right-hand propeller (one that turns clockwise in driving the boat forward) are:

- The boat is always under better control with headway, going forward, rather than with sternway, going backward, because of the effect of the propeller's discharge current on the rudder.

- Until the boat has gathered headway the stern has a tendency to swing to starboard, even with rudder amidships, as the propeller starts to turn ahead. With good headway, rudder angle is the principal factor in affecting control.

- When backing, there is a strong tendency to go to port, regardless of the rudder angle, except with full right rudder and considerable sternway. To back in a straight line you need a certain amount of right rudder which varies with the speed.

- When not moving, there is no rudder control, yet the stern can be kicked rapidly to port or starbord by turning the wheel and applying a brief surge of power before the boat has a chance to gather headway.

- With a left-hand propeller, the boat's reaction will be the opposite of a right-hand propeller. With two sterndrives having propellers turning in opposite directions, obviously, steering and maneuverability are improved.

- A boat having two engines or outdrives gives the skipper the means of throwing one side or the other ahead or astern. Much of a boat's maneuvering at low speed is done by controlling the two throttles rather than the wheel.

Use a Checklist

Before casting off, go through a checklist. Make sure you have enough fuel. Inspect the engine area, checking for water or fuel leaks, tight hose connections, and engine crankcase oil level, if applicable to your boat. With gasoline engines, check for any odor of fumes. With even the faintest trace of an odor, ventilate thoroughly before the engines are started; operate the bilge blower for at least four minutes to expel any gasoline vapors. It's also good practice to leave the blower running when the engine is running. Check the oil pressure and see that the cooling water is circulating. There should be a visible flow of water overboard, usually through the exhaust line. If the water doesn't circulate, check it out immediately. Check the battery. Run the bilge pump, if necessary, until the flow stops. Make sure you have enough lifesaving devices, one for everyone on board, and make sure you have the necessary emergency gear. Check the boat's trim. Check the weather forecast. Lower the outdrive or outboard motor into down position. Running either unit in the up position may cause damage. Make sure the gear-shift control is in neutral. Don't race a cold motor as it idles. And don't spend too much time warming up the engine. Long periods of idling are not good for the clutch. The engine will warm up better and quicker with the propeller engaged.

After you've shifted to forward, open the throttle gradually. Generally, normal cruising is done at two thirds to three quarters full throttle. Start slowly. In a high performance boat, you drop the drives down and drop the trim tabs down to get up on plane. When you're on plane, you bring the tabs up and the drives out and, as Cook explained, "sort of settle the boat down according to the water. You figure out where you want the tabs and the drives, and that is something you have to feel your way through as it varies with the wind and water conditions."

In returning to the dock, throttle down gradually to keep the boat under control. Give yourself plenty of room to reduce speed. When you think you have enough headway just to reach the dock, shift into neutral and use reverse power when necessary to slow the boat down as it approaches the dock. You should approach the dock at a 10- to 20-degree angle and slowly coast up to it, ideally losing all headway just as the bow is about the kiss the dock. That kind of landing takes practice. Until you have your docking procedure down, just take it slow and easy.

The dealer who sells you a high-performance boat should be responsible for showing you how to control it. Make a series of lessons part of your purchase agreement. The dealer or his mechanic can show you how and why the boat responds to changes of the trim tabs and drives, and after a few practice runs as copilot you will have acquired the essentials needed to start practicing on your own. Practice in open water, away from any other boats. After some fundamental training on the basics, it's time to get some experience, "preferably alone, with some friends nearby on another boat in case you do something stupid," advises Fred Kiekhaefer.

How Trim Tabs Work

In a high-performance boat, trim means control and efficiency. Achieving trim is obtaining the desired operating attitude by counteracting the force of the wind and sea. This is done with trim tabs, metal plates that extend from the transom, horizontal to the water, and are adjusted to control the boat's attitude. Five means of using trim tabs are explained by Kiekhaefer Aeromarine:

1) *Getting on plane.* During acceleration, tucking the drives under and dropping the tabs (bow down) brings the boat on plane without loss of visibility and with less effort. As the boat comes on plane, bring the tabs up so the bow won't plow, then trim the drives for the best performance. Using tabs, one can plane heavier loads —like a load of fuel, a full bait well, water skiers, or a half-dozen friends.

2) *Smoothing the ride.* In heavier water, a head sea can create an uncomfortable, jarring ride. Put the tabs to a middle position. As a wave throws the bow up, tabs dampen the boat's reaction, leveling and smoothing the ride. In a following sea, put the drives and the tabs up. This will allow the boat to lift, offsetting the waves that lift the stern. In milder water, some boats will gently porpoise. Don't react by trimming the drives down. Drop

the tabs instead, a touch at a time until the lope disappears.

3) *Correcting a list.* Listing may be caused by an unbalanced load. A little "down tab" on the side of the heavy load will level the ride. List also may occur in a quarter-following sea. Waves lift the stern unevenly, causing the boat to pitch forward and roll opposite the lift. If the starboard transom is lifting, drop a little port tab. This will remove the listing and produce a dryer ride.

4) *High-speed trim.* A fast boat without tabs may be "flighty." Tab down to get no more than a slight bow-up attitude. This way the stern reenters first if the boat leaves the water. Too much tab and you will land hard, bow first. Practice to achieve a level trajectory. Develop your high-speed skills in a variety of conditions starting in mild water and working up gradually.

5) *Low-speed trim.* In controlled speed zones, many boats start to fall off plane, thereby reducing visibility as the bow rises. Lowering both trim tabs will keep a boat on plane at legal, lower speeds while maintaining a level boat attitude.

At idle speed, bow steering (wandering from side to side) requires constant correction to maintain a heading. Dropping both tabs creates stern drag which improves tracking.

Tabs also reduce roll. When a boat is at rest or idle, the water level is above the tabs. A wave that normally would cause rolling must first move water out of the way—from above one tab and below the other. This dampens rolling.

In an inboard-powered performance boat, whether gasoline or diesel, it is important always to know the position of the trim tabs. Tempest Marine's Jerry Berton advises checking the boat's flotation before leaving the dock. Make sure the boat floats level and if it doesn't, adjust the weight.

"I don't like to use the trim tabs unless there is a crosswind or an uneven load where you have a lot of weight on one side of the boat and you need to balance it with the trim tabs," said

Berton. "Inevitably, if you run with the trim tabs down, you are creating a lot of drag. If you run with one trim tab down because there is so much weight on one side of the boat, you are effectively counterbalancing it by dragging this big flap through the water." Under these conditions, if the boat were to fly out of the water it can veer sharply on reentry as the tab hooks into the water. An unexpected shift in the weight also can cause the boat, with the trim tabs down, to heel severely.

When there is a stiff crosswind, however, trim tabs are the only way to keep the boat level. "If the wind is coming from the starboard side, you are turning the wheel to starboard to counterbalance it and this causes the boat to lean to that side," explained Berton, who ran the APBA paceboat for many years. "You need to tab it to create some drag to balance the boat. The tab acts like the flap on an airplane. Obviously, if you change course, you need to change the trim tab also."

If one does use the trim tabs in a big crosswind, make sure the boat is going slow enough to prevent it from flying out of the water. "Never run a high-speed boat with the trim tabs cocked, no matter what the angle of the waves is," Berton cautioned.

When running at high speed in big seas, a performance boat will fly, and when it comes down, if it reenters at even a slight angle, it can catch on the trim tab and this will cause the boat to hook. Basically, the trim tab then is acting like a rudder, turning the boat sideways. In a fast boat, you can be thrown to the side or spin the boat out. "That's not likely to happen in a big diesel boat because you normally are not flying out of the water, but typically in a gasoline-powered speed boat it could happen," he said.

A driver also should be aware that if he has to turn suddenly and the trim tabs are down, they can have an adverse effect on his steering.

Also, you should become familiar with the boat's reaction time to the lowering and raising of the trim tabs. "It takes time for the boat to react to the water flow," Berton pointed out. "If a person trims the boat down, he will see the indicator go to Four but nothing happens. He is expecting an instant reaction. So he keeps pushing the trim tabs down and all of a sudden he's down to Six. Now, because the trim tabs themselves are moving faster than the reaction of the boat, he has over-trimmed. If the driver's intention was to trim to counterbalance heeling to starboard, he's likely to find the boat now will lurch to port. You must trim gradually. The bigger the boat, the bigger the tab and the more gradual the trim should be," he said.

Trim tabs can be helpful in getting up on plane and traveling at low speeds in a harbor. If, in throttling to get up on plane, the boat's bow rises cutting off visibility, the trim tabs can be lowered to hold the bow down. And in a harbor's no-wake zone where speeds are restricted to 4 to 5 mph, boat wake can be reduced significantly by lowering the trim tabs. "At dis-placement speed with the tabs down, the boat will be level with the water and the stern won't be dragging," Berton noted.

Running in Heavy Seas

Trim tabs have distinct advantages and disadvantages when running in heavy seas. In a big sea condition, one is likely to take more water over the bow of the boat and one will want to run the boat slower. To run it slower, put the trim tabs down so the boat stays on plane easier at lower rpm. However, at the same time, the trim tabs are bringing the bow down, a situation one must be wary of.

"In heavy seas you have to slow down," said Betty Cook. "But then you have to feel there's a point where you go too slow and you bury yourself and then you're in for a very un-comfortable ride. You have to have the courage to give it a little more engine. You have to know how far to drop the tabs and drop the drives if you want to tuck them under. When the drives are up the props don't get as much bite. And with the tabs down they tend to keep the bow up a bit and keep it from plowing."

In 8- to 10-foot waves with high winds and a following sea, the boat will be going dead slow up one wave and down the back of another. "Inevitably, one wave comes along that is bigger than the others, which breaks the pattern. When you go sliding down the wave with your trim tabs down, the tabs will cause you to bury the boat's nose and get a giant wall of water over your boat," Berton explained. Consequently, in big seas, he said, it is best to stay off plane and plow through the water at a speed just greater than displacement speed so that the bow remains up. In severe conditions, you can drive at a slight angle to the waves to lessen the impact and in essence tack or zigzag toward your destination. Back off on the throttle until you are just maintaining headway. This is called "heaving to" and it's the most comfortable way to ride out a storm.

If the engines stop in severe weather, rig a sea anchor. The commercial ones are cone-shaped bags with a bridle to which you tie a long line. There is a trip line so when the emergency is over, you tip the parachute-like sea anchor and bring it back on board. The sea anchor holds the boat into the wind and sea. But you can only use a sea anchor on the open sea where you have room to drift downwind. If you don't have a sea anchor on board, in an emergency you can use any bulky material on a small boat and it will work.

The alternative to heaving to is to stay on plane without the trim tabs down so the bow always is in a positive angle. The resulting pounding, however, can be hard on the boat and the passengers, depending on the waves. "It takes more nerve to stay on plane," Berton continued. "As long as you're going fast enough to stay on plane, the boat will go from wave top to wave top at maybe thirty-five to thirty-eight miles an hour. But if you lose your confidence and bring the boat down to twenty-five miles an hour, then the boat might trip over the next wave and bury its bow."

Berton sums up his trim-tab philosophy this way: "A boat should be balanced to run with no trim tabs, unless there is a strong crosswind. If there is a big crosswind then you shouldn't be jumping the boat out of the water. Typically, when the boat is out of the water, it is subject to the effects of the wind. Even though you fly out straight, the wind can turn the boat and when you land, if the tabs are down, you can do an immediate ninety-degree turn and be thrown out of the boat. If you must use the trim tabs, keep the boat from flying."

Driving a Catamaran

The difference between driving a vee-hull and a catamaran at high speed, says Betty Cook, is that the catamaran is more sensitive. "They are easy to drive, but that's only true when they've got the kind of water and wind conditions that they need." Catamarans are fair-weather boats, performing best on flat waters. Even then they require a delicate hand at the helm.

"You can hook them very easily," said Cook who has raced six different catamarans from 30 to 40 feet in length. "You do not turn sharply with a cat because you can't lay it over on the chine and have it bite like a deep-vee. If you turn too sharply you can dive in one of those sponsons and you're in trouble. Instead, on a turn you put a little [of the sponson] in and take it out, put a little in and take it out."

Cook recalled that she turned too sharply in a Detroit race at a checkpoint that was almost a 180-degree turn. The sponson dug in and the "only serious thing that happened was the boat bogged down in the water. It took a while to get it straightened out and back up to speed and trim. But if it had been rough the sponson would have dug in and that could easily have flipped the boat."

The first time Cook drove a catamaran, she had "a devil of a time. It was an obstinate boat to begin with and when I got it, it was even more so," she recalled, laughing. She was given a piece of advice, though, that stayed with her through her years of racing these sensitive craft: "Act as if you have a bubble in the tunnel and you don't want it to break."

Running an Inlet

When an outgoing tide meets an onshore breeze the result can be a rough inlet. You may leave a calm inlet in the morning and return in the late afternoon to find the inlet has turned into a mass of cresting rollers through which you have to run to reach home. The sea breeze increases during the day. The sun heats the land mass and the rising warm air over land is replaced by the cooler air from the sea moving in as an onshore breeze. Generally, the velocity increases as the day goes on.

If the rollers are some distance apart, put the boat on the rear slope of a swell and ride it in. Adjust the throttle to keep the boat there. Don't go too near the top of the wave or the crest might pitchpole the boat. And don't fall into the trough between the seas or you might broach. In a broach, the boat is pushed sideways. Then the following sea picks up the stern and throws it to one side and rolls over the boat. If you feel the stern swinging out to the side, steer against it and increase the speed a bit to straighten the boat out.

Three Common Mishaps

Mishaps do occur on the water, though of course you try to prevent them. Three common mishaps are (1) running aground, (2) needing a tow, and (3) man overboard.

Everyone runs aground at one time or another. If you're in a small boat you often can push the boat off, if you haven't driven up hard and fast. Immediately after you hit, shift into reverse and apply power. You can try wake bouncing: Put the engine in reverse and hope the swells of passing wakes will lift you off. In a deep vee hull you also can heel the boat to one side in an attempt to work it off. If the tide is coming in, just wait patiently.

A small boat should be towed with the line attached to the towing eye on the boat's stem. And the boat being towed should supply the line. Before attaching towing lines to cleats, check to make sure the cleats are bolted through the deck or they may pull out under the strain. If a small boat is giving a tow to a big boat, it may be best to come up snug alongside, with plenty of fenders, in the manner of a tugboat.

If someone falls overboard, toss him the throwable flotation device you are required to have in the cockpit. Designate some-one on board to keep an eye on the person in the water. Instantly turn and circle back, shifting into neutral as you approach the person in the water, and bring him up over the side. If you are bringing him in over the stern swim platform or cavitation plate, kill the engine.

High-Performance Cruising

High-performance boats are opening up entirely new ways of going boating. As with a car, these boats can be driven long distances, with the skipper and crew dining and sleeping ashore at marina-style motels. With a larger high-performance boat, one brings all the amenities along. It can be a craft with a modest cabin arrangement or a megayacht on the leading edge of luxury and elegance, with everything from helicopter pads and Jacuzzis to entertainment centers and enough electronic gear to outfit a Navy submarine.

Float Plan

Big boat or small, fast or slow, some things remain the same. The Float Plan is one. Before you leave on a trip, advise a responsible person ashore of where you intend to cruise and when and where you expect to arrive. Give this person a complete description of your boat. In the event you fail to arrive, he or she will then be able to tell the authorities where to look for you and the type of boat to search for. Advise the person of any changes in your Float Plan as well as of your arrival, in order to prevent false alarms about your safety.

Reading the Weather

"The beauty of being out on the sea is that you can look up and see weather coming or going," noted Jerry Berton. Berton, based in Mamaroneck, New York, probably has more high-performance cruising miles under his hull than any other person. In recent years he has cruised with friends from Miami to

New York; Miami to Maine; Boston through the Reversing Falls to the top of the St. John's River in New Brunswick—and back; from New Orleans to Key West; and from San Francisco to Long Beach.

"A forecaster on a TV show can show you the weather map but it doesn't look real," he said. "On a boat you can see the weather approaching from a great distance, and on a speedboat you generally can run around it or run in on time. Whether you can outrun the weather depends on how fast your boat is and how fast the weather's moving. Sometimes it can just capture you in one stroke and there's nothing you can do about it."

It is important to know your local weather patterns and check the forecasts before leaving the dock. Most weather tends to come from the west, the direction of the prevailing winds. But not all of it. So keep an eye on the western and northwestern horizons, but don't forget the other quadrants. Large weather systems, such as cold fronts and low-pressure systems, are carefully tracked by satellite but they can change quickly, speeding up, slowing down, or dissipating. In the summer you have to think ahead to the afternoon weather; a morning forecast for scattered afternoon thunderstorms might degenerate into a mass of squalls.

When a cloud begins to thicken and grow vertically, it's likely to produce a small shower. If it continues to grow, a thunderstorm may be brewing. One thunderstorm can breed others, because at one stage of a storm the cooler air flows downward and spreads in all directions. If you are upwind of the storm, the cool airflow cancels out the prevailing wind. This is known as the calm before the storm. However, it doesn't necessarily mean the storm is coming your way. Winds on the downwind side are increased by the flow of air and can become gusty. Thunderstorms are mean and tricky. If you see one coming, run for safe harbor.

The best sources of weather information by radio are the continuous broadcasts by National Weather Service stations, generally on designated VHF channels, which can be picked up by any marine radio. There also are small, inexpensive weather radios that are used only to pick up the Weather Service channels. These are available from your marine dealer. Larger boats can carry weather fascimile machines, relatively compact units built for marine use that print out current satellite weather maps. These cover large areas, though, and might omit details useful in evaluating local conditions.

In addition, storm signals indicating hazardous conditions at sea are displayed at Coast Guard Stations, yacht clubs, and municipal facilities. You should not go out when the storm signals are raised. In order of the indicated ascending wind velocities, the storm signals are: One red flag means small-craft warnings; two red flags mean gale warnings; a square red flag with a black box means storm warnings; and two square red flags with black boxes means hurricane warning.

Cruising Tips

To cruise long distances without incident requires some advance planning as well as common sense. The goal is to be self-sufficient, to be able to cope with any problems that may arise, and to enjoy your travels. Here are some tips for a successful voyage:

- ALWAYS KNOW WHERE YOU ARE. Follow your progress on the chart. This is a safety precaution, as emergencies come up fast and you may need to put into shore in a hurry. It also will make your trip more interesting.

- USE HYDRAULIC STEERING. If you plan to be running at high speed for several hours at a time, you should have a hydraulic rather than a manual steering system. Hydraulic steering eliminates chatter through the wheel.

- MAKE SURE YOU HAVE THE APPROPRIATE BOAT. Make sure your boat is suitable for the planned journey. If you're thinking of going direct from New York to Martha's Vineyard in a 25-foot sport boat with a single engine, think again. On paper, running at a certain speed and with refills, you can make it. But the boat is too small for the distance and you'd be embarking on an endurance test. Instead, plan stops; run at a slower speed and preserve your equipment and yourself.

- ASSESS SPARE PARTS. While spare propellers are probably sufficient for local cruising, on a long cruise it is advisable to bring whatever part is likely to break—particularly with a performance boat, because parts are not available at every marina. As a general rule, take parts that do not require a haulout to repair. If something breaks that requires a haulout, the boat is usually out of the water overnight. And with overnight delivery, just about any part can be shipped in. In addition to the props, bring: starter motors, an alternator, and belts for the cooling pump. If you break the drive or the internals of the engine, the boat has to be hauled and there is no quick fix.

- KEEP A DAILY LOG. Logbooks with printed formats are available at marine supply stores. The purpose of a log is to record navigational data, such as the time you started, the time you reached your destination, the time you passed important navigational aids or landmarks, and your various headings and speeds with the time either changed. These data ensure you will be able to keep track of where you are. Also record the names of persons on board other than the usual family members or crew, and make notes of sea and weather conditions. Note any unusual events, such as trouble with your boat or assistance given to another craft. Also use the log to record your operating expenses such as fuel and dockage.

For those who are well equipped and well prepared, boating is an adventure. High-performance boating can provide some of the best in adventure. To be able to cruise comfortably at high speed puts many more playgrounds within your reach. And since a good offshore boat can cruise comfortably anywhere from 50 to 70 mph, just think of all the places you can go. Yes, you must take time to learn about the water and your boat. You must spend time keeping your engines in top shape—or make sure someone else does. The higher the power, the more precious the engine and the more care it needs—truly a case of high tech, high touch. Put in the time and the rewards are yours.

Part 5

Directory of High-Performance Builders

For the purpose of this listing, a high-performance boat is considered as one having either a deep vee or a tunnel hull (with the exception of Boston Whaler, which has an inverted W hull) and the ability to cruise at 50 mph or more. An offshore high-performance craft is generally regarded as one that is thirty feet or longer.

This listing includes some of the foremost production and custom builders in the United States in the high-performance field.

APACHE BOATS, INC.
2800 N. 30th Ave.
Hollywood, FL 33020

Mark McManus, general manager
(305)920–1455

Apache was formed in 1984 by
Jack Kramer, the father of racer Ben
Kramer. The firm builds quality 41-
and 47-foot deep-vees, both in race
and pleasure boat configurations,
which run 70 to 100 mph. Don
Aronow designed the 41 and built
the original hull. The 47 was
designed by Ben Kramer and Mark
McManus. Apache also builds a 41-
foot catamaran, in race and pleasure
boat versions. Standard power:
MerCruiser 2/575 hp. Optional
power to 2/800 hp.

ARONOW POWERBOATS
3030 N.E. 188th St.
North Miami Beach, FL 33180

Gary Garbrecht, president
(305) 931–1533

This is the former USA Racing
Team, Inc., founded in 1983 by Don
Aronow and run by the legendary
racer until his death in 1987. The
firm builds two fiberglass catamaran
models, 24- and 39-footers. The 39,

called Blue Thunder, is used by
U.S. Customs. Aronow Powerboats
added a monohull line in 1989 with
37-, 45-, and 47-foot deep vee hulls,
and a 40-foot raceboat. The builder
will install power and drives of the
buyer's choice.

ARRIVA
Division of U.S. Marine
P.O. Box 9022
Everett, WA 98206

Rick Manion, sales manager
(206) 435–2888

Arriva is the newest affiliate of
U.S. Marine, which is a Brunswick

275

company. U.S. Marine, the world's largest boatbuilder (producing 54,000 units in 1988), entered the high-performance field in 1989 with Arriva. Arriva is available in four models, ranging from 20 feet to 24 feet in length. The low-slung Arriva comes with MerCruiser sterndrive power from 230 to 330 hp, as well as power trim and tilt as standard gear. Arriva engines and hulls are factory matched.

BAJA BOATS, INC.
1520 Isaac Beal Rd.
Bucyrus, OH 44820

Doug Smith, president
(419) 562–5377

Baja, formed in 1969 by the Aeroglass Corporation, was acquired by Doug Smith in 1979. The company builds high-performance, deep vee boats 16 to 42 feet long, which are known for styling and performance. Ninety percent are equipped with sterndrive power and 10 percent outboard power. The boats are powered according to dealer specifications, with MerCruiser the dominant sterndrive. Top power in the Baja 42 is twin MerCruiser 630 V12 Lamborghini sterndrives.

BANANA BOAT, LTD.
1128 Narragansett Blvd.
Cranston, RI 02905

Ray Mooney, president
(401) 941–2000

Mooney purchased Banana Boat in 1977 from Charlie McCarthy, Offshore racer and trucking executive. The firm produces a 24-foot fiberglass Offshore raceboat, as well as pleasure boat versions of the racing hull. Banana Boat has a deep vee hull with a 24-degree deadrise that maintains its V shape from bow to stern. Standard power: single MerCruiser with full power trim; single or twin Mercury outboards with power trim.

BOSS RACING TEAM, INC.
2950 N.E. 188th St.
North Miami Beach, FL 33180

A. J. Roberts, Sr., president
(305) 937–0040

Boss was founded in 1988 by A. J. Roberts, Sr., former world champion Offshore racer and owner of Cougar Boats, to build race, patrol, and pleasure boats in catamaran and deep vee configurations. Boss has thirteen pleasure boat models, from an 18-foot, center-console open fishing boat to a 50-foot triple-engine luxury craft capable of 100 mph. With Roberts, boating is a family affair. When he won the world Class I title in 1985, he drove his son's boat—*A. J. Jr.'s Mr. Roberts*.

BOSTON WHALER, INC.
1149 Hingham St.
Rockland, MA 02370

W. C. Herman, vice-president of marketing
(617) 871–1400

Boston Whaler began in 1959 with a 13-footer that has become

276

one of the best-known and most prolific small boats in existence. This flattened W hull, designed by Ray Hunt and Whaler founder Richard Fisher, has evolved into the modern Whaler line. Whaler's high-performance entity is its Temptation series in 20-, 22- and 25-foot models. Built with Whaler's foam-core technique, the strong, unsinkable Temptations are backed by a ten-year transferable warranty.

CARRERA POWERBOAT
CORPORATION
13995 W. W. 139 Court
Miami, FL 33186

Roger Russell, vice-president
(305) 255–9334

Carrera was founded in 1977 by Humberto Picon, a racer who achieved success with his series of boats called *Damn Carrera*. Carrera offers five deep vee recreational models from 27 to 32 feet in length, in sport and center-console configurations. The 27 and 30 are based on raceboat hulls. Outboard or sterndrive power is available. Carrera's handlaid fiberglass laminated hull carries a lifetime warranty that also is transferable for ten years after purchase.

CARY MARINE, INC.
1 Grand Isle Drive
Grand Haven, MI 49417

Randy F. Postma, president
(616) 846–1501

Cary was started in the early 1970s by Elton Cary and Don Aronow, who helped design the original tooling. Cary, which built Aronow's first Cigarette design, was sold to a French company from which Randy Postma purchased the Cary 50 tooling in 1979. Postma redesigned the 50 and added a 32-footer, a 45-footer, and in 1989, a

65-footer. The luxurious 50, with suede interior and two staterooms, is powered by four V8 engines delivering 2,000 hp.

CELEBRITY BOATS, INC.
P.O. Box 394
Benton, IL 62812

Fred Claxton, president
(618) 439–9444

Fred Claxton started Celebrity in 1977 with an 18-foot sport boat model. Today Celebrity is one of the largest independent boatbuilders with a line of 18- to 29-foot sterndrive sport boats and cruisers. Celebrity entered the high-performance field in 1988 with the Andretti 259, named for racing car driver Mario Andretti. Power options include single 365-hp or twin 320-hp sterndrives to give this stylish, modified deep-vee speeds in excess of 65 mph.

CENTURY BOATS
6725 Bayline Drive
Panama City, FL 32404

A. L. Kirkland, Jr., chairman, CEO
(904) 769–0311

Founded in 1926 and known for its ski boats, Century went through seven different owners before being purchased in 1987 by Glasstream, a major independent builder owned by A. L. Kirkland, Jr. Century builds thirty models of cruisers and sport boats ranging from 16 to 36 feet. The company moved into high performance in 1988 with its 27-foot Ultra II, and entered club racing with a production boat, winning its regional class. Maximum power is 2/454 MerCruiser Magnums.

CHAPARRAL BOATS, INC.
P.O. Drawer 928
Nashville, GA 31639

Jim Lane, president
(912) 686–7481

Chaparral began in the mid-1960s in Fort Lauderdale, Florida, under the name Fiberglass Fabricators, Inc. In 1976, the company changed its name and moved to Georgia. Now a subsidiary of RPC Energy Services, Inc., the firm is a major production builder, turning out twenty-six models. Its high-performance entry is the sleek Villain, built in three

models from 20 to 30 feet in length, all powered by MerCruiser sterndrives.

CHECKMATE BOATS, INC.
P.O. Box 723
Bucyrus, OH 44820

William "Kit" Combs, president
(419) 562–5027

Checkmate was started in 1963 by Bill Combs, Kit Combs's father, to build small outboard boats. In the 1980s, Checkmate moved into sterndrive boats, using MerCruiser and OMC engines, and the company now turns out twenty models, ranging from 17-foot outboards to 30-foot offshore high-performance boats. Kit and his brother Mike compete in the Great Lakes Offshore races. And in 1986 and 1987, a Checkmate 28 won the Stock B world title.

CIGARETTE RACING TEAM, INC.
3131 N.E. 188th St.
North Miami Beach, FL 33180

Robert Gowens, president
(305) 931–4564

After the success with his prototype Cary Cigarette, Don Aronow formed Cigarette Racing Team in 1969 to build raceboats. Cigarette also evolved into a production builder with ruggedly sleek hulls that almost made its name generic for offshore high performance. Cleveland entrepreneur Jeffrey I. Friedman purchased Cigarette in 1984, becoming its fourth owner. Today Cigarette builds eight models from 21 to 42 feet in length. In 1989, its 38-foot Top Gun was replaced as flagship with a highly styled 42-foot sport boat.

DONZI MARINE CORPORATION
P.O. 987
Tellevast, FL 34270

Dick Genth, chairman and CEO
(813) 355–9355

Don Aronow founded Donzi in 1963 to produce the Donzi Classics, based on the raceboat hulls. By the time Dick Genth bought Donzi in 1985, this former racer had already set industry records with Thunderbird, Wellcraft, and Chris-Craft. Donzi, sold to OMC in 1988, now makes fifteen high-performance models from 17 to 33 feet long, with a 36-foot performance cruiser on line for 1990. The 30-foot Black Widow, new in 1988, features 2/340-hp King Cobra engines with racing drives.

DOUGLAS MARINE CORPORATION
P.O. Box 522
Douglas, MI 49406
Peter Hledin, president
(316) 857-4308

High Roller and *Dirty Laundry*, 1988 national winners of the Pro-Stock and Modified classes, are evidences of Douglas Marine's dominance on the racecourse, with its 24-foot Skater. Founded in 1979 by former racer Peter Hledin, Douglas's niche is the ultra-high–performance outboard market. The tunnel-hulled 24-foot Skater approaches 100 mph with twin 2.4 EFI Mercury outboards. The 21-, 24-, and 32-footers are equipped as race or pleasure boats with inboard or outboard power.

ELIMINATOR BOATS
10795 San Sevaine
Mira Loma, CA 91752

Bob Leach, president
(714) 681–1222

Founded by Bob Leach in 1972, Eliminator's first successful model was its 19-foot Daytona tunnel hull. Today the firm builds thirty-two models, both deep-vee and tunnel hulls, from 19 to 27 feet in length. Eliminator, regarded as a leading builder of recreational tunnel hulls, is also known for splashy gel-coat graphics. Its newest model is the 234 Edge tunnel hull, which runs 72 to 74 mph, with a single 7.4-liter MerCruiser Bravo engine.

FOUNTAIN POWERBOATS
P.O. Box 457
Washington, N.C. 27889

Reggie Fountain, president
(919) 975-2000

After winning world and national titles in the APBA Outboard Performance Craft Class,

Reggie Fountain started building an offshore powerboat called the Executioner in 1979. Since then, his quality deep vee hulls, capable of 90-plus mph speeds, have shared a unique bottom configuration, having a near-flat pad or planing surface. Fountain today builds eight models, ranging from the 27-foot Fever to the 40-foot Lightning. All carry a limited three-year warranty.

FOUR WINNS
905 Frisbie St.
Cadillac, MI 49601

John A. Winn, president, OMC
Boat Group
(616) 775–1351

Bill Winn, Sr., bought a small boat company called Safe-T-Mate in 1975, which he renamed Four Winns, the other three Winns being his sons John, Bill, and Charlie. Today the firm builds five types of boats: sport, deck, cuddy, cruiser, and Liberator performance series, 21 to 26 feet long. A division of OMC, Four Winns' power is OMC sterndrive, with the maximum on the Liberator 26 being twin 340-hp engines. All equipment carries a three-year transferable warranty.

GLASTRON, INC.
3150 IH 35 West
New Braunfels, TX 78130

Ernie Schmidt, president
(512) 625–7761

Founded in 1957 by Bob Hammond and Bill Gaston to build runabouts, Glastron became a division of Genmar Industries in 1987. Art Carlson, whose innovative designs originally sparked Glastron, returned in 1987 to create the firm's first high-performance line—the stylistic Carlson Signature Series. The first model, a 19-footer, has been the firm's sales leader since being introduced in 1988. A 28-foot model, with a 24-degree deadrise for offshore running, was introduced in 1989, with a 33-foot model to follow.

HARDIN MARINE
1665 S. Claudina Way
Anaheim, CA 92806

Victor K. Hardin, president
(714) 535–3640

The firm was started in 1968 by Victor K. Hardin and Barry Lieberman to build marine engines. In 1983, Hardin acquired the Tahiti and Caribbean boat lines to produce runabouts and ski boats, as well as Warrior deep vee high-performance craft in 24- and 28-foot models powered by MerCruiser sterndrives. The Warrior 28 features a 24-degree deadrise with power options, including twin 454 Magnums. Construction is of handlaid fiberglass with a multicolored gelcoat finish.

HARLEY BOAT CORPORATION
300 S. First Ave.
Bartow, FL 33830

Howard D. Harley, president
(813) 533–2800

Howard Harley started the firm in the early 1970s to manufacture aircraft components. In 1980, the company began building boats. Today Harley turns out twelve high-performance models, ranging from 27 to 54 feet in length. Harley carries aircraft technology into the marine field, using vacuum-molded Kevlar, Airex, and epoxy construction. The 42-foot Superstar's power options include triple or quadruple outboards, and twin gasoline or diesel engines.

HUSTLER INDUSTRIES, INC.
124 Springville Rd.
Hampton Bays, NY 11946

Paul Fiore, president
(516) 728–8282

In 1979, Paul Fiore and two partners formed Hustler as a hobby to build boats for themselves. The hobby grew into a business. Fiore bought out his partners, and today Hustler builds five high-performance craft, 21 to 40 feet long. Introduced in 1988, the 40, which sleeps six, runs over 90 mph with gasoline engines, and at 70 mph with diesel. The 32 runs 100 mph with good tracking. All have a full range of power options, from multiple outboards to Hustlimer Eliminator custom engines.

IMP BOATS, INC.
500 Lincoln
Iola, KS 66749

Don Vincent, president
(316) 365–5131

IMP has been building 18- to 31-feet-long powerboats for more than thirty years. In 1985, the company was acquired by Russo Industries. IMP's high-performance Eleganza series includes the 310, 255, and 235. The raceboat *Cheap Thrills*, using the 310 hull, has met success in Great Lakes Offshore competition. The Eleganza craft are constructed of handlaid fiberglass with a balsa core.

JAGUAR MARINE, INC.
1798 S.W. 31st Ave.
Pembroke Pines, FL 33009

Jack Clark, president
(305) 961–7693

Jack Clark started racing in 1984 with a 30-foot Chris-Craft catamaran and captured a string of victories that led to his being named rookie of the year. In 1985 he built his first boat, a 35-foot wooden tunnel hull, which sank in competition. After spending a year researching construction methods, he developed a vacuum-bagging method and started producing raceboats, turning out six to ten a year. One of Jaguar's 35-footers, John D'Elia's *Special Edition*, won the U.S. Open Class title in 1988. A 46-foot Superboat Class version was expected to make its debut in 1989.

JET SET MARINE
Route 73
Palmyra, NJ 08065

Dennis Fridmann, president
(609) 829–7956

Jet Set's custom line of deep vee offshore hulls called the Avanti was created by Dennis Fridmann, who started the firm in 1978. The Avantis consist of five models, ranging from 22 to 41 feet in length. The Avantis are constructed of handlaid fiberglass, with Kevlar and AME 4000 resin construction also available. All models are capable of speeds of 70 plus mph, and the 41 will cruise at 75 mph with a pair of 575-hp MerCruiser sterndrives.

MAELSTROM MARINE, INC.
5916 Sandsphil Rd.
Sarasota, FL 33582

Bernard Rice, president
(813) 371–0694

Bernard Rice founded Maelstrom in 1985 to build a 32-foot tunnel-hulled raceboat. His success is evidenced by *Main Attraction*, which won the Stock Class in the 1988 Key West worlds. In addition to the 100-plus mph tunnel hull, offered in race and pleasure boat versions, Maelstrom introduced a 23-foot sport boat, the first in a line of deep vee hulls in 1989. The tunnel hulls are made of bi- and tri-directional glass, vacuum-bagged over a foam core.

MAGNUM MARINE
CORPORATION
2900 N.E. 188th St.
North Miami Beach, FL 33180

Filippo M. Theodoli, president
(305) 931–4292

Don Aronow developed the Magnum line in 1963, starting with the 27 and 35, which went on to win Offshore titles. The Magnum 27, the father of the Cigarette, was the boat that started the modern era of offshore high performance. Filippo Theodoli and his wife, Katrin, purchased Magnum from Aronow in 1976. Today Magnum is one of the world's foremost luxury high-performance builders, with models ranging from a 27-footer to a 70-foot flybridge motoryacht, all capable of speeds in excess of 60 mph.

MANTA RACING, INC.
2405 S.W. 57th Ave.
Hollywood, FL 33023

Thomas L. Greco, Jr., president
(305) 963–5887

A former Offshore racer, Tom Greco started Manta in 1974. The firm now builds deep vee offshore hulls in 23-, 28-, and 32-foot models equipped as race or pleasure boats. The pleasure boat versions are available as center-console or sport boats, and take either outboard or sterndrive power. Mantas are proven on the racecourse. The 32-SM Manta won the world title in the Production Class in 1981 and 1982 as well as the Sportsman B Class in 1988.

MIDNIGHT EXPRESS, INC.
12900 N.W. 30th Ave.
Opa Locka, FL 33054

Byng Goode, president
(305) 688–6872

Byng Goode, former president of Cigarette Racing Team, started Midnight Express in 1979 to produce custom deep vee offshore powerboats. The line now consists of three models of deep-vees, a 32-footer, a 37-footer, and a 47-footer, available in both sport and open-console versions. The firm also produces a 37-foot catamaran. OMC and Mercury power options on the 37 deep-vee range from two to five outboards to 2/850-hp Cobra inboard engines with Stellings headers.

MIRAGE MARINE CORPORATION
P.O. Box 1001
Arlington, WA 98223

Rod Hubbart, president
(206) 435–5762

Mirage has become one of the fastest-growing boat companies in the West since it was formed in 1984. The firm now produces seventeen models from 17 to 27 feet in length in outboard and sterndrive versions, and with a full power train complement from MerCruiser. The high-performance 27-foot Intimidator features a 24-degree deadrise, and is rated for a maximum of 730 hp. Mirage also offers a lifetime hull warranty as standard with every sterndrive boat.

POWERPLAY
2709 N.W. 29th Terrace
Fort Lauderdale, FL 33311

Dan Weinstein, president
(305) 733–2500

Formed in 1980, Powerplay began as Powerplay Racing Team, which won the Class 2 national championship in 1982, and then developed into a production team. Powerplay produces two custom models, 25- and 33-footers, designed by racer Pete Huebner. With offshore deep vee hulls, the two models are available in sport and center-console configurations with one, two, and three outboard-engine combinations. They are constructed of high-pressure laminates; raceboat fabrication is used throughout.

PROGRESSION INDUSTRIES, INC.
515 Victoria Ave.
Copiague, NY 11726

Kevin Loughran, president
(516) 226–1431

Progression began with its first blueprints in 1983. The firm now produces its 24-foot Instigator and 29-foot Intense offshore performance boats in sterndrive and outboard configurations. Maximum power in the 24 is 500 hp, and in the 29, it is 600 hp. Progression boats are constructed of bi- and tri-directional glass, using AME 4000 resin and a balsa core. Kiekhaefer controls and VDO instruments are standard. The hulls carry a ten-year limited warranty.

REGAL MARINE INDUSTRIES, INC.
2300 Jetport Drive
Orlando, FL 32609

Paul Kuck, president
(305) 851–4360

Since Paul Kuck founded Regal in 1969, the firm has developed a full line of powerboats, including sport boats, cruisers, and Velocity high-performance craft. Steve Stepp, who drove his Velocity raceboats to a string of national titles and world records, began building them in 1978. Regal acquired the company in 1985, and now produces Velocity 22-, 23- and 30-foot models. All feature the HydroStepp hull, which incorporates a flat, narrow pad and a bilevel step transom, a race-tested configuration.

SEAHAWK MARINE, INC.
618 Broadway
Bedford, OH 44146

Max Condelli, president
(216) 232–0017

Seahawk raceboats captured two world and two national Offshore Modified Class titles in a four-year span. The original builder, Miami Offshore Powerboat, teamed up with Cleveland businessman Max Condelli to form Seahawk Marine, which began distributing six deep vee models, ranging from 22 to 38 feet, in the fall of 1988. Cofab, a matrix design using Kevlar and graphite fibers, is used in constructing the hulls, which carry a five-year transferable warranty.

SEA RAY BOATS, INC.
2600 Sea Ray Blvd.
Knoxville, TN 37914

John Hedberg, president
(615) 522–4181

C. N. Ray started Sea Ray in Detroit in 1959. In 1984, Ray sold 85 percent of the firm to his employees, and two years later he and the employees sold Sea Ray to Brunswick. Sea Ray is the second largest boatbuilder in the world, producing forty-five models, 16 to 50 feet in length. Sea Ray builds five high-performance Pachangas, 19 to 32 feet long. All have full MerCruiser power train options. On the 27, the 7.4-liter Bravo engine is standard with 2/454 Magnums the maximum.

STARFIRE BOATS
5955 W. Wells Park Rd.
West Jordan, UT 84084

Gil Freedman, president
(801) 569–1400

Founded in 1969 by Gil Freedman, Starfire is an independent builder turning out quality runabouts and family cruisers. In 1988, Starfire moved into high performance with the first in its Starchaser line, a 23-foot deep-vee that rises up on plane in 2.4 seconds with a stock 260-hp sterndrive. A cuddy version was added in 1989. Maximum power is one 7.4-liter, 365-hp MerCruiser Bravo One. Construction is handlaid fiberglass over Coremat with mahogany stringers.

SUPERBOATS, INC.
275 Dixon Ave.
Amityville, NY 11701

John Coen, president
(516) 842–1560

Superboats produces race and pleasure boats, ranging from 21 to 32 feet in length, with inboard and outboard models. All are deep vee hulls, except the 32 Supercat. Construction is handlaid fiberglass over a balsa core with AME 4000 resin. John Coen founded Superboats in 1973, starting with a 16-foot outboard. A Modified Class 32-foot Supercat raceboat will run 120 mph with twin small-block Chevrolet engines and NASCAR-style Buick heads.

SUTPHEN MARINE CORPORATION
923 E. 13th Ave.
Cape Coral, FL 33904

Richie Sutphen, president
(813) 574–1155

Ritchie Sutphen has been involved with racing boats—outboards, flat bottoms, inboards, even iceboats–for thirty-five years. He began building powerboats in 1968, and later spent four years racing on the Offshore circuit. In 1988, Sutphen fielded his first team in Unlimited competition. His offshore high-performance line, frequently found in club races, includes eight models, from 26 to 38 feet long and powered by outboard or sterndrive engines.

TEAM WARLOCK, INC.
4581 Eisenhower Circle
Anaheim, CA 92807

Tom Stolarz, president
(714) 777–3132

Tom Stolarz started closed circle racing in the early 1970s, building his own boats as well. A marine engineer, he then started designing offshore powerboats, leading to the creation of Team Warlock in 1985. Warlock's line ranges from a 23-foot deep vee hull to a unique 31-foot "catamaran." The 31 "catamaran" features a center pod flanked by two sponsons, similar to a trimaran, affording efficient performance throughout the speed range.

TEMPEST MARINE
3205 N.E. 188th St.
North Miami Beach, FL 33180

Adam Erdberg, president
(305) 937–4400

Tempest was formed in 1983 by Dick Simon, a South Florida entrepreneur, and Adam Erdberg, a naval architect, to build a rugged offshore boat. The result was the Tempest 44, a smooth-riding deep

vee hull, powered by twin 3208 Caterpillar diesels for performance and reliability. Today Tempest builds 32- and 38-foot models with sterndrive or outboard engines. Other performance diesel models include the 42 and 60, with 74- and 85-foot motor yachts introduced in 1988.

THUNDERBIRD PRODUCTS
P.O. Box, 501
Decatur, IN 46733

Scott Porter, president
(219) 724–9111

Thunderbird, a privately owned firm, manufactures the Formula high-performance powerboats. Formula was the first boat company created in the early 1960s by Don Aronow, who had immediate success with the Formula 233. Aronow sold Formula to Thunderbird, which has continued to build deep vee hulls of quality and performance. The line now includes performance and cruiser models from 20 to 35 feet long. The performance boats are powered by MerCruiser or Volvo sterndrives.

WEBB BOATS, INC.
P.O. Box 10
Collinsville, OK 74021

Brad Webb, president
(918) 371–2571

Webb is a family-owned firm started in 1971 by William Webb, whose three sons are involved in producing thirty-one models of Webbcraft. They include cuddy cabins, bow riders, and offshore powerboats, ranging from 19 to 35 feet long. In 1982, Webb was the first builder to offer a five-year hull warranty for an offshore boat. Its offshore deep vee line includes nine versions to 35 feet in length, all powered by MerCruiser or Volvo sterndrives. Maximum power option: twin 575-hp MerCruisers.

WELLCRAFT MARINE
1651 Whitfield Ave.
Sarasota, FL 34243

Robert Long, president
(813) 751–7884

Started as a regional boatbuilder in 1955, Wellcraft now is the largest division of Genmar Industries, Inc., and one of the world's largest boat manufacturers, producing more than fifty models of sport, fishing, and performance boats as well as cruisers. With its Nova and Scarab lines, Wellcraft is the leading supplier of performance boats. The Scarabs, ranging from 21 to 48 feet in length and designed by Larry

Smith, have a record of success in Offshore competition, capped by Don Johnson's 1988 Key West World Superboat victory.

XLEM TECHNOLOGIES
1149 Hastings Ave.
Traverse City, MI 49784

Steve Baum, president
(616) 020–0598

Formed in 1987 by Steve Baum, former World Champion Offshore racer, Xlem produces two high-tech versions of old-style "gentlemen's runabouts"—the 32-foot Classique and 38-foot Grand Classique. Crafted of a patented wood composite with a balsa core to resemble the mahogany speedboats of the 1930s, the Classiques reach speeds of 65 mph. Features include a five-year warranty covering the hull, which is vacuum-built without screws or staples, and the MerCruiser sterndrives.

APPENDIX

Glossary

Abeam: At right angles to the boat's centerline, usually outside the vessel

Aft: Toward the back of the boat

Ahead: Anything in front of you

Astern: Anything behind you

Athwartships: Running across the boat at right angles to the keel

Attitude: The orientation of the boat's centerline relative to the surface of the water. (*See also* TRIM.)

Beam: A distance across the boat from side to side

Beam, Maximum: The boat at its widest point

Below: Below the deck; the cabin area

Bilge: Lowest interior areas of the hull

Blown Hydro: A hydroplane with a supercharged engine

Blowover: To flip over

Blueprint: (1) A drawing showing details of the boat, engine, or any mechanical item. (2) To verify the specifications of an engine, propeller, or hull; to bring a piece of equipment to the highest specifications of tolerance; to fine-tune

Box-Stock Engine: An engine right out of the box, as delivered by the manufacturer; unmodified

Bow: Front end of the boat

Bow Steering: Excessive bow down-trim that causes the boat to steer by the entry portion of the keel, making control difficult. This usually can be corrected by adding rocker or moving weight aft.

Bulkheads: Vertical supports or partitions separating the boat's cabins

Catamaran: Twin-hulled craft

Cathedral Hull: An inverted W-type hull, similar to a tri-hull configuration (such as the Sea Sled, Boston Whaler), originated by Dick Cole. Opposite of a DIHEDRAL hull

Cavitation: The sudden formation and collapse of low-pressure bubbles in water caused by a rotating propeller, resulting in loss of thrust and propeller wear

Cavitation Plate: A horizontal plate directly over the propeller; found in outboards and sterndrives to help prevent ventilation

Cetane Number: A measure that expresses the combustion ability of a diesel fuel

Chart: A nautical map

Chine: The sharp angle at the intersection of the boat's topsides and its bottom

Chine Walking: A condition in which the boat oscillates from side to side at high speed

Choke: A valve on a carburetor that enriches the fuel mixture to aid in starting a gasoline engine

Cleat: A fitting to which a line under strain is secured

Compression Ratio: A measure of how much the fuel charge in an engine cylinder is compressed before it is ignited

Corrosion: The chemical deterioration of a metal. (*See* GALVANIZE and ELECTROLYTIC CORROSION.)

Current: River or tidal flow of water

Dead Reckoning: Calculating a boat's position based on the course, speed, and time the boat has been under way

Deadrise: The angle formed at the centerline between the bottom panel of the boat and a horizontal plane, usually measured at the transom

Deck: Floor; on a raceboat, the forward top of the boat

Deep-Vee: A hull with a deadrise angle of 16 degrees or greater

Delta-Conic: Hull shape created by Harry L. Schoell, which features planing area in shape of a delta with a conical forward section and broad chines above the waterline

Dial In: To adjust the drive height, gear ratio, and propeller size to optimum performance

Diesel: An internal-combustion process that ignites fuel by the heat of compression rather than by a spark

Dihedral: The upward or downward inclination of an aircraft wing from true horizontal; in geometry, the angle formed by two intersecting planes; an early term for a deep vee hull

Displacement: (1) The weight of the water displaced by a floating hull. (2) The total cubic content of the volume traversed by the pistons of an engine in one revolution

Displacement Hull: A boat supported by its own buoyancy while it is under way

Draft: Maximum depth of the hull

Drift: Deviation of a boat from a planned course due to the action of the wind or current

Glossary

Dry Stack Storage: A slip ashore in a storage building

Dynamometer: A machine used to measure the amount of torque at a specific rpm in engine horsepower output

Ebb: Outgoing tide

Electrolytic Corrosion: A condition in which two different metals, electrically connected, deteriorate because of the flow of electric current; can be avoided by fitting a sacrificial anode, i.e. zinc

Fathom: Six feet, a measure of depth

Fatigue: The failure of a metal, or of people, after being subjected to repeated stresses

Feather: To adjust the throttles to maintain proper rpm when the propellers go in and out of the water as a boat jumps from wave to wave

Flood: Incoming tide

Forward: Facing the bow

Freeboard: Height of topsides from the sheerline to the waterline

Fuel Cell: A flexible, foam-filled fuel tank

Galvanize: To coat steel with zinc to prevent corrosion

Gasket: A soft material between two mating (joined) surfaces, used to prevent leaking

Ground Tackle: All the gear used for anchoring

Gunwale: The upper edge of the side of a boat

Hatch: Deck opening

Header: A tubular manifold in which the length of the exhaust pipes is equalized or tuned for efficiency

Heaving-To: In a storm, a powerboat heads into the seas, or nearly so, and reduces speed to the minimum necessary to retain control

Hook: (1) To have a sponson snag a wave rather than ride over it. (2) A concave curvature of the aft section of a boat's underbody, causing it to ride in a bow-down position, which provides less lift but better tracking, the opposite of rocker

Hull: The main body of the boat excluding cabins, masts, and all internal fittings such as engines

Hump: The semiplaning speed in which the bow is trimmed up and the boat is dragging a large wake. (*See* PLANE.)

Hydrofoils: Structures called foils, usually fitted below the hull and designed to give lift, which permit the boat to "fly" just above the water surface with little drag and at increased speeds, much like the wings of an airplane

Hydroplane: A powerboat designed for racing, with lift provided by sponsons, special planing surfaces at each side of the hull

Inboard: (1) An automotive engine mounted inside the hull. (2) In from the rail of the boat

Jet Drive: A method of propulsion in which a boat is driven forward by the reaction of a high-velocity jet of water expelled aft

Keel: Major central structural member of the hull, usually the center and lowest part of the hull running fore and aft

Knot: The speed of one nautical mile in one hour, equivalent to 1.15 statute miles per hour

Leeward: The side of a boat away from the wind

Line: On a boat, a rope is always a line

Locker: A closet. Hanging locker is a clothes closet.

Magneto: A self-contained generator usually found on outboard motors to supply voltage for ignition

Marlinespike: A pointed tool for splicing line

Marlinespike Seamanship: Knowledge of tying knots. Basic knots to know: bowline, square knot, cleat hitch, eyesplice, clove hitch, backsplice, needle whipping

Modified Deep-Vee: A hull with less deadrise, 16 to 18 degrees, than an offshore or racing hull, which may have 20 to 24 degrees. A modified deep-vee will have greater lateral stability.

Multihull: A boat having more than one hull, such as a catamaran, which has two hulls, or a trimaran, which has three hulls

Nautical Mile: A measure of distance used on salt-water charts (statute miles are used on Great Lakes charts), equal to 6,076 feet or 1.15 statute miles

Octane Number: A measure of the combustion characteristic of gasoline

Offshore Powerboat: Generally a boat having a deep vee or tunnel hull 30 feet or longer that is used for high-speed travel offshore

Optimize: To set up and fine-tune the best combination of engines, drives, and propellers

Outboard: (1) An engine mounted on the transom. (2) Beyond the rail of a boat

Overhead: Ceiling in a boat

Pickle Fork: A tunnel hull in which the sponsons extend beyond the most forward point of the hull, resembling a pickle fork

Piston: A solid cylinder or disk that fits into a larger cylinder and moves back and forth under pressure

Pitch: (1) The theoretical distance a propeller should move forward in one revolution, expressed in inches. (2) The rising and falling of a bow in a sea

Plane: To rise partly out of the water, as a planing hull does at high speeds. A boat rises on plane when its displacement is supported by hydrodynamic lift. To reach plane, a boat starts in a displacement mode and, with acceleration, passes through semi-planing or hump speed, in which the boat is trimmed up in the bow and dragging a large wake. Once through the hump, the boat levels off on plane.

Planing Hull: A hull designed so that forward speed creates lift, reducing wetted surface and increasing speed

Porpoise: The rhythmic rise and fall that a boat may exhibit when the center of gravity is forward of the center of buoyancy. The solution has generally been to move the principal weight, the engines, as far to the stern as possible, moving the boat's center of gravity aft and over the planing surface or over the center of hydrodynamic lift.

Port: Left side of boat when facing forward

Propeller: A device used to transform rotative power into thrust

Rocker: A convex curvature of the aftmost section of a boat's underbody. As a boat rises up on plane, the rocker causes it to tilt back slightly onto the trailing edge, increasing lift and reducing wetted surface. The opposite of hook

Rode: The anchor line

Rollover: To roll 360 degrees

Set: The direction in which the current flows

Sheer: The intersection between hull and deck when looking at the boat's side

Slack: Period between flood and ebb when current is not flowing

Sponson: One of two hulls in a twin-hulled craft; one of two hull extensions forward of the hull in an Unlimited raceboat. (*See* PICKLE FORK.)

Spring Line: A line leading from the boat's stern to forward on the dock, or from the boat's bow to aft on dock to prevent boat from moving ahead or astern

Stabilizer Wing: A horizontal raised section over the stern that gives a high-speed boat, such as an Unlimited, additional control

Stacking: A condition created by an opposing wind and current in which the waves are held up by the wind, making them larger; also known as "wind over tide." This can lead to stuffing the bow when you are running with the wind and increases the odds for a blowover when you are running against the wind.

Starboard: Right side of boat, facing forward

Statute Mile: A distance equal to 5,280 feet. (*See* NAUTICAL MILE.)

Step: A transverse break in the planing surface, intended to reduce skin friction; a step ends a planing surface

Stepped Hull: A hull with two or more support areas with a step between them that permit moving weight forward without running the risk of porpoising

Stern: Back end of a boat

Sterndrive: Propulsion system with inboard engine attached to outboard drive and propeller; steering is done by turning outboard unit. Also called an outdrive or inboard/outboard (I/O)

Strake: A longitudinal strip, usually triangular, on the planing surface, running more or less parallel to the keel and used to help increase lift and to provide tracking ability

Stringer: A longitudinal hull support

Stuff: Nosedive into a wave

Stuffing Box: An enclosure of the propeller shaft to prevent leakage where the shaft passes through the hull

Supercharge: To force air or a mixture of air and fuel into a combustion chamber of an engine under pressure

Supercharger: A blower or compressor driven by the engine for supplying air under high pressure to the engine's cylinders

Surface Drive: A drive in which the propeller runs on the surface of the water, half immersed

Synchronize: To cause two engines to run at the same rpm

Tachometer: An instrument used to measure the rotational speed of a shaft or an engine

Tide: Rise or fall of water

Timing: Adjusting the precise moment when ignition or fuel injection occurs in an engine

Topsides: Side of a boat between the waterline and the deck. (*See* FREE-BOARD.)

Torque: A twisting force

Track: The ability of a high-speed boat to maintain a straight course without using the steering wheel. Tracking is a factor of the strakes.

Transom: Flat area across a stern

Transom Lift: A phenomenon in which the force of the blades of a surface propeller slapping the water lifts the transom of the boat

Tri-Hull: General term for boats having a rounded bow and hull shape in the form of an inverted W. This design provides good lateral stability and a comfortable ride in choppy water. (*See* CATHEDRAL HULL.)

Trim: Longitudinal attitude of the boat; adjustable by shifting ballast fore and aft. When driving a boat it will usually trim up by the bow as speed increases and then level off once the boat gets on plane.

Trim Tabs: Metal plates that extend from the transom, horizontal to the water, which are adjusted to control the boat's trim

Tunnel Hull: A catamaran hull in which the tunnel between the two sponfrmtsons is used to generate lift

Turbine: A mechanical device that generates power by simple rotation

Turbocharge: To force air or a mixture of air and fuel into the combustion chamber of an engine by means of the energy in the exhaust

Unblown Hydro: A hydroplane without a supercharged engine

Unlimited Hydroplane: The fastest class of raceboats, has a minimum length of 28 feet and unlimited power

Vapor Lock: Fuel flow stoppage caused by air bubbles in the fuel line

Veer: A clockwise shift in wind direction. Counterclockwise is called "backing".

Ventilated Step: A step exposed to air on its vertical face to disrupt suction and thus increase speed

Ventilation: A condition in which surface air or exhaust gases are drawn downward from the water surface into the propeller causing it to overrev and lose its bite

Windward: Toward the wind

Yaw: (1) A condition in which the stern is moved to either side by following sea. (2) To steer an erratic course

American Power Boat Association Records Unlimited Racing Commission Past National Champion Drivers

Year	Driver	Boat Driven	Races Won
1988	Tom D'Eath	Miss Budweiser	4
1987	Jim Kropfeld	Miss Budweiser	5
1986	Jim Kropfeld	Miss Budweiser	3
1985	Chip Hanauer	Miller American	5
1984	Jim Kropfeld	Miss Budweiser	6
1983	Chip Hanauer	Atlas Van Lines	3
1982	Chip Hanauer	Atlas Van Lines	5
1981	Dean Chenoweth	Miss Budweiser	6
1980	Dean Chenoweth	Miss Budweiser	5
1979	Bill Muncey	Atlas Van Lines	7
1978	Bill Muncey	Atlas Van Lines	6
1977	Mickey Remund	Miss Budweiser	3
1976	Bill Muncey	Atlas Van Lines	5
1975	Billy Schumacher	Ms. Everett Weisfield's	2
1974	George Henley	Pay 'n Pak	7
1973	Mickey Remund	Pay 'n Pak	4
1972	Bill Muncey	Atlas Van Lines	6
1971	Dean Chenoweth	Miss Budweiser	2
1970	Dean Chenoweth	Miss Budweiser	4
1969	Bill Sterett, Sr.	Miss Budweiser	4
1968	Billy Schumacher	Miss Bardahl	4
1967	Billy Schumacher	Miss Bardahl	6
1966	Mira Slovak	Tahoe Miss	4
1965	Ron Musson	Miss Bardahl	4

Year	Driver	Boat Driven	Races Won
1964	Ron Musson	*Miss Bardahl*	4
1963	Bill Cantrell	*Gale V*	0
1962	Bill Muncey	*Miss Century 21*	5
1961	Bill Muncey	*Miss Century 21*	4
1960	Bill Muncey	*Miss Thriftway*	4
1959	Bill Stead	*Maverick*	5
1958	Mira Slovak	*Miss Bardahl* *Miss Burien*	3
1957	Jack Regas	*Hawaii Kai III*	5
1956	Russ Schleeh	*Shanty I*	3
1955	Lee Schoenith	*Gale V* *Wha Hoppen Too*	1
1954	Lee Schoenith	*Gale V*	4
1953	Lee Schoenith	*Gale II*	1
1952	Chuck Thompson	*Miss Pepsi*	3
1951	Chuck Thompson	*Miss Pepsi*	5
1950	Danny Foster	*Such Crust* *Delphine X*	2
1949	Bill Cantrell	*My Sweetie*	7
1948	Dan Arena	*Such Crust*	2
1947	Danny Foster	*Miss Pepsi V*	6
1946	Guy Lombardo	*Tempo VI*	2

APBA Gold Cup

Boat Name, Owner, Driver, Overall Race Average mph, Race Location

1988 *Miss Circus Circus*, Fran Muncey, Jim Prevost (heats 1, 2) and Chip Hanauer (heats 3, 4), 123.756, Evansville, IN

1987 *Miller American*, Fran Muncey, Chip Hanauer, 127.620, San Diego, CA

1986 *Miller American*, Fran Muncey, Chip Hanauer, 116.523, Detroit, MI

1985 *Miller American*, Fran Muncey and Jim Lucero, Chip Hanauer, 120.643, Seattle, WA

1984 *Atlas Van Lines*, Fran Muncey and Jim Lucero, Chip Hanauer, 130.175, Tri-Cities, WA

1983 *Atlas Van Lines*, Fran Muncey and Jim Lucero, Chip Hanauer, 118.507, Evansville, IN

1982 *Atlas Van Lines*, Fran Muncey, Chip Hanauer, 120.050, Detroit, MI

1981 *Miss Budweiser*, Bernie Little, Dean Chenoweth, 116.932, Seattle, WA

1980 *Miss Budweiser*, Bernie Little, Dean Chenoweth, 106.932, Madison, IN

1979 *Atlas Van Lines*, Bill Muncey, Bill Muncey, 100.765, Madison, IN

1978 *Atlas Van Lines*, Bill Muncey, Bill Muncey, 111.412, Owensboro, KY

1977 *Atlas Van Lines*, Bill Muncey, Bill Muncey, 111.822, Tri-Cities, WA

1976 *Miss U.S.*, George Simon, Tom D'Eath, 100.412, Detroit, MI

1975 *Pay 'n Pak*, Dave Heerensperger, George Henley, 108.921, Tri-Cities, WA

1974 *Pay 'n Pak*, Dave Heerensperger, George Henley, 104.428, Seattle, WA

1973 *Miss Budweiser*, Bernie Little and Tom Friedkin, Dean Chenoweth, 99.043, Tri-Cities, WA

1972 *Atlas Van Lines*, Joe Schoenith, Bill Muncey, 104.277, Detroit, MI

1971 *Miss Madison, City of Madison, Ind.*, Jim McCormick, 98.043, Madison, IN

1970 *Miss Budweiser*, Bernie Little and Tom Friedkin, Dean Chenoweth, 99.562, San Diego, CA

1969 *Miss Budweiser*, Bernie Little and Tom Friedkin, Bill Sterett, Sr., 98.504, San Diego, CA

1968 *Miss Bardahl*, Ole Bardahl, Bill Schumacher, 108.173, Detroit, MI

1967 *Miss Bardahl*, Ole Bardahl, Bill Schumacher, 101.484, Seattle, WA

1966 *Tahoe Miss*, Bill Harrah, Mira Slovak, 93.019, Detroit, MI

1965 *Miss Bardahl*, Ole Bardahl, Ron Musson, 103.132, Seattle, WA

1964 *Miss Bardahl*, Ole Bardahl, Ron Musson, 103.433, Detroit, MI

1963 *Miss Bardahl*, Ole Bardahl, Ron Musson, 105.124, Detroit, MI

1962 *Miss Century 21*, Willard Rhodes, Bill Muncey, 100.71, Seattle, WA

1961 *Miss Century 21*, Willard Rhodes, Bill Muncey, 99.678, Reno, NV

1960 No contest

1959 *Maverick*, Bill Waggoner, Bill Stead, 104.481, Seattle, WA

1957 *Miss Thriftaway*, Willard Rhodes, Bill Muncey, 101.787, Seattle, WA

1956 *Miss Thriftaway*, Willard Rhodes, Bill Muncey, 96.552, Detroit, MI

1955 *Gale V*, Joe Schoenith, Lee Schoenith, 99.552, Seattle, WA

1954 *Slo-Mo-Shun IV*, Stan Sayres, Joe Taggart, and Lou Fageol, 92.613, Seattle, WA

1953 *Slo-Mo-Shun IV*, Stan Sayres, Joe Taggart, and Lou Fageol, 99.108, Seattle, WA

1952 *Slo-Mo-Shun IV*, Stan Sayres, Stan Dollar, 79.923, Seattle, WA

1951 *Slo-Mo-Shun V*, Stan Sayres, Lou Fageol, 90.871, Seattle, WA

1950 *Slo-Mo-Shun IV*, Stan Sayres, Ted Jones, 78.216, Detroit, MI

1949 *My Sweetie*, Ed Gregory and Ed Schoenherr, Bill Contrell, 73.612, Detroit, MI

1948 *Miss Great Lakes*, Albin Fallon, Danny Foster, 46.845, Detroit, MI

1947 *Miss Pepsi V*, Roy and Walter Dossin, Danny Foster, Jamaica Bay, NY

1946 *Tempo VI*, Guy Lombardo, driver and owner, 68.132, Detroit, MI

1942–1945   No contests

1941   *My Sin*, Zalmon G. Simmons, Jr., driver and owner, 52.509, Red Bank, NJ

1940   *Hotsy Totsy III*, Sidney Allen, driver and owner, 48.295, Northport, NY

1939   *My Sin*, Zalmon G. Simmons, Jr., driver and owner, 66.133, Detroit, MI

1938   *Alagi*, Count Theo Rossi, driver and owner, 64.340, Detroit, MI

1937   *Notre Dame*, Herb Mendelson, Clell Perry, 63.675, Detroit, MI

1936   *Impshi*, Horace E. Dodge, Jr., Kaye Don, 45.735, Lake George, NY

1935   *El Lagarto*, George Reis, driver and owner, 55.056, Lake George, NY

1934   *El Lagarto*, George Reis, driver and owner, 55.000, Lake George, NY

1933   *El Lagarto*, George Reis, driver and owner, 56.260, Lake George, NY

1932   *Delphine IV*, Horace E. Dodge, Jr., Bill Horn, 57.775, Montauk, NY

1931   *Hotsy Totsy*, Vic Kliesrath and R. F. Hoyt, Vic Kliesrath, 53.602, Montauk, NY

1930   *Hotsy Totsy*, Vic Kliesrath, driver and owner, 52.673, Red Bank, NJ

1929   *Imp*, Richard F. Hoyt, driver and owner, 48.662, Red Bank, NJ

1928   No contest

1927   *Greenwich Folly*, George Townsend, driver and owner, 47.662, Greenwich, CT

1926   *Greenwich Folly*, George Townsend, driver and owner, 47.984, Greenwich, CT

1925   *Baby Bootlegger*, Caleb Bragg, driver and owner, 47.240, Port Washington, NY

1924   *Baby Bootlegger*, Caleb Bragg, driver and owner, 45.302, Detroit, MI

1923   *Packard Chriscraft*, J. G. Vincent, Caleb Bragg, 43.867, Detroit, MI

1922   *Packard Chriscraft*, J.G. Vincent, driver and owner, 40.253, Detroit, MI

1921   *Miss America I*, Gar Wood, driver and owner, 52.825, Detroit, MI

1920   *Miss America I*, Gar Wood, driver and owner, 62.022, Detroit, MI

1919   *Miss Detroit III*, Gar Wood, driver and owner, 42.748, Detroit, MI

1918   *Miss Detroit II*, Detroit yachtsmen, Gar Wood, 51.619, Detroit, MI

1917   *Miss Detroit II*, Gar Wood, driver and owner, 54.410, Mississippi River, MN

1916   *Miss Minneapolis*, Miss Minneapolis P.B.A., Bernard Smith, 48.860, Detroit, MI

1915   *Miss Detroit*, Miss Detroit P.B.A., Jack Beebe (heat 1) and Johnny Milot (heats 2, 3), 37.656, Port Washington, NY

1914   *Baby Speed Demon II*, Mrs. J. Stuard Blackton, Sr., Bob Edgren (heats 1, 3), and Jim Blackton, Jr. (heat 2), 48.458, Lake George, NY

1913   *Ankle Deep*, Casimir S. Mankowski, driver and owner, 42.779, Alexandria Bay, NY

1912   *P.D.Q. II*, A. G. Miles, driver and owner, 39.462, Alexandria Bay, NY

1911   *MIT II*, J. H. Hayden, driver and owner, 37.000, Alexandria Bay, NY

1910   *Dixie III*, F. K. Burnham, driver and owner, 32.473, Alexandria Bay, NY

1909   *Dixie II*, E. J. Schroeder, driver and owner, 29.590, Alexandria Bay, NY

1908   *Dixie II*, E. J. Schroeder, driver and owner, 29.938, Chippewa Bay, NY

1907   *Chip II*, Jonathan Wainwright, driver and owner, 23.903, Chippewa Bay, NY

1906   *Chip II*, Jonathan Wainwright, driver and owner, 25.000, Chippewa Bay, NY

1905   *Chip I*, Jonathan Wainwright, driver and owner, 15.000, Chippewa Bay, NY

1904   (Sept.) *Vingt-Et-Un II*, Willis Sharpe Kilmer, 24.900, Hudson River, NY

1904   (June) *Standard*, Carl and Eugene Riotte, Carl C. Riotte, 23.160, Hudson River, NY

Unlimited Hydroplane Hall of Fame

The Unlimited Hydroplane Hall of Fame and Museum, Inc., is a nonprofit organization, located in Seattle and affiliated with the Unlimited Racing Commission, that is dedicated to preserving the sport's history.

1950	Stay Sayres	1963	Bill Harrah
1951	Jerry Bryant	1963	Harry Leduc
1952	Bill Cantrell	1964	Ron Musson
1953	Joe Taggart	1980	Dean Chenoweth
1954	Lou Fageol	1980	Dave Heerensperger
1955	Les Staudacher	1980	Bernie Little
1956	Ted Jones	1980	Jim Lucero
1957	Bill Muncey	1980	Lee Schoenith
1958	Mike Welsch	1980	Bill Schumacher
1959	Stan Donogh	1983	Fred Alter
1960	Willard Rhodes	1983	O. H. Frisbie
1961	Jack Regas	1983	Chuck Hickling
1961	Jim Spinner	1983	Shirley Mendelson McDonald
1962	Mira Slovak		
1963	Ole Bardahl	1983	Leo Vandenberg

Unlimited Hydroplane World Records

Race Records

60-MILE RACE, 2½-MILE COURSE: 120.643 miles per hour; boat, *Miller American*; year, 1985; driver, Chip Hanauer; at Seattle, WA

48-MILE RACE, 2½-MILE COURSE: 116.644; *Mr. Pringle's*; 1988; Scott Pierce, Evansville, IN

37½-MILE RACE, 2½-MILE COURSE: 134.631; *Miss Budweiser*; 1988; Tom D'Eath, Tri-Cities, WA

35-MILE RACE, 2½-MILE COURSE: 122.785; *Mr. Pringle's*; 1988; Scott Pierce, Madison, IN

30-MILE RACE, 2-MILE COURSE: 128.792; *Miller American*; 1986; Chip Hanauer, Syracuse, NY

28-MILE RACE, 2-MILE COURSE: 124.458; *Mr. Pringle's*; 1988; Scott Pierce, Las Vegas, NV

Heat Records

15-MILE HEAT, 2½-MILE COURSE: 133.551; *Miss Budweiser*; 1984; Jim Kropfeld, Tri-Cities, WA

12½-MILE HEAT, 2½-MILE COURSE: 136.745; *Miss Budweiser*; Tom D'Eath, Tri-Cities, WA

12-MILE HEAT, 2-MILE COURSE: 129.104; *Miss Budweiser*; 1988; Tom D'Eath, Evansville, IN

10-MILE HEAT, 2-MILE COURSE: 134.617; *Miss Budweiser*; 1986; Jim Kropfeld, Syracuse, NY

7½-MILE HEAT, 2½-MILE COURSE: 129.752; *Competition Specialties*; 1988; Larry Lauterbach, Madison, IN

6-MILE HEAT, 2-MILE COURSE: 143.785; *Mr. Pringle's*; 1988; Scott Pierce, Las Vegas, NV

Competition Lap Records

2½-MILE LAP: 146.460; *Miss Budweiser*; 1987; Jim Kropfeld, Tri-Cities, WA

2-MILE LAP: 139.968; *Miss Budweiser*; 1988; Tom D'Eath, Evansville, IN

1⅔-MILE LAP: none certified

Qualification Lap Records

2½-MILE QUALIFICATION LAP: 156.169; *Miss Budweiser*; 1988; Tom D'Eath, San Diego, CA

2-MILE QUALIFICATION LAP: 146.909; *Miller High Life*; 1988; Chip Hanauer, Evansville, IN

1⅔-MILE QUALIFICATION LAP: 136.110; *Miss Budweiser*; 1988; Jim Kropfeld, Miami, FL

Straightaway Records

MILE: 200.419; *Miss U.S. I*; 1962; Roy Duby, Guntersville, AL

KILOMETER: 198.168; *Miss U.S. I*; 1962; Roy Duby, Guntersville, AL

World Straightaway Records for Propeller-Driven Boats

Date	Boat & Driver	Site	Speed
4/17/62	*Miss U.S. I,* Roy Duby	Guntersville, AL	200.419
2/16/60	*Miss Thriftway,* Bill Muncey	Seattle, WA	192.001
11/19/57	*Hawaii Kai III,* Jack Regas	Seattle, WA	187.627
11/01/57	*Miss Supertest II,* Art Asbury	Picton, Ontario	184.494
7/07/52	*Slo-Mo-Shun IV,* Stan Sayres	Seattle, WA	178.497
6/26/50	*Slo-Mo-Shun IV,* Stan Sayres	Seattle, WA	160.323
8/19/39	*Bluebird II,* Malcolm Campbell	Lake Coniston, Scotland	141.740
9/17/38	*Bluebird,* Malcolm Campbell	Lake Halliwil, England	130.910
9/2/37	*Bluebird,* Malcolm Campbell	Lake Maggiore, Switzerland	129.500
9/20/32	*Miss America X,* Gar Wood	Detroit, MI	124.915

Date	Boat & Driver	Site	Speed
7/18/32	*Miss England III,* Kaye Don	Loch Lomond, Scotland	119.810
2/5/32	*Miss America X,* Gar Wood	Miami Beach, FL	111.712
7/9/31	*Miss England II,* Kaye Don	Lake Garda, Italy	110.223
4/24/31	*Miss England II,* Kaye Don	Parana, Argentina	103.490
4/16/31	*Miss America IX,* Gar Wood	Miami Beach, FL	103.069
3/20/31	*Miss America IX,* Gar Wood	Miami Beach, FL	102.256
6/13/30	*Miss England II,* Henry Seagrave	Lake Windermere, England	98.760
3/23/29	*Miss America VII,* Gar Wood	Miami Beach, FL	93.123
9/5/28	*Miss America VII,* George Wood	Detroit, MI	92.838

Offshore Racing Commission World Championships

Year	Driver	Country	Boat Name
		Superboat*	
Three-Race Series			
1988	Don Johnson	USA	*Gentry Eagle*
At Key West, FL, World Cup			
1987	Tom Gentry	USA	*Gentry Turbo Eagle*
At Key West, FL			
1986	Al Copeland, Sr.	USA	*Popeyes/diet Coke*
1985	George Morales	USA	*Maggie's MerCruiser Special*
1984	George Morales	USA	*MerCruiser Special*
1983	George Morales	USA	*MerCruiser Special*

*Superboat is not a recognized UIM class.

302

Year	Driver	Country	Boat Name
		Open Class/UIM Class 1	

Three-Race Series

1988	Fabio Buzzi	Italy	*Cesa 1882*

At Guernsey, England

1987	Steve Curtis	England	*Cougar*

At Key West, FL

1986	Antonio Giofredi	Italy	*Mededil*
1985	A. J. Roberts, Sr.	USA	*A. J. Jr's Mr. Roberts*
1984	Alberto Petri	Italy	*Miura*
1983	Tony Garcia	USA	*Arneson Special*

APBA Expanded Format

1982	Renato della Valle	Italy	*Ego Rothmans*
1981	Jerry Jacoby	USA	*Ajac Hawk*

Single Race Format

1980	Michel Meynard	USA	*Fayva Shoes*
1979	Betty Cook	USA	*Kaama*
1978	Francesco Cosentino	Italy	*Alitalia Uno*
1977	Betty Cook	USA	*Kaama*

World Circuit Format

1976	Tom Gentry	USA	*American Eagle*
1975	Wally Franz	Brazil	*Pangare Gringo*
1974	Carlo Bonomi	Italy	*Dry Martini*
1973	Carlo Bonomi	Italy	*Dry Martini*
1972	Bobby Rautbord	USA	*Fino*
1971	Bill Wishnick	USA	*Boss O'Nova II*
1970	Vincenzo Balestrieri	Italy	*Black Tornado*
1969	Don Aronow	USA	*The Cigarette*
1968	Vincenzo Balestrieri	Italy	*Tornado*
1967	Don Aronow	USA	*Maltese Magnum*
1966	Jim Wynne	USA	*Thunderbird/Ghost Rider*
1965	Dick Bertram	USA	*Brave Moppie*
1964	Jim Wynne	USA	*Wyn-Bil/Donzi-Doozy/Setimo Velo/Coronet/Wyn-Bil*

Production Classes

1988 (at Guernsey, England)
      Modified/UIM Class II, Roger Fletcher, England

1987 (at Key West, FL)
      Modified/UIM Class II, Peter J. Hidalgo, USA

Year	Class	Champion
1987	Pro-Stock	Anthony Caligure
	Stock A	Richard H. Felson
	Stock B	Jeff Kalibat
1986	Modified/UIM II	John D'Elia
	Pro-Stock	Nicky Cutro, Jr.
	Stock A	Bob Erickson
	Stock B	Jeff Calibat
1985	Modified/UIM II	Chris Lavin
	Pro-Stock	Rob Weinstein
	Stock A	John D'Elia, Jr.
	Stock B	Jeff Kalibat
1984	International	Ben Kramer
	Modified/UIM II	Emilio Riganti
	Modified Vee	Justo Jay
	Pro-Stock	Peter Aitkin
	Club	Jeff Kalibat
1983	Sport	Henry Ryan
	Modified	Robert Kehrig
	Pro-Stock	Peter Aitkin
	V-B	Franz Kneissel
	V-A	Nicky Cutro, Jr.
1982	Sport	Willy Diaz
	Modified	Chuck Jepson
	Pro-Stock	Lance Ruble
1981	Sport	Willy Diaz
	Modified	Randy Sosa
	Pro-Stock	Lance Ruble
1980	Sport	Steve Baum
	Modified	Tim Sheehan
	Production	Dave Albert

United States National Champions

1988	Superboat	Al Copeland, *Popeyes*
	Open	John D'Elia, *Special Edition*
	Modified	Joe Mach, *Dirty Laundry*

	Pro-Stock	Tom Akoury, *High Roller*
	Stock	Derek Simons, *Bermuda's Racing*
1987	Superboat	Al Copeland, *Popeyes/diet Coke*
	Open	Bob Kaiser, *ACR Systems*
	Modified	John D'Elia, *Special Edition*
	Pro-Stock	Nick Cutro, Jr., *Boardwalk/Trump's Castle*
	Stock A	Richard Felsen, *High Risk*
	Stock B	Joe Sorrentino, *Fully Involved*
1986	Superboat	Al Copeland, *Popeyes/diet Coke*
	Open	Ben Kramer, *Team Apache*
	Modified	John D'Elia, *Special Edition*
	Pro-Stock	Dominick Palombi, *What-a-Package*
	Stock A	Bob Erickson, *AME 4000 Express*
	Stock B	Bill Kaye, *Captain Maintained*
	Sportsman D	Carlos Capilla, *Danger Zone*
	Sportsman C	Peter Hidalgo, *Miami's Best*
	Sportsman B	John Sheels, *Ocean Outboard*
	Sportsman A	Lloyd Gootenberg, *Lucky Strike*
1985	Superboat	Al Copeland, *Popeyes/diet Coke* (1)
	Open	Sal Magluta, *Seahawk* (UI)
	Modified	Chris Lavin, *Jesse James*
	Pro-Stock	John Emmons, *Town & Country Auto*
	Stock A	Bob Erickson, *Mercury Racing*
	Stock B	Bill Kaye, *Captain Maintained*
	Sportsman C	Rolando Pieiga, *Miami's Best*
	Sportsman B	Robert Zieger, *Mariah*
	Sportsman A	Keith Staub, *Chick A Bob Ranch*
1984	Offshore I (Superboat)	Al Copeland, *Popeyes/diet Coke*
	Offshore II (International)	Sal Magluta, *Seahawk*
	Offshore III (Modified)	Mark Lavin, *Jesse James*
	Offshore IV (Modified Vee)	Casey Cnossen, *Hustler*
	Offshore V (Pro-Stock)	Jack Clark, *Thriller*
	Offshore VI (Club)	Gene Whipp, *Team Gulfwind*
1983	Offshore I (driver-Open)	George Morales, *Fayva*
	Offshore I (boat-Open)	Michelob Light, *Tom Gentry*
	Offshore II* (Sport)	Butch Ryan, *Express*
	Offshore III* (Modified)	Bob Sheer, *Sheer Terror*
	Offshore IV* (Pro-Stock)	Peter Aitkin, *Black Duck*
	Offshore V-B*	Jeff Kalibat, *K & K Ghost*
	Offshore VI (Club)	Walter Beasley, *Tabu*

*Driver and Boat championships

1982	Offshore I (Open)	Jerry Jacoby
	Offshore II (Sport)	Dan Weinstein
	Offshore III (Modified)	Sal Magluta
	Offshore IV (Pro-Stock)	Pete Aitkin

1981	Open	Betty Cook
	Sport	Gary Stuewe
	Modified	Randy Sosa
	Pro-Stock	Dave Albert
1980	Open	Bill Elswick
	Open II	Bill Peacock
	Modified	Tim Sheehan
	Sport	Dick Carlson
	Production	Dave Albert
1979	Open I	Betty Cook
	Performance I (Sport)	Dan Patrona
	Performance II (Modified)	Tim Sheehan
	Performance III (Production)	Jeff Brown
1978	Overall Open	Betty Cook
	Open I	Betty Cook
	Performance I (Sport)	Stan Pike
	Performance II (Modified)	Tom Murphy, Jr.
	Performance III (Production)	Bill Gazell
1977	Overall Open	Joel Halpern
	Overall Production	Sandy Black
	Open I	Joel Halpern
	Open III	Vaughn Szarka
	Production I	Jessup "Jay" Smith
	Production II	Bill Gazell
	Production III	Cal Barnett
	Modified IV	A. Pete Smith
	Sport V	Sandy Black
1976	Overall Open	Joel Halpern
	Overall Production	Marty King
	Open II	Dick DeWitt
	Open V	Joel Halpern
	Production I	Russell Zablocki
	Production II	Kimberly Young
	Modified III	David L. Owen
	Modified IV	Marty King
	Sport	Marvin Marter, Jr.
1975	Overall	Sandy Satullo
	Open I	Bob Brown
	Open II	Dick DeWitt
	Open III	Bill Vogel, Jr.
	Open IV	Wallace Cole, Jr.
	Open V	Sandy Satullo
	Production I	George Rossi
	Production II	Allen Allweiss
	Modified III	Sam Altese
	Modified IV	Wayne Vicker
	Sport V	Ken Black
	Sport VI	Preston Henn

306

1974	Overall Open	Arthur W. Norris
	Open I	Dick DeWitt
	Open II	Robert J. Sinclair
	Open III	William K. Vogel
	Open V	Arthur W. Norris
	Overall Sports	Jean-Claude Simon
	Sports I	Robert E. Brown
	Sports II	Jean-Claude Simon
	Overall Production	Tom Adams
	Production II	Donald G. Penkoff
	Production IV	Tom Adams
	Production Cruiser	James R. Solum
1973	Inboard	Bob Magoon
	Outboard	Randy Rabe
1972	Inboard	Bob Magoon
	Outboard	Steve Shere
1971	Inboard	Bob Magoon
	Outboard	Willie C. Meyers
1970	Inboard	Bill Wishnick
	Outboard	Bob Magoon
1969	Inboard	Don Aronow
	Outboard	Patrick Duffy
1968	Inboard	Don Aronow
	Outboard	Bob Magoon
1967	Inboard	Don Aronow
	Outboard	John Stenback
1966	Inboard	Peter Rothschild
	Outboard	Jerome G. Langer

1988 Key West Offshore World Cup

Class	Boat Name	Driver
Superboat:	*Gentry Eagle*	Don Johnson
Open:	*Gancia dei Gancia*	Stefano Casiraghi
Modified:	*Dirty Laundry*	Joe Mach
Pro-Stock:	*Konkrete Kat*	Ray Tresch
Stock:	*Main Attraction*	Paul Kesselring

The Key West World Cup was also the world championship for the Superboat Class and the national championship for the APBA Sportsman classes.

Sportsman A:	*Snakebite*	Richard Misiti
Sportsman B:	*Fever*	Joseph Srgo

Sportsman C: *Break Out*   Al Gerstenberger
Sportsman D: *Razz*   Pete Markey

Harmsworth International
Trophy Races

Driver, Nationality, Boat, Race Site, Average Speed
   1987–1988   No contests

Trophy Switched from Offshore to Outboard Tunnel Drivers in Team Racing Format:

1986   Mike Seebold,   USA, Bristol, England

1985   J. Hill, J. Jones, T. Williams, M. Wilson, Great Britain, Bristol, England, and Nassau, Bahamas

1984   J. Hill, J. Jones, M. Wilson, Great Britian, Bristol, England, and Nassau, Bahamas

Trophy Awarded to Offshore Driver with Highest Points in International Series of Races:

1983   George Morales, USA, *Fayva Shoes*

1982   Al Copeland, USA, *Popeyes*

1981   Bill Clauser, USA, *Satisfaction*

1980   Bill Elswick, USA, *Longshot* and *Satisfaction*

Trophy Awarded to British Driver with Highest Points in International Series of Races:

1979   Derek Pobjoy, England, *Uno Mint*

1978   Doug Bricker, Australia, *Taurus*

1977   Michael Doxford, England, *Limit Up*

1962–1976   No contests

1961   Bob Hayward, Canada, *Miss Supertest III*, Lake Ontario, Canada, 100.2 mph

1960   Bob Hayward, Canada, *Miss Supertest III*, Lake Ontario, Canada, 116.3

1959   Bob Hayward, Canada, *Miss Supertest III*, Detroit River, MI, 104.0

1957–1958   No contests

1956   Russ Shleeh, USA, *Shanty I*, Detroit River, MI, 90.2

1951–1955   No contests

1950   Lou Fageol, USA, *Slo-Mo-Shun IV*, Detroit River, MI, 100.6

1949 Stan Dollar, USA, *Skip-A-Long*, Detroit River, MI, 94.1

1934–1948 No contests

1933 Gar Wood, USA, *Miss America X*, St. Clair River, MI, 86.8

1932 Gar Wood, USA, *Miss America X*, Lake St. Clair, MI, 78.4

1931 No contest

1930 Gar Wood, USA, *Miss America IX*, Detroit River, MI, 77.1

1929 Gar Wood, USA, *Miss America VIII*, Detroit River, MI, 75.2

1928 Gar Wood, USA, *Miss America VII*, Detroit River, MI, 59.3

1927 No contest

1926 Gar Wood, USA, Detroit River, MI, 61

1922–1925 No contests

1921 Gar Wood, USA, Detroit River, MI, 59.7

1920 Gar Wood, USA, *Miss America I*, Osborne Bay, England, 61.4

1914–1919 No contests

1913 Tommy Sopwith, Sr., England, *Maple Leaf IV*, Osborne Bay, England, 56.4

1912 Tommy Sopwith, Sr., England, *Maple Leaf IV*, Huntington Bay, NY, 43.1

1911 Fred Burnham, USA, *Dixie IV*, Huntington Bay, NY, 40.2

1910 Fred Burnham, USA, *Dixie III*, Huntington Bay, NY, 36

1909 No contest

1908 Barclay Pearce, USA, *Dixie II*, Huntington Bay, NY, 34.

1907 Barclay Pearce, USA, *Dixie I*, Solent, England, 31.7

1906 Lionel de Rothschild, England, *Yarrow-Napier*, Solent, England, 15.5

1905 John Montague, England, *Napier II*, Arachon, France, 26

1904 Henri Brasier, France, *Trèfle-a-Quatre*, Solent, England, 26.6

1903 E. Campbell Muir, England, *Napier I*, Queenstown, Ireland, 24.9

APBA Offshore Straightaway Kilo Records

Class, Mph, Date, Location, Boat Name, Driver, Hull, Engine

SUPERBOAT 148.238, March 8, 1987, New Orleans, LA, *Gentry Turbo Eagle*, Tom Gentry, Cougar, Gentry Turbo Marine

OPEN 138.512, March 8, 1987, New Orleans, LA, *Popeyes/diet Coke*, Al Copeland, Cougar, Mercury

PRO-STOCK   110.360, July 1, 1988, Sarasota, FL, *High Roller*, Tom Akoury, Douglas Skater, Mercury

STOCK A   102.452, March 8, 1987, New Orleans, LA, *AME 4000 Express*, Bob Erickson, Skater, Mercury

STOCK B   80.480, July 3, 1987, Sarasota, FL, *Right Choice*, Joseph M. Clark, Velocity, Mercury

SPORTSMAN A   84.310, July 1, 1988, Sarasota, FL, *Team Gulf Wind*, Gene Whipp, Velocity, MerCruiser

SPORTSMAN B   82.045, July 3, 1987, Sarasota, FL, *Catnip*, Greg Den Boer, Eliminator, Chevrolet

SPORTSMAN C   99.416, July 1, 1988, Sarasota, FL, *Rajah*, Rajah R. Rodgers, Skater, Mercury

SPORTSMAN D   80.225, July 1, 1988, Sarasota, FL, *US-1 Boat Mfg.*, Berny Gonzalez, Shadow, Mercury

APBA Offshore Course Average Speed Records

Class, Driver, Boat Name, Date, Place, Speed (mph)

SUPERBOAT   Al Copeland, *Popeyes/diet Coke*, July 3, 1988, Sarasota, FL, 109.69 mph

OPEN (UIM CLASS I)   John D'Elia, *Special Edition*, July 3, 1988, Sarasota, FL, 109.45

MODIFIED (UIM CLASS II)   Ed Colyer, *Team Skater*, July 3, 1988, Sarasota, FL, 106.88

PRO-STOCK   Tom Akoury, *High Roller*, July 3, 1988, Sarasota, FL, 101.17

STOCK   Richard Felsen, *High Risk*, July 3, 1988, Sarasota, FL, 90.34

Distance Races

362.3-Mile Miami–Nassau–Miami Searace

Miami, FL, to Nassau, Bahamas, and return

Year	Driver	Country	Boat
1988	Carlo Bonomi, Jr.	Italy	*Gancia Dei Gancia*
1987	Ted Theodoli	USA	*Maltese Magnum*
1986	Ted Theodoli	USA	*General's Titan*

Searace 100

Miami, FL, to Gun Cay, Bahamas

1988	Norman Silverman	USA	*Rebellious*

Transatlantic Record Runs

Ambrose Light, NY–Bishop Rock, England

1986 *Virgin Atlantic II*, England, 3 days, 10 hours, 31 minutes
1952 Liner S.S. *United States*, USA, 3 days, 12 hours, 40 minutes

APBA Special Event Record Runs

Name of Event and Where Run, Date, Time, Driver, Hull, Engines

Miami–Nassau–Miami: Miami, FL, to Nassau, Bahamas, and return; June 3, 1988; 05:19:58, Tom Gentry; Vospers; T-MTU/Turbine

Miami–New York: Miami, FL, to New York; June 18–19, 1988; 19:17:23 (1,093-mile course, average speed 56.64 mph); Tom Gentry; Vospers; T-MTU/Turbine

Heartland Express: Minneapolis, MN, to New Orleans, LA; June 27–July 2, 1988; 50:21:00; Mike Ward, Jim Boonstra, Terry Stephenitch; Barretta Phaser 230; Chevrolet 350 with Volvo Dual Prop

Mississippi River Race: New Orleans, LA, to Memphis, TN, to St. Louis, MO; September 3–4, 1988; 14:55:03; Roy L. Fulton; Starcraft, Yamaha

Budweiser Challenge Cup/Mississippi River Race: New Orleans, LA, to Memphis, TN, to St. Louis, MO; September 5–6, 1987; 19:51:09; Don Johnson; Wellcraft Scarab; Lamborghini/MerCruiser

Assault on the Great Lakes: Chicago, IL, to Detroit, MI; May 16, 1983; 12:34:41; Michael E. Reagan; Wellcraft Scarab; Evinrude V8

Assault on the Inside Passage: Ketchikan, AK, to Seattle, WA; June 8, 1984; 23:55:21; Michael E. Reagan; Wellcraft Scarab; Evinrude V8

Assault for the Gold: Long Beach, CA, to San Francisco, CA, and return; July 7, 1984; 19:21:39; Michael E. Reagan; Wellcraft Scarab, Evinrude V8

Scorpion Powerboat Miami–NY Record Challenge (Outboard): Miami, FL, to New York, NY; August 17–19, 1984; 40:02; Julio De Varona; Scorpion; Mercury

Miss Liberty Challenge Cup: New York, NY, to Albany, NY; August 29, 1984; 01:57; Betty Cook and Kathy Genth; Chris-Craft Cat, Kaama

Miss Liberty Challenge Cup: New York, NY, to Albany, NY, and return; August 29, 1984; 04:22; Betty Cook and Kathy Genth; Chris-Craft Cat; Kaama

For Further Reading

Boating Facts and Feats. Peter Johnson. New York: Sterling Publishing Co., 1976.

Chapman Piloting, Seamanship & Small Boat Handling. Elbert S. Maloney. New York: Hearst Marine Books, 1989.

The Complete Book of Pleasure Boat Engines. Ernest A. Zadig. Englewood Cliffs, N.J.: Prentice-Hall, Inc., 1980.

Dhows to Deltas. Renato "Sonny" Levi. Lymington, England: Nautical Publishing Company, Ltd., Nautical House, 1971.

Fast Fighting Boats 1870–1945. Harald Fock. Lymington, England: Nautical Publishing Company, Ltd., Nautical House, 1978.

Gas, Gasoline and Oil-Engines. Gardner D. Hiscox. New York: The Norman W. Henley Publishing Co., 1915.

High Speed Small Craft. Peter Du Cane. Newton Abbot, England: David and Charles, Ltd., 1974.

Naval Architecture of Planing Hulls. Lindsay Lord, NA. Cambridge, Md.: Cornell Maritime Press, Inc., 1963.

Powerboat. Kevin Desmond. New York: Orion Books, 1988.

The Powerboat Handbook. Jim Martenhoff. New York: Winchester Press, 1975.

Thunderboating with Bill Muncey. Tony Hogg. Newport Beach, Calif.: Tony Hogg Publications, 1978.

There also are a number of magazines that carry articles on high-performance powerboats. These include: *Boating, Motor Boating & Sailing, Nautical Quarterly, Powerboat*, and *Power and Motor Yacht*.